Praise for *Untie the Strong Woman* .

"With passionate and lyrical stories and prayers, and her own brilliant artwork, Clarissa Pinkola Estés shares her intensely personal lifelong relationship with the Blessed Virgin Mary. With holiness and humor, Dr. Estés invites all willing souls to join her on this joyful journey with Mary, a journey to a new kind of mercy, an ever-replenished strength, and a profound freedom of spirit, heart, imagination, and love. This book is nourishing, uplifting, courageous, and creative, teaching us how to wear our toughness on the inside and our softness on the outside, with Mary always there to guide us, encourage us, comfort us, and push us a bit when necessary. As Dr. Estés says: 'I fully admit: Her fingerprints are all over me. Perhaps they are all over you, too. I hope so.'"

—DIANE SCHOEMPERLEN
Author of *Our Lady of the Lost and Found:*
A Novel of Mary, Faith, and Friendship

"Estés powerfully transmits the Divine Feminine's oceanic currents of unconditional love, enlivening every corner of the cosmos and our own hearts, transporting us to precious times, places, and memories when we have been touched by Her piercing tenderness and majesty."

—MICHAEL BERNARD BECKWITH
Author of *Spiritual Liberation: Fulfilling Your Soul's Potential*

"All of us have been awaiting Estés next book—and she has delivered—with depth, understanding, courage, humor, and fine storytelling. There's no one that doesn't need a gulp, a hit, a stroke of the Divine Mother—drink it up in these pages. Beautifully illustrated, full of poems and direct teachings, this is indispensable material."

—NATALIE GOLDBERG
Author of *Old Friend from Far Away: The Practice of Writing Memoir*
and *Writing Down the Bones: Freeing the Writer Within*

"Outrageously warm, intelligent, witty, and brave. In these pages, Clarissa Pinkola Estés delivers our souls straight into the love of the divine feminine, and what freedom and joy result!"

—REGINALD A. RAY
Author of *Touching Enlightenment: Finding Realization in the Body*

"Those who know that the future of the world depends on the full restoration of the Sacred Feminine in all its tenderness, passion, divine ferocity, and surrendered persistence will find in Clarissa Pinkola Estés's sublime new book the deepest kind of help and the highest inspiration. Clarissa Pinkola Estés fuses in her being three unique gifts—that of a great poet on fire with love for all creation, that of a visionary whose whole life is grounded in unfolding revelation, and that of a fierce and compassionate activist for justice in all realms. She is our most profound guide into the mysteries of the Mother, at a time when such guidance breathes the oxygen of our survival."

—ANDREW HARVEY
Author of *The Return of the Mother* and
The Hope: A Guide to Sacred Activism

"To *Untie the Strong Woman,* Dr. Estés writes with a sharpened axe through the heart, and her Madonnas are born full grown from the writer's brow. This epic book by Dr. Estés gives us the key, and the vision to unlock the mysteries of the Strong Woman and know the Madonna of our time. Like the word made flesh, these thousand written portraits of the Madonna would take me one hundred lifetimes to paint. In the presence of the Divine, I am just a barbarian viewing the world through the eyes of a painter, with my only salvation being to create beneath the radiant glow of Our Lady's Love for the Wild Soul."

—GEORGE YEPES
Painter/Master Muralist

UNTIE
the
STRONG
WOMAN

UNTIE the STRONG WOMAN

Blessed Mother's Immaculate Love for the Wild Soul

Clarissa Pinkola Estés, PhD

Boulder, Colorado

Sounds True, Inc.
Boulder, CO 80306

Sounds True is a trademark of Sounds True, Inc.

Published 2011.

Book design: Karen Polaski
Cover painting: Virgen de Guadalupe © 2009 All rights reserved, George Yepes, georgeyepes.com

Printed in Korea

Library of Congress Cataloging-in-Publication Data

Estés, Clarissa Pinkola.
  Untie the strong woman : Blessed Mother's immaculate love for the wild soul / by Clarissa Pinkola Estés.
        p. cm.
Includes index.
ISBN 978-1-60407-635-6
1. Mary, Blessed Virgin, Saint. I. Title.
BT603.E88 2011
232.91—dc22
            2011010338

10 9 8 7 6 5 4 3 2 1

UNTIE
the
STRONG
WOMAN

For Paul Marsh, *compadre*, foreign agent to scribes worldwide,
and soul in Spirit. You carried this manuscript
about Our Lady across the world—
from the Rocky Mountains in America
to dear waiting hands in an Italian city
in sight of the Alps on a clear day.
A city that long ago placed *La Madunina*, the little Madonna,
atop a spire, she acting as the city's guiding force.
Ever the languages scholar,
you said the city's name, Milano,
came from ancient Celts and old Latin *Mediolanum*
said to mean *center-heart sanctuary.*
Here we thought was a perfect doorway
to first bring this work through.
That favored line by Kafka most lovers of language know by heart:
. . . *ein Buch muß die Axt sein für das gefrorene Meer in uns.*
A book is to be an axe to chop open the frozen sea inside us.
Just so. The illustrious little Madonna atop Milano Cathedral
overlooking the city stands radiant and open-handed, her starred halo
blazes, and she has a fierce lance with sharpened blade of Cross to do
just that for us, to axe open the modern freeze inside us
so we are freed to flow forth in the best time-honored ways . . .
all of us souls
who walk with or will someday walk with La Nuestra Señora,
The Great Woman, Holy Mother,
holding her close
no matter her name,
garb,
race,
or
face.

◀ *La Madunina,* Milano, Italy

Table of Contents

REST SWEET SLEEP QUIET PEACE FRIENDS SOOTHING HEART HEALING BEAUTIFUL DREAMS

Totus tuus ego sum Maria

BLESSED MOTHER IMMACULATE HEART MI MADRE MIRROR OF HEAVEN , IVORY TOWER, ARBOL DE LA VIDA,
STAR OF THE OCEAN, PLEASE PRAY FOR ME RESTORE ME STRENGTHEN ME HEAL ME... MY GRATITUDE IS YOURS
FOREVER , I AM TOTUS TUUS-

Our Ancestral Great Mother

Opening Blessing: *Totus Tuus,* I Belong to You, Blessed Mother

With needles and thread, soft red felt, and white ink, I carefully appliquéd and shaped words, extra leaves, branches, and birds onto a bought quilt to hang over my bed to serve as a doorway to sleep.

I named this doorway *Totus Tuus ego sum María,* for it is a love letter to the Great Woman, a letter constantly being written and delivered, a letter from the heart that says, "I am yours completely *mi Madre.* Please pray for me and stay with me Blessed Mother."

In a world that is often heart-stopping in horror and breath-taking in beauty, but too often scraped down to the bone by those who leak scorn with such soul-sick pride, it is the Blessed Mother, who is so unspeakably gracious with brilliant inspirations that pour into us—if we listen, if we watch for them.

Thus, there is such blessed reason to seek out and remain near this great teaching force known worldwide as Our Lady, *La Nuestra Señora,* and most especially called with loyalty and love, Our Mother, Our Holy Mother. Our very own.

◀ Ex-voto: "Our Lady's Blessing Quilt for Beautiful Dreams"

She is known by many names and many images, and has appeared in different epochs of time, to people across the world, in exactly the shapes and images the soul would most readily understand her, apprehend her, be able to embrace her and be embraced by her.

She wears a thousand names, thousands of skin tones, thousands of costumes to represent her being patroness of deserts, mountains, stars, streams, and oceans. If there are more than six billion people on earth, then thereby she comes to us in literally billions of images. Yet at her center is only one great Immaculate Heart.

Since we staggered out of the Mist eons ago, we have had irrevocable claim to Great Mother. Since time out of mind, nowhere is there a feminine force of more compassion and understanding about the oddities and lovability of the wild and wondrous variations to be found in human beings.

Nowhere is there found a greater exemplar, teacher, mentor than she who is called amongst many other true names, Seat of Wisdom.

In Blessed Mother's view, all are lovable; all souls are accepted, all carry a sweetness of heart, are beautiful to the eyes; worthy of consciousness, of being inspired, being helped, being comforted and protected—even if other mere humans believe foolishly or blindly to the contrary.

If, following in the pathways laid down in the stories of the "old believers," if after the old God Yahweh Jehovah who seemed to spend inordinate time creating and destroying, thence came to us in huge contrast, the God of Love—then Our Blessed Mother is the ultimate Mother Who Gave Birth to Love.

She is the Mother who ascended whole, the Mother who has lived through wars, conquests, conscriptions. The Mother who has been outlawed, done outrage to, squelched, carpet bombed, hidden, stabbed, stripped, burnt, plasticized, and dismissed.

Yet she survived—*in* us and *for* us—no matter who raised a hand against her or attempted to undermine her endless reach. She is writ into every sacred book, every document of the mysteries, every parchment that details her as Wind, Fire, Warrior, Heart of Gold, *La que sabe*, the One Who Knows, and more.

And most of all, she is writ into our very souls. Our longings for her, our desires to know her, to be changed by her, to follow her ways of acute insight, her sheltering ways, her trust in goodness—these are the evidences that she exists, that she continues to live as a huge, not always invisible but palpably felt, force in our world right now.

Even when she was *una desaparecida,* disappeared by thugs and dictators over the many decades of the so-called Cold War, which was really a time of darkness meant to destroy the voice of souls across vast lands, we dreamt of her at night regardless.

We saw her colors and her flowers, her roses, morning glories, lilies, bluebells, marigolds, and more appear at the side of the darkest roads, despite being told she was gone and never existed to begin with.

We espied her on the roadway through the trees. Our Lady of the Birch Grove basilicas, Our Lady of the Sycamores, Our Lady of the Shrine of the Pines, Our Lady of the Redwood Cathedrals. She remained with us, even though outlawed for us to even think of her, to even imagine her. She was there nonetheless, for she is the quintessential Mother who does not, will not, leave her children behind.

Even when her cottages and groves and *vías,* pilgrimage roads, were erased from maps, or renamed, or plowed under, she appeared to us in our travails and moments of white-heat creating anyway—pulling something stubborn from the ground of us, helping us to let die what must die, helping us to let live what must live.

She will share her breath with us when we feel we have lost ours. She will warm us when we are too cold, and cool us down when we are too hot—in emotion, in spirit, in mind, in ideation, in desire, in judgment, in the creative life of the soul. She tells us to be gentle, but she will tell us too, "Be friendly, but never tame."

All we have to do is ask and she will be there in ways that we may see/feel immediately. Or, we may have to reach toward her, apprehending her in a new, not at first completely comfortable way.

St. Francis of Assisi was said to have rushed from cave to cave crying out in lamentation that he had just lost his God and could not find Him any more. But God told Francis He'd been there all along, that Francis had to learn to see God in all His many guises.

Thus, all we have to do is heart-call and she will make her way through walls and across water, under mountains and through iron or gilded bars to make herself known. All we have to do is *remember* her, and she is instantly with us—teaching, re-centering us in her spiritual outlook, hiding us, comforting us, helping us to truly see—like what is called in old

Yiddish a *mensch,* one who is innately wise. In Buddhism this is referred to as *bodhi,* a knowing place. We Latinos call this being *ser humano,* one who has learned through travail to become a true human being.

Our Lady is Compassion personified, and shows up wherever she beholds human spirit and soul in heartbreak, in injury, in fatigue, and also when the road is long and the gold of the soul's charisms and talents weigh heavy in creative life, or when the life of the family or work are raveled. Especially so then, she bends to tend to the needful soul.

She will show up in our thoughts, our dreams, our inner knowings, our sudden awarenesses . . . with the most useful spare wheel, the lever, the spiritual muscle, the needle and thread, the warp and the weft, the clay, the materia, the music, the nourishment, the difficult insight into, the brilliant thought, the doorway to new attitude, the exact encouraging word needed.

She is here with us, has always been here with us, will always be with us no matter which "here" we cross over or into.

By this work, I hope to make her more visible to those who have not yet seen her, make warm invitation to those who have been estranged from her, or who have traveled far away from her for far too long, help calm a little those who wish to fossilize her living being, and help mend a little those who have been shamed for asserting she not only exists, but is central to their being and has informed their strivings to follow sacred life in ways that nourish the soul deeply, and that may or may not show in public in obvious ways.

This work was written to let others who love her so and those who have been with her for a lifetime, and those who have as yet unnamed yearnings for the Holy—know they are on the right path—that often steep and winding path of following her.

Thus, for all souls, these enclosed stories, prayers, and images I've written here about her exemplary ways, her charges to us, her ancient ways in our modern times, are meant to be windows blasted through the thick concrete walls that some cultures have built around and over her living presence to sequester her, to "disappear her" via only appearances duly "pre-approved," allowing her to only say previously vetted words.

This work is formed especially to let any soul who longs toward her, walks with her, dreams toward her . . . to know they are surrounded by fellow travelers who do not "believe" she walks with us: From our bones outward, we who are fellow travelers *know* her and *experience* her up front and cheek-to-cheek. We are, together, all of us, the sparkling flashes of light on her ocean of love. We are together the flashing of innumerable stars on her mantle. You are not alone. We are together—with and within—her.

This work is in the tradition I was raised and consecrated in—to her, Our Blessed Mother. As a young child, out in the rural lands where we all lived, I was taken before the altar in a tiny chapel the size of a kitchen. My elderly immigrant family women in their big broken-down shoes, and two even more elderly nuns in their dusty black skirts and veils, were my sponsoresses.

I have always had the suspicion that our consecration to Blessed Mother derived from the most creakingly old ethnic traditions in the Old Country villages. And that perhaps consecrating little girls to Holy Mother for life, pledging these wild-haired, jumping-rope, winged little girls to solemn vows to Our Lady—vows of Chastity, Obedience, and Loyalty for life, when only six years of age—was likely not done in congregations that were more melting-potted, more tidy, and reserved—not so get-down-gritty immigrant.

However, I took my troth with all the seriousness of a child as bride of Espírito Santo—a child's bright calm heart—and I try to carry that troth with the same child-heart now—succeeding, failing, trying again. Like most muddy angels, I have to strive, not to be devoted to La Señora, for that is easy, but to remember to live what is known—which includes being dazzled by learning her, to see her concretely, how she speaks to all—if they choose to have a listening ear and a listening heart. I so hope they do and will, and that I do and will, *siempre,* always.

Thus, I have tried hard to live the beautiful devotion I was given to carry in this rough-cut and cracked earthen vessel I am made of. In this work, I hope to share with you what that journey with her has been like—certain windows into the interior of the sacred—that will help to introduce Blessed Mother to those who have inklings of her but yet too, little experience.

I hope to re-introduce her to those who have wandered away perhaps, but are seeking the literal mother-lode again, and for those too, who have lifetime devotions to her, I hope to delight and strengthen and deepen all.

May these words awaken a little bit to a good amount, any unused corner of the heart, any portion that feels friendless. If anything, Blessed Mother is indeed that: the ultimate friend to the friendless one.

Thus, if I may, I would like to not "end" this chapter, but to *abre la puerta,* open the door— by blessing you. If you'd like to receive this, just incline your head a bit, and open your hand, your palm up, in whatever way is comfortable, or place your open palm over your heart or over whatever of your body or life needs strength, care, healing. This is how I was taught by the old believers of my immigrant families to receive Blessed Mother's healing grace.

BLESSED MOTHER BLESSING[1]

My prayer for, and to, and over the crown of your life is this . . .

We lift you up so your soul can be seen by Mother Mercy,
she who checks doorways, sees through cracks
and into corners where souls often hide, seeking refuge.
She who is the Immaculate Heart sees you easily,
greets you warmly, remembers you with love,
for she is
the Mirror of Heaven,
the Tower of Ivory,
Obsidian Blade,
Star of the Waters,
Seat of Wisdom . . .

We lift you up so Blessed Mother can see
all that you need now
in order to bring goodness and contentment,
healing and health,
understanding and love

—to you and to your beloveds—
in every possible way.

And especially, may all these be given to you
in ways you can most easily see and understand . . .

and in ways you can put to immediate good use.

We lift you up because you were knitted up
in your earthly mother's womb by One Greater . . .
not only born already blessed . . .
but also born as a blessing on all of us . . .

Do not forget this,
for we have not forgotten you.
And neither and never has your Greater Mother.

Let you walk now forward into this day,
both deeply blessed and blessing others
with the magnitude of Our Holy Mother's love.

Aymen

. . . which means in the old language—Let it be so.

CHAPTER ONE

Meeting the Lady in Red

The First Time Ever
I Saw Your Face

We were going to something called a lake. I was so joy-jolted.

No longer young enough to wear just skin and nothing more, after four years of age I had to wear strange scratchy clothes. I thought wearing clothes was like being in prison . . . and I now wore shoes that never bent right in the ten places a foot bends naturally.

My hand-me-down clothes included skirts that hung down to my ankles, or else were too tight in the neck and arms. It was like being a mermaid caught in a net that bound you, crunched you, choked you, tied you down, left deep red circles all over your wrists and ankles, your waist and neck.

But today it was early winter, and I was dressed in two itchy-baggy handmade sweaters, and woolen leggings that had elastic bands that went under my black rubber boots—the ones with the silver jingle clasps to buckle me shut into them. I had been buried into a big brown coat that swirled around my boots and a too-small hat that pinched my fine fly-away hair in the elastic.

But, I was puppy happy, for we all were being taken "for a drive," meaning spending precious coins on gasoline just to treat others by going fast in a rusty

---

◀ "Red Woman Lake"

old car. This time we were going to "drive fast" so our uncle could show off the "new-used" car with four mismatched tires that he'd won in a poker game with other immigrants in some smoky hallway.

So, we veered down the road to the Great Lake, Michigan, a huge inland ocean not far from the little village of six hundred people where we lived in what were called saltboxes, meaning four rooms arranged in a small square.

At the lake, it was even more icy-cold as everyone piled out of the hulk of a car. Within a few moments everyone looked like they had red cherry juice on their cheeks and noses, which went nicely with all their flashing gold teeth.

As the grown-ups toasted each other with bright yellow liquid in tiny etched glasses, as they all stood laughing on the high bluffs overlooking the sunset on the lake, as the cold wind blew away their steaming words to each other—I, as the only child present, slipped away unnoticed.

I went down three long concrete staircases, holding onto the iron-pipe handrail high above my head. One step down, then my other foot to the same step, then again, one step down, bringing my other foot to the same step—and thus I made it to the very bottom and onto the wet brown beach.

This was the first time I had ever seen big water since I left my mother's womb. The waves in the Great Lake, Michigan, were the size of big bolts of red and yellow lace in the late sun—waves rushing into shore, breaking apart, but with the strength of lace having brawn enough to move tree trunks and parts lost off ships. Bringing those big objects in and slamming them onto the shore, and then gently taking them out again, over and over.

I came from grandmothers who made lace with what seemed like hundreds of bobbins and threads trailing—and when I saw the lace on the waves, I wanted to go out into the lake where I imagined there might be old women somehow, watery old women, making all this red and yellow lace in the deep.

So with full open heart, I ran right into the cold lake, my rubber boots filling with heavy water immediately. I could feel some spirit under the water wanting to take my legs away from me.

And that's when I first saw her, the lady in the water coming toward me. The sky behind her red with sunset, and a sudden Holy Spirit white bird flying through the air over her head, a sliver moon already in the rose-yellow-clouded sky. The lady wore a long red mantle with many, many golden spangles, and on her head was a beautiful golden crown.

I cannot explain this: I felt I was seeing a long-lost relative that I so loved, and had missed so dearly for an eternity. I was so glad to see her I tried to run farther into the water toward her, but she was calling to me, "No, no! Don't run toward me. I came to run after you. Turn around, run away from me!"

She was playing a game with me. I understood now, and turned before the next wave crashed. I ran laughing, heavy booted and all, falling palms down through water that had no bottom, water going straight up my nose, but I rose choking, coughing, slog-running some more. I ran lopsided inland, gaining my breath; it was so cold outside, so burning cold inside my body. But I was still laughing, laughing, running all wobbly, and then stopping to see if the lady was catching up.

She was. She ran after me bent over with her hands out fluffing the air behind my back, the way you would shoo a gosling.

I ran more—laughing, laughing, colder, colder, wobbling more and more. I fell down in the sand, laughing as though crazy drunk, scrabbled my way upright again; the lady ran behind me chasing me high up onto the wet sandy mounds—away from the big water and toward the long concrete stairs.

I glanced upward and saw my relatives galloping full speed down the stairs sideways. Men in mustaches, women with pocketbooks swinging wildly. I had vaguely heard them earlier as they seemed to be bellowing across the divide, "No! no!" to someone, but now their voices came into full focus, and they were somehow shouting and cooing to me at the same time, "Yes, yes, come to us, run to us. That's right, come to us."

I remember being taken off my feet as someone grabbed me by the coat sleeve and arm so hard it left painful black-purple on my skin later. Then someone hit me. Hard. For running into the water, they said.

I was cold as ice, shivering and crying now. I was carried up the stairs like a weeping cord of wood under someone's arm. But I held my arms out toward the Great Mother Lake Michigan. Blinded by tears, opening and closing my fingers, I cried out "Lady, Lady . . ."

For punishment, they put me in jail, setting me down hard in the dark backseat of the car by myself. I tried to roll down the heavy window to tearfully tell them about the lady, the beautiful lady in the water. Soon several someones piled into the backseat and stripped off my drenched clothes, then wrapped me in a dark blanket that smelled of motor oil.

"There was no lady," they barked. No lady in red. "No laytee!" they snapped in their heavily accented English. "No laytee wett golten croon." No lady with a golden crown. Only the same old red lighthouse that had always been there on the lake. A lighthouse that had a widow's walk on top. It only looked like a crown. There was no crown, "no croon," no lady in red.

I stopped trying to tell them, for they warned I'd be punished worse if I told any more stories.

But, I had seen the Lady. I had seen her.

And she had seen me.

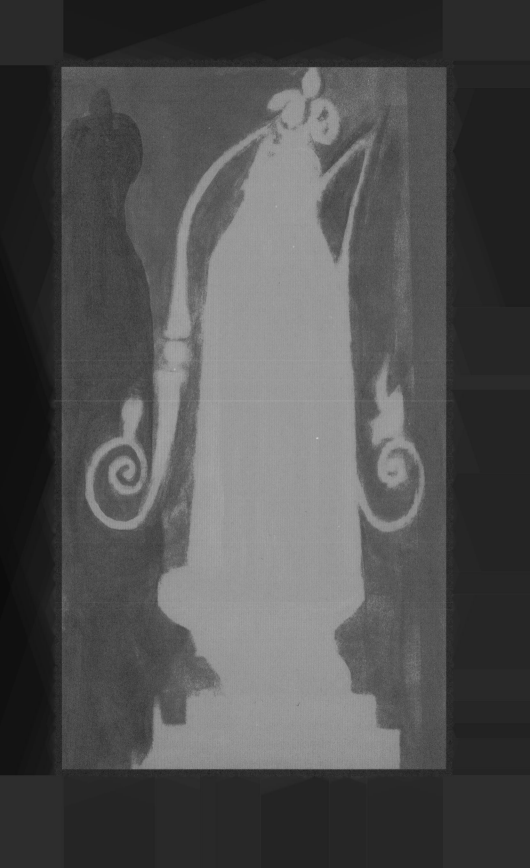

Blessed Mother, Woman of Many Faces, Many Names: I know you as Our Holy Elder, a nearly unheard of depiction of you. But/And in the old stories, you, as aged Mary, climbed the hills to Artemis' Ephesus where you held forth: "teaching by being." Some old believers report, as at Cana, you continued to enjoin sacred tribal dances.

Today, June 2011, the day of completing this book, and after near 2 millennia of peoples across the world crying out in pain, it has been decreed worldwide, by Christian authorities, that herewith Christian missionaries are to "reject all forms of violence ... including the violation or destruction of places of worship, sacred symbols or texts" belonging to others.

If so, true reason for Hallelujah: may it come into being for all groups. All. That all swords are this very day hammered into plow blades... to plant new life instead of harming life.

CHAPTER TWO

How the Great Woman Was Erased:
Our Part in Restoring Her

Untie the Strong Woman

My grandmother Katerin said that if you listened to stories about Mother
Maria for nine weeks straight without interruption . . .

Or if you prayed the rosary for nine days straight without your mind
wandering once . . .

Or if you walked to one of Mama Marushka's shrines in the woods for
nine nights in a row—nine being the number of months Blessed Mother
carried the living Cristo before giving birth to the Light of the world . . .

If you did any of these, Blessed Mother would appear to you and answer
any question you might have about how to live on earth fully ensouled.

But my grandmother also said there was a shortcut.

Need.

That any human being needing comfort, vision, guidance, or strength
was heard by the Immaculate Heart . . . and thus, Blessed Mother would
immediately arrive with veils flying, to place us under her mantle for protection, to give us that one thing the world often longs for so: the warmth
of the mother's compassionate touch.

◀ Ex-voto: "Elder Holy Mother, That She Be Known And Shown Unfrozen"

I know you and I have seen many statues of Our Lady, lovingly made yet erasing all her Semitic features, or her Asian, Inuit, Nahua, Polynesian, tribal European, Celtic, African, Las Americas, indigenous ones.

I don't think envisioning *Nuestra Madre,* Our Mother, was meant to be one racial preference only. Perhaps in the beginning, "whitening" her, as in ancient alchemical poetics, was a symbolic attempt to show that the color white and purity are often seen as complementary in Western imagination.

Thus, for centuries, she was heavily painted as light-skinned, with blonde or light brown hair, and often with blue eyes like princesses in fairy tales, who were often portrayed with nearly identical coloring. But it isn't an issue of color exactly; it's an issue of paling her in every way until she appears frozen, anemic, and half-erased. Our Mary, María, Mir-yam, Guadalupe, over the eons also came to be spoken about in more and more hushed tones:

She's pure, you know. Demure.
As they say, so content, so gentle,
so quiet, so passive, so submissive.

Yet, I must say, "No!" I say she is instead: "Fire!"
Fire of love
Fire of hope
Fire of compassion
and we are her bloodline.

I hope, with deepest love,
that you also know the Mary,
María, Mir-yam, Guadalupe
of wilder heart, of long journeys
with a blurred map, of night fires
at the far encampment,
that you know Our Lady
who in the old stories,
when nearly all the apostles ran away . . .
she stayed . . . and stayed.

No demure little cabbage, that woman. No paltry, well-behaved carbon dot. No follower of worldly orders. Quite the contrary. *Our exemplar.* Blessed Mother, she who is renowned as the one able to wear the flaming, exploding fire-lakes of the Sun.

I have a little white porcelain statue of Mary that some good soul hand-painted carefully in a factory of thousands of porcelain Marys on a conveyor belt—tiny gold curlicues on the selvages of her mantle. And lovely.

But the Mother I most often carry with me everywhere is the woods-woman *La Nuestra Señora,* Our Lady Guadalupe, she whose mantle is fashioned of moss from the north side of trees at sunset, she who has star shards caught in her wild silver hair. Her gown is soft, coarse-woven cloth with the thorns and weed seeds and petals of wild roses caught in it.

She has dirty hands from growing things earthy, and from her day and night work alongside her hard-working sons and daughters, their children, their elders, all.

LA GUADALUPE IS NO SYMMETRICAL THING WITH PALMS EQUALLY OUTSTRETCHED AND FROZEN IN TIME

She is ever in motion.
If there is emotion, she is there.
If there is commotion, she is there.
If there is elation, she is there.
Impatience, she is there.
Fatigue, she is there.
Fear, unrest, sorrow,
Beauty, inspiration,
She is there.

And she *is* demure in a sense, yes, but different from those who would fade her essence into an anemia: Yes, she *is* demure as in demurring, that is, refusing to be contained and made small.

And she *is* calm, yes, but not without will to rise again and again. Instead, yes, she is calm as the mighty ocean is calm as it moves in enormous troughs and pinnacles, its huge waves like a heartbeat: easy, intentional, muscular.

And she *is* pure, yes, but not as in never going dark, never having doubt, never taking a wrong turn for a time, but rather pure, yes, as a gemstone is cut into a hundred sparkling facets—that kind of pure, meaning gem-cut by travail, adventure, and challenge—and yet fully without a streak of dead glass in any facet.

Despite all travail, diminishments, scorn, hounding, ridicule, Holy Mother still burns pure-fire bright.

THE STORY OF THOSE WHO ATTEMPT TO MAKE GIANTS DIMINUTIVE

I often think of Guadalupe, Blessed Mother, with regard to an illustrated novel, Gulliver's Travels *by Jonathan Swift. The book carried a picture of Gulliver pinioned to the ground.* Gulliver had become a quasi-prisoner of the Lilliputians, a tiny people only six inches high. They criticized Gulliver, amongst other things, for being in several ways "too big."

So, they tied him crisscross over all his limbs, and took him down with ropes wrapped around brass nails driven into pallet and ground.

The tiny Lilliputians stood on Gulliver's chest and felt they had tied down the leviathan, the behemoth. But Gulliver just simply sat up—and all his bonds burst, and all the tiny Lilliputians flew off, catapulting into the grass.

The giant lumbered off with the trivial rope-strings trailing behind. The Lilliputians shook their heads—as usual—trying to make sense of the Gulliver figure that was, in form, similar to themselves in body—but in an entirely other way, so very unlike themselves.

I think many can understand this push to pare down the numinous, the infinitely larger, the unfamiliar, the unknown, the "other," the *different.*

Mystery can be overwhelming. Touching Divinity can seem like all one's atoms composing mind and body have suddenly been rearranged. Divine mystery is supposed to be overwhelming in order to knock out the ego who tends to use smallest mind—attempting to critique and cripple everything it cannot imagine or immediately grasp.

Many old institutions and cultures unwittingly trade their love of verve, inherent in the Divine, for calcified and rote forms of being that "minimize the magnitude" of the thousands of talents carried in holiness by the creative soul. Some, attempting to magnify the minimus, "the little man"—that is, the flimsy, the mean, the least well-formed and least well-informed egos of human beings, politics, and matters in general.

Then it becomes not only our calling, but our troth, our sacred promise given from the very first moment we ever saw the soul be assaulted in anyone, by anyone—to untie the Strong Woman—to unleash whatever of her profound gifts continually pour into us through our shared bloodline with her. We learn to study her life stories, and thereby learn how to plan and enact our own customized versions of a blessed *Imitatio Maria*[1] in and on this world. Not just for now. For all of our days, and for all the people and creatures and "matters that matter."

Too often, the only relationship we have been taught/told/offered to have with Blessed Mother is either none—through silence about her rich bloodline with us—or else one in which we must agree to bind her down into a small and handle-able form. This diminishes her: she is made into the quiescent "good girl" in phony opposition to having another woman, The Magdalene, be the less quiescent "bad girl."

These are distortions of both holy women's origins and gifts. Untie them both, then.

I have listened to some few theologians speak about Our Lady as though she is an appendage to a group of historical facts. Neither is she, as some charge, a superstition. She is not an obedient building made of cement, marble, or bricks. She is not to be used as a length of holy wire to bind us all into docility, severing the other thousands of traits given by Creator to us all for being beautifully and reasonably human and soulful.

Holy Mother is not meant to be a fence: Holy Mother is a gate.

SHE SPECIALIZES IN LOVE LESSONS THAT STRENGTHEN RATHER THAN WEAKEN

I remember a well-known book reviewer scorning an author who had urged readers to ask for consultation with Holy Mother. The reviewer dismissed this suggestion as pure nonsense.

I have never come closer to flying cross-country, pouncing on said critic's crate-for-a-desk, and calling for a plague of frogs to take over her entire office, as in the old fairy tale "One-Eye, Two-Eyes, and Three-Eyes."[2] In the tale, whenever the criticizer opened her mouth to speak, from that day forward, lizards, toads, and snakes dropped from her lips.

Ay! I was almost more horrified by my own horrible reaction than by the critic's jaded take on supplicating the Blessed Mother. Almost.

Yet, I had understood Guadalupe to say into my heart at that very moment of my hurt and pique, something like this: "All are mine, all belong to me whether they know me or not, whether they practice a devotion or not."

And that too, that oceanic generosity of the Mother—so unusual in our modern cultures, which endlessly use war rhetoric and death terms nearly exclusively for most everything—that turned most of my ire into undertaking a far more merciful attitude—for the sake of self-knowledge, for peace, for mercy on others.

This is one of the messages of Blessed Mother: Even when someone strikes out at what matters to one's heart and soul, we should not let intrusive matters go by; rather, though we should approach with calm red living heart, rather than frazzled fried heart . . . or no heart at all.

And this too, I believe: we can allow ourselves the inspiration to develop "the grace to embrace," even when that embrace is not returned. This kind of sometimes startling intelligence can occur when the Strong Woman is untied.

BEING *WITH*, SEEING *WITH*, THE GREAT WOMAN

As a little child, I felt I was called to the priesthood. A priesthood that perhaps does not exist for me in this world codified as it is.

Yet, for certain the charisms granted to me, and my promise given to Creator, was and is to try as hard as I can, to take Holy Mother and her works into the world as much as I'm able—and through her also the works of her precious Child—to offer these into the yearning, bright, creative, and sometimes ruined worlds that so need Love and Inclusion—to help gently remind that we all are here to walk together—each in his and her own customized ways of goodness.

So I take *mi* Guadalupe everywhere, to one soul, to gatherings, retreats, schools, the street, and churches, some of which are, but some of which are not, Roman Catholic. I take her to those who are kind enough to ask me to give the sermon, or make space for me to heal and bless others with my hands during that special set-aside time in a temple or *temenos*, this last being a place dedicated as "sacred space"—as in a grove, a sick-room, a meditative state.

I tell about her world, her life, her daughters and sons, and always there is at least one someone who says, "We don't 'believe in' her." Or, "How can you believe in this?"

And I say, "I do not believe in her. I know her. Face-to-face, skin to skin. *Mi madre*. She is my mother. Nuestra Madre. Our Mother."

Very often I am asked how a soul just coming to truly be with Our Lady might think about María, *Nuestra Madre Grande.* I say:

HOW TO COMPREHEND HER, BE CLOSE TO HER

The exotic locale is not necessary to apprehend her. She is found in a shard of glass, in a broken curb, in a hurt heart, and in any soul knowing or unknowing, yet crazy in love with the mysteries, with the divine spark, the creative fire—and not quite so in love with mundane and petty challenges only.

Think of her not in the ways you've been told/sold.
Rather, seek her with your own eyes without blinders
and your own heart without shutters.
Look low instead of high.
Look right under your nose.
She comes in many guises and disguises.
Hidden, right out in the open.
And you will know her immediately by her immaculate
and undivided heart for humanity.

This is the Guadalupe I think you know of, or sense, or want to know, or are very close to for years now. Our Lady is joy-centric and sorrow-mending. She is one who is present in every way. In so understanding one's own pull to the Holy Woman, thus do we untie the Strong Woman.

Here, please allow me to pray strength into your hands and heart—and inspiration and daring—and fire—to lift the Great Woman away from whichever Lilliputians have tied her down into more manageable form.

No matter which dissertation or diminution she has been tied down by, she is greater than any Lilliputian mind by far.

The moment we ask for her,
see her, converse with her, love her—
she gracefully rises up
against all her ropes,

and they burst open whilst
the pins fly in all directions.

With much love, some levity, and certainly deep longing,
together let us all sit up too,
let us bust through all the ropes
and make all the pins fly too—
untying ourselves as we also untie the Strong Woman.

May it be deeply so for you.
May it be so for me, also.
May it be so for all of us, ever.

CHAPTER THREE

She Is the Inspiratus *for Souls Who Suffer*

The Drunkard
and The Lady

F ifteen years ago, I moved all my thousands of books and writings to a tiny blue house. From the viewpoint of some "moderns," there's one fast way to become an instant eccentric in any increasingly gentrified neighborhood in the desert Southwest: that is, to create a shrine to La Nuestra Señora de Guadalupe in the old, time-honored tradition of many Latino immigrants—by burying a bathtub in your front yard with only half its length showing above ground, then putting a sweet statue of Guadalupe inside the arch of the tub and planting some perennial flowers where the porcelain ends and the earth begins.

Some strongly suggest brightly colored plastic roses be placed there too: for long ago, Guadalupe miraculously made roses appear in the wintertime, and this is as close as miracle-challenged Latinas like me are probably ever likely to have roses blooming during the winter.

You can imagine: either the tub or the Guadalupe can cause all kinds of "v.s.z.q.," "very serious zoning questions," to rise up amongst those who do not yet understand that each homeplace needs a guardian of the soul(s) who live there—a guardian at the gate, so to speak, outdoors, under the open sky, to warn away some and to welcome most.

Despite the fact that I could imagine neighborhood people gossiping about the lady with the bathtub tipped end up in her front yard, I began mentioning that I was looking for a workman to come help me dig a hole for the old claw-foot tub I'd spotted at the plumbing salvage joint.

I planned and drew, and pretty soon had a half-way presentable drawing of said tub and the small concrete statue of Blessed Guadalupe I'd come by.

Because the statue really was made of asphalt molded around a rod of rebar and I could not carry her about all by myself, I called her "She Who Can Hardly Be Lifted," even though La Señora, in reality, ever lifts all others easily, no matter how much their problems or their hopes weigh.

Now I only needed a willing soul with strong muscles to help me dig down into the stubborn earth there, to a depth of more than three feet in order to seat a six-foot tub on end.

As an old believer, and trusting that whatever good we are seeking is also seeking us, I prayed for the right "strong soul with shovel," to please stumble across my path, find *mi* Guadalupe and me, and help us to create her shrine.

THE DRUNKEN MAN APPEARS

Well, the stumble part came true nearly right away. I was soon brought face-to-face with a drunken man who said he'd heard I was "looking for someone to build something."

I hesitantly showed him my drawings, and he boasted that he was just the right "muscle and might" needed to make a bathtub grotto for Guadalupe.

Really G!d?[1] *This was the "right man" for whom I'd prayed? The one who should find me and my concrete Guadalupe and help us? Who says G!d has no humor?* I had sort of been expecting a courtly old gent or perhaps a woman elder in the trades, who just did little side jobs now that they were in their venerable eighties.

But this man, unsteady on his feet, was only about forty-five years old, even though he looked about nine hundred years old, had bad pasty skin, dirty hair, and unshaven gray-and-brown beard hairs all sprouting in different directions. And as men who have been in some part of their lives *los borrachos,* or heavy chronic drinkers—when older and still drinking hard—he also had that stale next-day odor coming through his pores. Even when more or less sober for a few hours, older bodies often can't purify as quickly as they once did, and that humus smell of leaf-rot hangs around the person, like a cloud filled with wafts of sour sweat mixed with the smell of whiskey.

The helper whom I'd prayed would find me and my concrete Guadalupe was all this and more. He didn't just have the drinking sickness. The drinking sickness had him.

He'd drank everything: pulque, tequila, rum, shots, shooters, keggers, and moonshine. Like most souls with this illness, he'd never met an alcohol demon that didn't sweet-talk him half-senseless inside an hour's time.

But the drunken man also came with a credible recommendation about his masonry skills from someone whom I trusted on earth—and on the recommendation of someone whom I trusted in Heaven: she who whispered into my heart, "Yes, this is the exact one I sent to you."

And so, with my chin to my shoulder in a little self-doubt, I said, Yes. Even though a less promising partnership could hardly be imagined. Yet, something else seemed present too . . . something of invisible import.

WE PROCEEDED TO BUILD THE IMPORTANT PARTS FIRST

No talk about money or design. We began in the old way—by trading stories: First the topographical stories, then the middle-deep ones, and finally the "want to set my hair afire and go screaming down the road forever" stories, the toughest ones to hear and tell.

Of the last: This man who'd stumbled into my life was a stone-mason by trade, and a soul who in childhood had lived in institutions that had broken his spirit bones and his actual bones, and left him for dead.

You could see that he was physically strong from the waist up, from a lifetime of heaving brick and slapping frosting, of working plumb lines to perfection.

Yet. One leg was the leg of a strong man—but the other leg was the leg of a boy, thinner than thin, with an ankle like a child's. He drag-limped whenever he took a step. It was from the polio.

When he was eight years old, his parents, already down-and-out, left him at the polio people's door. His parents did not come back. Busted up in spirit and pinned for years afterward into foster care, and then unhooked and re-hung in various orphanages, the boy who survived polio became one of the children who kept brew under the cot, the only mother many would ever have to help them make it through the nights.

In those times, abandoned children didn't smoke dope or take methamphetamine. They did Mother Beer. Mother Chianti. Mother Thunderbird. Cheap. Ten percent good in one way and 100 percent lethal in every other.

These were the arterial stories inside stone-mason man when he came to me limping, red-rimmed and bleary-eyed, smelly, slurring, unsteady— and somehow radiant. Seriously radiant. Anyone with the eyes to see could see there was something in his darkness, far back in a little room— there was a tiny candle lit and wavering in the wind.

THE MEREST BEGINNING OF THE
"TRANSFORMATIVE MOMENT"

Thus, we continued. How long would it take to make a grotto to Guadalupe? Just a little while, was his answer. Stone-mason man and I drew plans on lots of pizza-stained paper napkins. He had the drinking disease so bad, his preferred meeting place was a saloon. It was okay, for I too come from people who frequented and ran tiny corner saloons, and who had the same sicknesses from spirits that are fatal to the soul. I myself was not a stranger to Bill W.

As I told him stories about La Guadalupe, Our Blessed Mother, we worked our way from meeting at the scarred-up bar to meeting at a yellow oak table on the restaurant side of the saloon. I could see that it was talking about La Señora, Guadalupe, which caused this small progression from drink only, to actual food and drink.

And stone-mason man's awkward and not unpainful re-centering into a holier heart, a greater than human heart alone, continued as we continued. Gradually.

I told him the story of Our Lady at the Hill at Tepeyac, how she chose to appear to little thin-legged Don Diego, whose real name was his tribal Nahuatl name. (The Spanish called the Nahua people Aztecs.) His real name, long form, was Cuauhtlatoatzin—Speaking Eagle is one translation.

At my description of the little frail Indian man, and at the sound of the intricate-sounding name, Cuauhtlatoatzin, stone-mason man's ears perked up. And stayed up. You could see that something deep inside him was listening. Some meaningful connection that had been put to sleep for far too long was clearly awakening.

I told him how this little sweet man Cuauhtlatoatzin, Don Diego, had witnessed indescribable horror during the conquest of our ancestral people, yet somehow had survived with an unruined heart. How Cuauhtlatoatzin was still remembered amongst many of the elders today, as being afraid of all the "higher-ups," how he had been beaten and hurt bad, seen his own relatives and neighbors slaughtered and mutilated right before his eyes. He had seen all who survived then treated with scorn and flogging, indeed flaying, afterward—and those allowed to live only did so by trying to act "worthy"—that is, by taking the only way out—by becoming a slave, a bowing and scraping, shuffling, eyes-ever-lowered slave.

As I shined light on the under-stories behind the mystique of Guadalupe, stone-mason man took on the authentic visage of a child instead of that of a battered circus bear.

I told about how Cuauhtlatoatzin's, Don Diego's, story appeared to have been cleaned up by various minds that were supposed to be looking out for Don Diego's and Guadalupe's numinous legacy, but somewhere some made wrong turns into budgets and brio for publicity's sake.

Stone-mason man nodded a weary warrior's nod, and said he understood that kind of sell-out completely, had seen it many times.

HE WANTED TO KNOW, WHAT DID DON DIEGO, CUAUHTLATOATZIN, REALLY LOOK LIKE?

I told him that despite all sell-outs, overwritings, mistakes, and veerings, nonetheless, what undergirds numinous stories is incorrupt. Like the soul, numinous stories can be dented, scorched, dismembered, but they can never be killed. The real story still remains in any heart that has the eyes to see it, the ears to hear it, the guts to strive to shelter it . . . and follow it.

That was when stone-mason man asked what Don Diego really looked like. I wanted to say, "He looked like you, dear soul; he looked exactly like you. Crippled from the illnesses and the beatings, with long memories shredded into blood-red ribbons, yet heartfully alive. He looked just like you."

But I didn't say that. I didn't want to scare away this eagle who'd landed on the porch rail with such trust. I told a different truth instead: That in reality, if one wanted to know what little Don Diego really was like, don't listen to the claptrap about him being "the good Aztec who was converted to Christianity"—that is, at the point of a Spanish hardened-steel Toledo sword.

Instead, look at Holocaust survivors like Elie Wiesel; look into his face, his eyes, his imperfectly-perfect heart, and see the Sorrow of the Ages and the Determination of the Universe inside him. Look at any war survivors still alive today who somehow have not collapsed into insanity, bitterness or unmediated rage from all they endured, who still see the goodness in others and still strive to put an entire soul of a people back together, including everyone—not just one's own tribe—but conquerors and conquered, both and all.

That is Cuauhtlatoatzin. That is Don Diego personified. That is the eagle speaking with eagle-eyed insight. Real of heart, beleaguered, barely escaping with his life. No cleaned-up Indian with a good conduct medal. Instead a vulnerable and venerable heart on earth, who tried, as a result of Guadalupe's appearance to him, to bridge what seemed a cultural chasm of extreme opposites—to bring the souls of the conquered and the souls of the conquerors together in peace, all in one place.

And that gathering place of peace was not in the palaces of the Spanish bishops that were encrusted, both bishops and palaces, with the gold and jewels looted from the tribes. Rather, the ultimate gathering place was on the plain dirt ground of the Hill of Tepeyac— the exact place where the Great Woman appeared to the one considered far beneath the ruling class of the New World. She chose not to appear to gilded men, but to he who represented the people she held dear: the in-some-way abandoned, the in-some-way unloved, the "untouchables."

By then, stone-mason man had bowed his head and did that thing men sometimes do when they feel tears coming up out of their old ancestral graves again. He put on his sunglasses even though we were indoors. He pinched the bridge of his nose as though he was thinking deep thoughts, when in fact, he was weeping inside. Deeply.

And thus the grotto project grew on ancient and modern memories— and tears.

THE HANDS OF THE STONE-MASON

So we went on together he and I, telling story after story: about how the enslaved Nahua people had died at the walls of the churches they had built for their conquerors, how the conquerors ordered the Nahua to tear down their own temples, but leave the stone footers in place and build the new church walls atop those.

We spoke of how the bones of those who died demolishing and rebuilding became part of the cathedral walls themselves. Many a person gazing on those stone vaults would never know that human beings were carelessly interred there. To this, stone-mason man just nodded, saying, "I understand completely."

Meanwhile, the Guadalupe grotto project had grown way beyond "the bathtub concept." That had been left behind on the drafting room/ saloon room floor months earlier. The grotto now had a round water well that stone-mason man called "young Mary's well." It has a resting pond with a little fountain, a shapely flagstone walkway, and a scale duplicate of the original part of the Basilica of Our Lady of Guadalupe in Mexico City. Yes, really.

And yes, the neighbors were gossiping away like chickens disturbed by the mere photograph of a fox. They peered over the wall to see what the crazy people were up to.

But then, another structural problem arose. The little but lead-heavy concrete Guadalupe statue I'd brought to put inside the grotto was too small in comparison to the now much larger arch of the scale-size basilica. So stone-mason man proposed he create a larger Guadalupe, in scale.

"Don't make her bony. Please, could you make her round, like a real woman?" I asked. And dear youngest daughter agreed to sit in hot sun draped with mantle of old blanket to be posed as first model for Our Lady seated.

And so he began with chicken wire over an extravagant armature, then covered that over, as they say in the trades, "giving skin" in a creamy *café y ocre* colored stucco. Over weeks, he fashioned her in our image of her, with flowing wide hips and a beautiful lush bosom, articulate hands and big feet. Perfect round woman.

Stone-mason man's reverence for Guadalupe grew as he worked on her face and hands and feet, sculpting and taking away and adding until he made them all with such love. I overheard him as he whispered to the stones as he laid them, "This is for us, for her." And now as he spoke to her as he created her: "There my dear ... there and there," as he patted the plaster on gently, carving it away with a wooden spatula wherever needed to shape the most shapely shapes.

A softness had come into him. A pride. A willingness to be seen in all his woundedness, a courage to be seen as tender. These were the inward, incontestable changes that began to glow in him outwardly now.

There were material changes too. He began to shave daily. He came to work dragging bucket and metal tools as usual, but now his hair was washed and still wet every morning. For work, he wore his hair long in a braid down his back, or else rolled up at the back of his neck like a samurai. He worked naked from the waist up all through the summer. His back, his arms, his shoulders, his face became as coppery as Our Lady's skin—a hidden shared bloodline that could only be seen after exposure to sunlight.

He used his hands tenderly to build all the intricacies—like the white lilies made of metal for her to hold in her arms. To the flowers, he added little pipes in the blossoms for water to flow through. These were the same hands that years before had carried a rifle in Vietnam and had used that rifle for the horrors of what war rifles are used for—that time of his life being one he could still barely mumble more than a few words about.

Yet those same hands became the very ones that fashioned a little copper dome for Our Lady's grotto. Those hands that had wrapped more around a shot glass or a beer can or a whiskey bottle than around people who could love him truly. With those same hands, this stone-mason transformed a blank piece of earth into a tiny but fine *refugio,* shelter for La Señora, Our Lady.

And I kept feeding him. Food and more food. Stories and more stories.

As she and her grotto came into more magnitude in the small front yard of a nothing tiny blue house in the middle of a neighborhood of much bigger houses overshadowing—so did stone-mason man's heart and soul surface more and more clearly, despite all that had overshadowed him.

And as he worked, Our Lady took greater shape, but more so, in his hands, in his so able and creative hands, she became more and more visible *to him.*

MIRACLE-CITO[3] AT THE GROTTO

There's no other way to say it than just straight out. Less than halfway through the making of the grotto, stone-mason man stopped drinking.

Quit stone cold. Just stopped.

There was no "intervention," no packing him off to rehab (though goodness knows these might have helped greatly long before). I had spoken quietly to him one night about how the broken glass liner in my heart rattled when I saw his great beauty and creativity so deeply marred by his alcoholic haze.

But that only let him know he was loved, noticed, asked after by someone who cared.

It was more than that. Part was certainly his building the grotto, finding passionate devotion to something that mattered more to him than what had, time out of mind, made him into the least of himself—"the lying devil in the bottom of the bottle."

But the rest of how-why, I think, is, as my beloved madwomen in black (our nuns) used to say about the spiritually incomprehensible: "It's a mystery." Perhaps some part of stone-mason man's miraculous right turn away from drinking himself dead was this too: That little house where we built the grotto was literally what used to be called *"a broken-dream house."*

There were very few "broken-dream houses" left on the roads in the neighborhood—tiny houses set back all the way to the alley where the trash cans and incinerators of eld were kept. These alley houses were handmade rather than builder-designed.

Therefore, each one still in existence was wildly idiosyncratic, often with a sleeping porch and no insulation, and the entire house built on a sill plate straight atop the ground without foundation or crawl space.

My little blue broken-dream house was made of cement block, stuccoed over to look kind of like a plain lady with lots of pancake makeup on. This little cottage had ancient black-iron pipe for plumbing, and with no basement, the big, silver, aluminum-painted iron furnace squatted practically right in the living room.

These oddly built little houses were eventually called "broken-dream houses" because their owners long ago had planned to build this tiny one-bedroom-no-garage house, and live in it until enough money could be saved back to build "the big house" out front—usually, a two-bed-room, one-bath, one-story brick bungalow.

But, for some, the money never materialized; the owners fell on rough times, and that dream of the "big house out front" never came to be.

The parallel in all this was not lost on stone-mason man nor on me, that such a beautiful Guadalupe shrine, and also such beauty from stone-mason man's own soul, could surface perhaps only at The House of Broken Dreams. Had the "big house" been built, there'd have been no room for Guadalupe or her grotto. Or stone-mason man's huge bedraggled spirit to find its way home to him again.

Sometimes, emptiness is not vacancy, but rather a long gestation. Gestation by ego's measure is most often too long. But, by soul's measure, the length of the waiting and making within, before what is being created shows on the outside, is ever just right.

THE GROTTO PROJECT THAT WAS TO TAKE ONLY EIGHT WEEKS

Building the grotto stretched and stretched into a year-long project, with daily small details lovingly made, and more and ever-more stories exchanged between stone-mason man and myself. He began calling me "Sis." It was easy to call him "my brother."

Let's just say although the grotto was finally completed in one sense, it is not finished even yet. For who can ever be finished with Our Lady?

We can be finished with the ways of the world, finished with those who want to diminish us, finished with those substances that try to steal our souls, finished with relationships and works that make us smaller rather than expansive—but where would one start in order to be finished with *her*? How would one know one was done-done? When are we old enough to stop being Our Mother's child, to be done with needing "a blessing mother" to hold her hands over our lives?

Never.

This thereby became one of the clearest messages from Guadalupe, La Lupita, during the time my brother and I poured all our scar tissue into making the invisible armatures for the grotto, for our lives. Though her messages could be made fancy or defined by hundred-dollar words—in the end, Guadalupe is the humble, quintessential mother who does not encourage her sons and daughters who have been broken to walk as weaklings in this world.

Rather, she calls for those broken to walk as warriors. For those who are devoted to speak *of her* and *for her* in this world, she asks that they enact her holy heart by unfurling the ancient virtues of strength and sheltering, speaking up, standing up, taking action, and creating works in her name and in that of the God of Love she brought to Earth, and especially, intervening for the sake of goodness and mercy.

It is not by accident that she is called La Conquista, the Mother of the Conquered, for she pours her strength especially into us who have at least once in our lives been deeply stunned and staggered, harmfully shocked and pulled down, painfully intruded upon and left for dead.

Even yet in the midst of all our bandages and broken spirit-bones, she calls us to stop mis-thinking that we stand alone in our challenges, when in fact, she ever stands with us. We ought ever flee to her side, ever hide under her shoulder, ever shelter under her inviolate mantle, ever be guided by her wisdom so hard-won—for she too bore miracles, menacings, and sufferings in her life. She too lost everything precious to her soul in the darkened world of human fools, foibles, and frailties of spirit.

And yet: she still stands, radiant in the light, Vessel of Wisdom Pouring, calling to us to remember that to summon her we need do nothing complex. We need only remember her. We need only call her by the heart-name every human being has set into their very souls before they ever came to earth, that one word each of us knew before we could even feed ourselves, before we could even walk.

The Very First Word inscribed into the hearts of all of humanity across the entire planet:

Ma

Mama

Mami

Madre

Mamo

Mommie

Makuahine

Maji

Majka

Moer

MànaAnya

Móthair

Maman

Máti

Mére

Okaasan

Mutter

Mor

Mari

Motina

Matka

Mother

The Grotto of La Conquista

The Well of Mary

CHAPTER FOUR

In Humble, Helpless Love with Her

Guadalupe Is a
Girl Gang Leader In Heaven

In my family traditions, as in some parts of the Hebrew tradition and in the street-Christian traditions, there is a long legacy of speaking of and to the holy people as though one has a brother–sister relationship with them, rather than a vassal–serf or a lord–subject relationship. There is also the tradition of "received words"—a song, prayer, poem that is sought—and often granted by spiritual means.

This is a resistance prayer-poem at heart, saying in many different ways that others, no matter who they are, are not allowed to define or distort for political reasons, the people's personal experiences with the belovedly holy.

To each soul on earth, Holy Mother appears as each soul can best apprehend her and embrace her, so that each soul is individually invited to be washed in her ferocious and tender compassion, and to be filled to the trembling meniscus with her love.

This is an excerpt of a long chant in praise of Our Lady of Guadalupe.

◀ Ex-voto: "Nuestra Señora de los Cuchillos, Our Lady of the Knives"

GUADALUPE IS A GIRL GANG LEADER IN HEAVEN

Guadalupe, *La nuestra Señora,* Our Holy Mother,
is a girl gang leader in Heaven.

I know for a fact she is Pachuca
and wears the sign of *La loca* on her hand.

Guadalupe is a girl gang leader in Heaven,
this I know for I come from people who eat
with knives—no forks—just knives.

I come from people who sit on curbs to talk—
and stare down cars that want to park there.

I come from people who drag a chair
into the middle of the sidewalk
and sit all day staring straight into the sun
without blinking.
They say this is good medicine for their eyes.

The Virgin Mary is a girl gang leader in Heaven.
She is a Hell's Angel and she rides a Harley.
This I know for I come from people
who think axle grease is holy water.
They hold Mass out in the driveway
under the hood on Saturdays.
The engine is their altar.
They genuflect and say prayers all day,
and baptize themselves in crankcase oil.
The soles of their shoes
always smell like gasoline.
I come from people who think Confession
a necessity only the moment before a head-on collision.

Guadalupe is a girl gang leader in Heaven,
and I know this for certain
because I come from people who
have the kind of *abuelita* who,

when you tell her about the musical *Grease,*
she runs around like a squirrel in snagged stockings
yelling that her grand daughter told her
about this great new movie called *El vaselino.*

I come from the kind of grandfather
whose eyes are a thousand years old,
but his teeth are brand new,
less than two years old those dentures.
They make all his teeth the same length and size.
His face from the nose up is old,
his face from the mouth down is young.

I come from the kind of old people
who can sit on the edge of straight-back chairs
without touching their backs to the slats,
who can sit there without moving for a long time.
They just sit straight-backed and proud
breathing in and out like frail paper bags.

I come from people who in the night,
call the old ones down the dream chute
into our bedrooms so we can hear the old truths.
They tell us that the story the Spaniards told
is a great slander against our people,
that part the foreigners love to tell
about our habit of human sacrifice.
That is false. We have always valued life.

The *conquistadores* mistook our greatest story
about the great spirit warrior who was killed
by those who could not stand his loving radiance.
In the story his heart is cut out and
his murderers threw his body into a *cenote,*
a sacred well.
He died and was burned and then buried.

In the great myth he resurrected three days later,
and as the old ones of the family say,
Who cares what side he was on? He was God.

The Conquerors had no understanding of the God,
known by this "people of God."
And they were so enraged by the "witches"
they thought they saw in the tribal healers,
in the singers and poets,
that they extended their murderous Inquisition
to the New World there and then,
and these foreigners forced
the priests and the storytellers and the old people
up onto the stairs of the stone towers, they forced the
people to kill their own in the most heinous of crimes
against the soul.

And this is what the old ones say, the ones who
were there and come down to tell us the old stories
on *Día de los Muertos.*

I come from people who hunt in the winter for their food,
and are always arrested for poaching.
They try to get arrested together
so they can sit around in jail
telling the old stories,
crying together and singing
at the tops of their lungs.

I come from people who were and are crammed
into immigration and deportation shelters,
sitting there with shivering metal price tags
shot through their earlobes
like the cattle in the slaughter house.
$2,000 dollars to go back or come here,
either way, to the con-man Coyote,
it makes no difference.
He will leave thousands of souls
who cannot read nor write
in the desert
with a gas-station road map made of thin paper,
and one old gallon milk container of water.
The Coyote will not tell you it is 800 miles
through a riverless desert
to Los Angeles.

And yet, many will make it.
Even though it ought not be so.
But the Mojave Desert is said to be
Our Lady's turf, and that desert
is said to bear more miracles per square mile
than most any other place on earth.

I am Mexican by nature, a Magyar,
a Swabian, a Roma by nurture.
And Guadalupe is the one who looks after
fools such as we . . . the crossers of deserts
of many kinds, banging the empty water jug
against our tired legs, staggering, following
to the left of the sunrise, to the right of the sunset,
making out of the little map we were given
a sombrero of blue and red highways
to shelter our heads from the heat.

And in that desert live
some of what the United Statesians
call red-tailed hawks . . . but we know
this is Our Lady of Guadalupe wearing her red dress,
with the black pregnancy belt dotted around her waist . . .
And she shows us that wherever there is fresh dead prey
there is water in that prey.
She shows us a certain kind of flying insect
which knows which cactus is storing a watery slush
at its base.

She shows us wherever there are birds of a certain kind,
there is water . . .
hidden water in the rock bowls far under the mesas . . .
And in following her, our La Señora, we crawl
on our bellies under the low sand ledges, and
we find her hidden water there, drop our faces full into her hand,
and drink deep of her clear, cool bounty . . .

Even with so much against us
we have chances to find our ways out of the desert,
and we most often do find our ways back to life again . . .

by peering to find her and follow her
in all her many disguises:
water, north star, moonlight
through the darkness.

Guadalupe is a girl gang leader in Heaven.
I know for a fact that she is Pachuca
and wears the sign of *La loca* on her hand . . .
Sometimes she drives a four on the floor with a bonnet
and blue dot taillights, prowling the deserts and
the roadways to find souls just like us.

And I pray to her,
I pray to her,
I pray to her, *Mío Dío, Dío Mío,*
because she is the strongest woman I know.

★
"Rise
up!
even
after
bloodshed...
especially
after
bloodshed,"
says
La Conquista,
Our Lady
of the
Conquered

CHAPTER FIVE

Rise Up! Even From Bloodshed, Says La Conquista,
Our Lady of The Conquered

Massacre of the Dreamers: The Maíz Mother

DREAMS: STILL WE SHALL RISE

If one were to cease dreaming bold dreams,
then bold actions on earth would also cease.

Wild dreams are the primary fuel
for the engine of Doing.

Wild dreams are the golden fuse
For the life-force of Being.

If it cannot be dreamt,
it cannot be done.

Rise up!
No pre-empting,

◄ Ex-voto: "Rise Up After Bloodshed"

Rather, seed everywhere,
the most beautiful,
the most wild dreams
roared up by the Soul.

BACKGROUND: MYSTERIOUS ETERNAL
LIFE OF THE MOTHER

This we know: All our ancestors, and sometimes we too in modern times, have lived through an unspeakable, nearly unbearable something: an event so sudden, so destructive it seemed it would annihilate the life-giving force.

Yet still, at the center of a grief-stricken heart, there is ever a golden field—alive, flourishing with enough soul to feed all who come there. This inextinguishable heart of Love protects life-force essence there, even while all else stands in ruins.

We are green plants in this golden field. Despite death of dreams or dreamers, despite bloodshed, the essence in us is protected somehow, nurtured anew by one who cannot be destroyed. The Mother, giver of new life, will be called back to give us life time and again by love and longing for her—and by her love and longing for the people.

The oldest nations, oldest tribal people, have always known Our Lady. They knew her by one or more of her thousands of names.

Thus, in Cholula, in Tlaxcala, and elsewhere in Mexico, still today, live poor farmers who continue to tassel corn by hand, just as their ancestors did for the Mother in centuries previous. They remember Blessed Mother from before the conquest, before savage subjugations were perpetrated upon most all tribal peoples, beginning in 1519.

Farming people considered then, as now, the Life Force in seeds of all kinds—as blessings from the Mother who cares for all, who feeds all.

The people held on to their understandings and memories of the Great Woman, even though those intent on power tried to subvert her mightily.

It happened this way: By 1519, in Spain, Spanish royalty had banned Jews, forcing many to convert to Christianity against their will. Spain had already opened a bloody Inquisition. Now, they financed crews and wooden ships to sail from Europe to *Aztlán,* one of the ancient names for Mexico. Thus, *conquistadores* dragged themselves and their horses through the riptides and onto shore at the beautiful untouched harbors in what is now the Yucatán, Mexico.

Next, by killing unarmed indigenous people, by pitting tribes against one another through deceit, by threatening to starve or kill frightened families if they refused to let their daughters be abducted (and if their sons refused conscription), the conquerors built a patronage to buy loyalty. The armed "soldiers" from "Old World" Europe said they had rights to lay claim to all human beings in the Americas. They would in later histories be called "explorers." But that alone they assuredly were not.

They came with explicit missions to appropriate land, mineral wealth, gold, gems, children, young women, able-bodied tribespeople. Summarily, they carried out terrorisms they deemed effective to take all those, as well as to dishearten the people's souls. All the easier then to enslave these many, favoring the few, but overall capturing, without ransom, every soul.

Invaders called themselves conquistadores, but in reality, they represented only a tiny mercenary group from a hugely compassionate, warm nation of peoples in Spain—where some claimed "noble birth" but most were still serf-like farmers, often living under oppressive local rule themselves.

Yet, conquistadores alone could not have toppled the highly developed cultures of the Americas. The mercenaries were soon joined by waves of clergy and others claiming high social status from Spain, Greece, Italy, and elsewhere in Europe, all saying they thereby had "rights" over those born in the Americas.

In the 1500s, 1600s, and 1700s, hordes of "settlers" rushed to stake out land and slaves in the Americas, claiming to be religious, but seeming not to realize that even the largest, loudest golden crucifix *cannot* hide the dement nor insatiable greed of a grasping heart.

Thus, pretending their vanities were in fact virtues, opportunists pressed down now on the militarily occupied indigenous peoples. This devastation is sometimes still referred to in Mexico as the Mexican Inquisition.

Pressing their religion down over the indigenous people as they had done to Jews in Old World Europe, the invading men and women rolled over the Caribbean islands and Central and South America, setting themselves up to live in kingly sloth—whilst doling out beatings, mutilations, murderous punishments, and claiming native women, children, and men as their chattel.

By using fire, sword, sledgehammer, and defacement (thereby destroying the history, art, cultures of the people), in Mexico as elsewhere, enormous ancient libraries were destroyed on purpose—those carrying the poetry, science, biology, zoology, fertility songs, dances, family stories, war histories, mythos, storehouse counts, weather cycles, astronomy—all the provinces traditionally belonging to Holy Mother. (Only five codexes, out of literally millions of scrolls, managed to survive the conquest: two are facsimiles, and none detail one word about the Mother, nor the Father of Life, nor the Holy Child carried in hearts of *los indios,* the indigenous people, for centuries.)

MOTHER, AN IRONY OF IRONIES

Perhaps it is an unredeemed aspect of human nature to try to dilute and/ or deny wholesale slaughters of humans, destruction of cultures, after the fact. Similar to Holocaust deniers regarding World War II, Armenia, Cambodia, the slaughter of Masurian and Swabian tribes, and what has been done to the Kurds and hundreds of other tribes—there are some today who wish to erase memory of this cold-blooded invasion of the Americas too, thereby attempting to rename evil, "good."

But in our own time, watching the destruction of Zimbabwe by dictator Robert Mugabe, the ruin of Burma by dictator Than Shwe, the horror of colonizations in Haiti by invaders and then abject plunder by dictators Papa Doc, Baby Doc Duvalier and ex-wife Michèle Bennett, seeing in our time other lands and people nearly destroyed utterly—we have had front row seats in our time, witnessing with wide open eyes that it only takes a handful of thugs to overwhelm and harm literally millions.

Thus knowing the reality of the "abject least" of human nature, we clearly witness, in our own times, dictators' predictable terrorist ploys that they use to smash and conquer, their offhanded murders of souls who try to protect truth and innocence, their unopposed greed for lucre and for enslaving human beings. The old stories about the horrific acts and the actual purposes behind the conquest of the Americas must be left standing as a brutal set of stories that are egregious, and true.

Redemption of severe wrongs doesn't come through whitewashing *merde,* excrement, but by lifting up the life-force, lifting it up out of the mud, pain, and blood, so it can truly shine again and be properly and reverently held, no matter what else.

Holy Mother and the Holy People were deposed in the conquest but are regarded in modern churches across the Americas, now with new names, many different from the ancient names. When I came to Cholula in the 1960s, many people there, as elsewhere, recognized the Mother by old names, new names—really by any name, as their beloved

Holy Woman. They knew her because they *know* her, regardless of visage painted on, regardless of moniker.

There is another way the people kept Mother and the Holy People alive in memory in the midst of invasion. Oddly, conquest carries a specific trait in small aggressive groups bent on overwhelming a people: an "edifice-building frenzy" is often unleashed. Invaders attempt to overwrite the standing culture, so the people's iconic ideals are supposedly wiped out, forgotten, and the conquerors' values are the only ones to be seen.

We have observed this in our own time in various countries—most notably with the flurry of building edifices in Germany under Hitler, in Romania under Ceausescu, during post–World War II Soviet Union. In each you see that a small group or one person alone ordered huge demolitions of current cultural ways of life, such as the burning down, damming and flooding, and dismantling of villages, farmlands, and equipment, the carting off and slaughtering of livestock.

These demolitions force huge migrations of agricultural peoples to live in concrete-block high-rises in cities, with no central well or river. Venerable shrines and beautiful forms built by older cultures are pulled down and replaced by those which are considered the "state's" greatest buildings—meant to glorify a narrow idea or person.

Too, invaders in Mexico and the Americas pressed the remaining indigenous people into labor, making them demolish their own holy temples, figurative statues, frescos, and stelae. This included ordering slave laborers to destroy millions of shrines, temples, statuary, and painted figures of the Mother, and the artful representations of her many gifts to all human beings.

Instead, atop those exact sites and ancient holy places, the laborers were ordered often to build the extravagant palaces and buildings to please the invaders—and to create statuary reflecting European faces instead of the faces of the people.

Today, there is a sweet irony to this that must make Blessed Mother gently smile: Under most of the thousands of conquest-era churches in Mexico built by slave labor, one can see church walls soaring, yes. But the roots, the very stones of the foundations—which are often twenty and thirty feet or more high above ground, and yards deep—are the exact same stone foundation walls laid for Mother and her Family, for her temples and shrines.

These stone-walled foundations were laid with beautiful precision for the Nahua Holy People, long before *conquistadores* ever stumbled across the Americas.

Thus, the Mother has, all these centuries since the conquest, remained at the base of hundreds of thousands of churches erected across all the Americas: Holy Mother remains as foundation, as the very root of whatever lies atop her.

Most observers do not realize that long before the conquest, Aztec peoples, Mayas, Inca, all built new pyramids atop older pyramids, a seeming logical engineering tactic for stability of such tall structures.

Except the old people I spoke with at sites revealed that while this also had to do with engineering, the real purpose of building over buildings in the olden days was to give honor to "the feet." In other words, to venerate what the "new" ever stands on, grows from the Holy taproot.

Thus, thousands of conquest churches may be seen as not covering over exactly, but rather as being held up by, embraced by Holy Mother, by her nourishing root.

Perhaps you can imagine the ones who ordered new edifices thinking they were wiping out a culture they deemed alien, while those doing the building were thinking that Our Holy Mother is vast enough, deep enough, to hold this new edifice.

Maybe an ancient indigenous foreman, though a slave himself, convinced a Spanish builder to use the old foundations of the Holy People's temples. Perhaps a Spanish builder agreed, seeing the overt advantage of stability and the ideal underlying—to preserve old values and devotion to Mother and her kin, by building upon her strength.

Regardless, the people of the Americas kept Holy Mother alive in the foundations under the largest edifices, for the people understood, as with a green plant, that what matters most is rootedness; what truly holds up, nourishes and supports all else is underground.

Thus, no matter what or who else tries to occlude her, builds atop her, shuts her behind a wall, she is still here. All who have eyes to see, see her. All who have ears to hear, hear her.

Just as it is blessedly meant to be.

THE OLD MOTHER DREAMS HERSELF EVER NEW

Maybe we dream new dreams just for ourselves. But, for certain, we also dream old dreams, recycle dreams dreamt by others who lived long before we were born. We appear to be eidetically similar to some of our ancestors in this way: Our ancestors' gifts and dreams did not die when their lives were cut away horrifically, or too soon, or even at the end of a long life.

Amongst our people, no matter which tribal groups we come from (and some come from several tribal groups all at once), amongst all far-back people we have, there were dreamers who dreamed the present, past, and future.

The showers of sparks given off by their best dreams and understandings are somehow in us too—in impulses, in sudden inspirations, in that which sometimes seems to flare in us with extra fire for doing and being... and for bringing the soul back from walking only in the land of the dead.

Even though one generation passes from this earth, somehow many of each generation's hopes, ideas, and dreams seem to seek ground in generations following. Even if destroyed or buried, each generation's best ancestral ideals call to us across time, seeping up through the modern ground of our being like some inexhaustible artesian spring that undergirds our existence.

So too with memory of Holy Mother. The old ways and goodnesses knock to be let in, and then can be brought through us, and we can then seek to put them to work in new ways in our own time.

Whatever good we are seeking is also seeking us. Any good we have ever known in our family of humankind, will find us again. The psyche is a universe unto itself in which nothing good is ever truly lost. Any lost or missing parts to the Holy, we will dream again. We will ever dream the Holy anew.

Most everywhere I walked in and around Cholula and its tiny barrios, I was invited into homes that were one room only: three walls with a clean dirt floor. As in many places in the Americas amongst humble people, the fourth wall might be a violently blooming purple jacaranda tree, or a wavering blue mountain in the distance.

In small courtyards during heat of noon, and over *limón*-drenched *comidas,* biggest meal of the day, I learned how devoted many were to Holy Mother. Here she is known, too, by apocryphal and anecdotal narratives that have been handed down in oral tradition for centuries.

Some people still remember Blessed Mother by the name *Xilonen,* sometimes calling her *Santa Xilonen, La Madre del Maíz, Madre Maízeles,* Mother of the Corn Fields, some saying she is their image of La Nuestra Señora de Guadalupe.

Asunción, my sweet little guide to fields and flowers on the land there, told me that *La Morenita* (Our Little Brown Lady) is *La Mujer Grande* (Woman of Magnitude), that she survived the conquest even though so much and so many human beings did not.

As I lay one night in an under-the-tree sleeping room with a leafy star-leaking canopy for a roof, I could hear Asunción and other old women and old men "dreaming out loud," as they called it, or in other words, remembering how "it once was."

One of their stories I loved most was about the bones of Our Lady of Guadalupe walking amongst our people in different barrios, putting on different *trajes típicas,* "costumes," because each neighborhood recognized her image differently.

Thus, in this roadside she wore *ytatls,* scarlet puffs of yarn on either side of her head. In another village down from Cholula, she was veiled against dust storms that came up on new plowed fields where she could often be seen swirling just above the land. In another, she was shorn to show when she was grieving. In another she was completely depilated to show nothing corrupt could cling to her.

Elsewhere she was understood as a child looking to her own mother, another saintly being. In yet another village, she wore rattling turtle-shell belts. In another she was dressed in clematis, climbing buttercup, orangest orange marigolds. In another, she was perpetually pregnant with the tiny One, sometimes called *El Mañuelito,* sometimes called *Niño Jesús,* Child Jesus.

I thought this made sense entirely to soul: Great Woman, Holy Maria, Mer Mother, *La Nuestra Señora, La Mera Mera* (the End-All and Be-All) would in her mercy, appear decorated, gowned, featured as each soul on earth would, could, did, does . . . best understand her out of all her many guises.

Different images, different art. Different people. Dark complected, light eyed, dark eyed, copper skinned, blue eyed, red haired, white skinned, large nosed, little nosed, but one thing constant: her hands, her always generous hands.

Same soul. Same beautiful soul, Our Mother. Same Holy Mother. Same.

IF SHE WERE LOST OVER TIME, WE WOULD DREAM HER UP AGAIN

You know how night dreams sometimes seem to offer arresting information? Yes. It occurs to us all. When we have been traveling or thinking, learning or reading intently during the day, suddenly our night dreams may appear more vivid than usual. It is as if our unconscious chooses some small detail we have been thinking about or seeing with our mind's eyes and then soul dreams the larger view to us, not so we can exactly "know" something beyond the obvious, but so we can remember something important to soul—sometimes one's own soul; sometimes the soul of a beloved; sometimes the souls of family or tribe; and sometimes, perhaps, the soul of the world.

Such a happening occurred as I drove the Pan-American Highway from Denver, Colorado, to the tip of Panama's Darien jungle:

I'd driven long, stopping, staying, moving on. In reality, I had been feeling so sad from weeks of hearing so many old stories, carrying a deep motif of grotesque death by *conquistadores* and by those who came with and after to enslave and occupy.

So, one night, sleeping just at the edge of cornfields outside Cholula, cornfields smelling so sharply green, I dreamt Xilonen's, Maíz Mother's, other name.

I do not know if this was an old name in actuality that dream-maker translated into Spanish, or a new name come to earth, or no-name from the ether. I dreamt Great Woman, Maíz Mother, was also called *Las Sedas,* which would translate as "Silken Hair."

In my dream, I saw how gently Las Sedas wrapped her beautiful moist golden hair completely around each cylinder of corn inside its green leaves. I understood in the dream that her corn-silk hair was soothing to the tender kernels, protecting them. She was keeping the kernels at just the right temperature so they could flourish, instead of burning to death under the fiery sun.

Las Sedas, sweet mother indeed to smallest forms of life. A tender mother who used her silken hair to soothe and protect the juicy, the growing, the innocent, the not-ready-yet fruits, as well as those ready for nourishing harvest.

In a moment's lucidity in the dream, I thought, *It's just like back home.* One of the old grizzled truck farmers where I grew up would let us kids run through his tall cornfields. But, he'd caution us ragamuffins to not peel back any leaves from corn ears, or else that brace of corn would be harmed.

I could see back in time in my dream to cornfields of my childhood—cornstalks wearing their little green coats with yellow silk linings to keep from being burnt by the sun: this being their only protection against turning from sweet and tender to dried out and deadened.

But next in my dream, I saw sweet Xilonen not so sweet, not so easy to look at; rather, in her eyes, some combination of love and a fiery fierceness.

She was holding out her hand to show something. Come closer. In her palm was terrible beauty, a golden kernel of corn dripping with bright red blood.

I could feel my heart leap in pain, in excitement, both. This I began to understand: Somehow, even though enormous fields of maíz plants were destroyed in the fires of conquest—including kernels of living beings who were human and animal, including kernels that were plants and flowers—even though all those were destroyed, as long as there was left one last kernel of corn, that last kernel would be nourished by the very blood of people wrongfully cut down.

This one last kernel of corn was somehow the Mother, an eternal, elemental seed-corn that would lie in dirt and be pushed down by soldiers—yet from her, from this single seed, ten thousand seeds would spring up, and those ten thousand would seed tens of thousands more each. This replication producing new life would never cease.

People would be fed. The people would thrive again. What had been killed would come back in full dancing, waving, flourishing forms.

All this coming from one seed nourished by the blood of the slain.

I awakened barely holding on to what I thought I understood of this dream. We used to have contests at our 4-H fairs for counting seeds. I knew from my rural upbringing that each ear of corn has 700 to 800 kernels, and even the smallest midget corn has at least 400. Imagine what could come from one corn seed taking root, producing at minimum eight ears, or 64,000 seeds of corn, from a single plant in one growing season!

I wouldn't forget the bloody history, what the very dirt carried in Tlaxcala, Cholula, Puebla. Yet in the dream, Mother from time out of mind said that even bloodshed meant to murder everything holy, will nourish this miraculous seed that in turn will nourish the people.

I could somehow see this applied to the broken places in my own life, too. At the same time, I considered what would happen if we could all be a little like Las Sedas, protecting, wrapping with tenderness what is left of ourselves and others after a long travail, even if there is only one pitiful little seed left to us, a seed covered in blood, at that.

How brilliant an attitude it may be to turn from dead ruins at some well-warranted time, and focus on what is left bloodied. I thought Las

Sedas was also showing that the fundament survives even through bloodshed, heartbreak, burning, abandonment, betrayal, being cut down. Like temple foundations upon which conquest churches were built, there will always be the fundament; there will always be the last seed—for it represents Our Mother, The Inextinguishable One.

I prayed on, asking, "Aren't we all people who have been in some time and place, plowed under in one way or another, yet have managed to bear being taken down till there was only one bloody scrap left us? Isn't there a 'Somewhere' in us or near us, where Something rises to shelter the one last seed left to our souls?"

The next day, I told Asunción and her wreath of friends about my dream of *Las Sedas*. They were so quiet, so somber, I thought for a moment I had accidentally offended them, that they were disapproving. That wasn't it. They were stunned. "Who are you?" they asked. "Who are you, really?" And then they proceeded not to even listen to my stuttering as I tried to answer such a difficult simple question. They were already planning a feast day for Las Sedas.

They knew just the right foods: fresh maize cut from the cob with a sharp knife, pomegranate juice, some gentle chocolate, a nice *masa* tamale-like treat made with *Las Sedas'* leaves.

By evening, they had sent me to an *oracionadora*, a prayer-maker, to make a prayer for *La Fiesta de Las Sedas*. The prayer we made ran close to this: "*Santa Sedas,* please help us to take pride and dignity from surviving however our blood has been spilled, to behold the one last seed clearly. Please help us to multiply all goodness, all kindness, all sheltering. Help us to protect *the one last good thing, that all sweetness may grow from one seed into many seeds, helping us all.*"

NOW, TO THE PAST AGAIN,
TO UNDERSTAND MORE ABOUT
THE INDESTRUCTIBILITY OF THE MOTHER

I wondered too, if the one golden seed covered in blood *Las Sedas* held in her palm had survived another bloodshed other than the conquest, one said to have occurred in the heart of what some call pre-conquest Mexico, just as the thug-invaders were landing on Mexico's east coast.

A tragic blood-letting is said to have occurred just before armies from the Old World descended. Night dreams were considered intelligence then. Night dreams, as we see in our time too, can warn, can show how to protect. Night dreams were understood as sent by the Mother and the Holy People, who love their children, of many kinds and hues and pelts. These messages are delivered when the gates to the soul are fully open—in sleep.

This persistent legend refers back to a horrific event unleashed by the Emperor of the Aztec people himself, *el cacique,* the king-emperor, Motecuzoma Xocoyotzin, also known as Moctezuma. The story unrolls this way: The central leader of the Aztecas, in his anguish, harmed the children of the Mother by doing violence to dreams.

Listen . . .

MASSACRE OF THE DREAMERS

Long ago, for as far as one could see on fertile plains, old Mexico's land was covered in green fields of maíz, an ancient breed of corn bursting with energy and strength for the people.

Long ago this wild corn came in colors: gold, red, blue, white, black, sometimes kernels of many colors mixed together under one husk. Sometimes kernels were uniform in shape, sometimes naturally irregular.

Unlike foreign invaders yet to come who would judge native people as "not acceptable," maíz was considered a Great Mother who did not discriminate against, but rather, who loved and fed all her children—who, just like her, came in many sizes, shapes, and colors.

At the time, Mother Maíz was known amongst some ancient Nahua (Aztec) tribes as Xilonen. In holy memory, Xilonen was wife to Tezcatlipoca, icon of Memory. Memory and the Mother were united as a force, beloved by those who knew their stories. One would always *remember* one's Mother; the Mother would always *remember* her children.

Moctezuma, then the sovereign of the greatest city in Mexico, Tenochtitlán, had been hearing rumors about pale-skinned warriors descending fully armed from the east coast of Mexico.

Uncertain what to do or believe, a troubled Moctezuma sent for the tribal dreamers from all the villages across his empire.

Overland from hundreds of miles away came the dreamers, dressed in their belts, bells, leathers, mother-handed linen, feathered capes, their gourds, jade stones, quipis, knotted counting strings, their bark prayer scrolls, their walking sticks, staffs of authority, labrets piercing their lips, their tattooed skin.

These muscled travelers—old, middle-aged, and very young— streamed forth from every valley, every volcano, from every cave with painted bed for healing sufferings, from every stone fortress, from noble family lines, from poorest dusty villages. All carried the mirror of dreams.

Thus came the legions of dreamers to the floating island city of the Mexican empire, Tenochtitlán. They came before a highly interested Moctezuma, and he commanded the dreamers tell him the dreams they had been dreaming—about that most mysterious thing imaginable: The Future.

In *curanderismo,* the ancient healing ways that were constantly weaving in any newly found effective remedies alongside ancient time-tested ones, the "Future" can be understood in dreams as a wide open plain of possibilities. By a preponderance of dream people dreaming similar images repeatedly, it was understood that one trajectory or another might well come to pass—for a family, for a group, for an entire nation.

The tribal dreamers took their callings to dream "for the people of this world" as their serious troth with the holiest of Holy—to care for, educate, and protect the wisdom of souls, just as their Mother had taught them to protect the wisdom of plants and animals.

Tribal dreamers strived to lead lives of right conduct, without rancor or vengeance, so they could remain clear instead of clouded, so they could hear, sense, and see the messages sent between heaven and earth on the mirror of dreams. So they could fulfill their promises to be lucid messengers.

Dreams: this tiny but potent set of doorways. The prayers of dreamers still asked the highest Source that dream-vision be granted to the dreamer, along with a honeyed mouth to speak truth and an immaculate heart to see through—as the heart is considered a great lens of clarity able to hover over the past, present, future, finite, and infinite. And last, thereby the dreamers asked grace to record accurately what possibilities were seen in dreams.

Even though Moctezuma had already heard rumors of immense change bearing down upon the Nahua empire, he is said to have dearly wanted to be told otherwise.

As a ruling elitist, he wished the world he had put together by feast, by threat, by marriages, by war, would never end.

But the tribal dreamers were honest souls. They could not falsely support Moctezuma's fantasy.

The dreamers, instead, remained true to the dreams they had been given from a force greater. It is said they told Moctezuma that they dreamed he—and all Aztlán—would fall, that great fires would explode, huge stones would crash to earth, blood would run, the very soul of Mexico would suffer enormously.

Hearing this, what Moctezuma next ordered to be carried out could perhaps be understood as a horrendous decision by a man in abject fear, heartache, hubris. Not wishing to be deposed, he may have tried to do something no man can do: Pretend to be Creator . . . for he attempted to stop time, to turn time backward.

It is said he schemed how to stop dreamers from dreaming what he didn't want them to dream. That if he could just stop the dreamers from inaugurating preparation for this huge change rolling toward all the tribal groups, he could stop the end of his world as he once knew it.

In the many stories I have heard about this event, to his own end, Moctezuma did the unconscionable in full knowledge.

He ordered the slaughter of all the dreamers.

Moctezuma is said to have walked in a lake of blood amongst the bodies of murdered dreamers, weeping over the loss of "my beautiful dreamers."

But dead they were, lying in their blood like soft brown decorated stones in a bright red river. Dead they remained. He murdered every last dreamer who had spoken his or her dream aloud . . . and the end of an empire was at hand, a far more ruthless world was opening, and the current world as all once knew it would be crushed.

Moctezuma, last leader of many peoples of Mexico, had caused the red blood from every last gentle, innocent dreamer to sink into the sands of the island city. This blood of the dreamers was carried underground far and wide; it is said, it trickled and flowed, carried by rain and rivers for hundreds and thousands of miles.

And not far away in time—not far away in hectares—there advanced on horseback then, men girded in armor made of thick cotton batting overlaid with leathern scales, wearing scabbards holding sword blades made of Toledo steel, with leather saddles squeaking, stirrup buckles jingling. "The strangers," the ones Moctezuma most feared. They advanced from the east regardless.

Relentlessly so.

The massacre of the dreamers caused every village across the empire to lose their dreamer who dreamed not just for themselves, but for the health of the tribe, for everyone.

By killing holy people, Moctezuma helped to silence the living, walking, talking spiritual libraries of the empire.

Entire tribal groups lost their messengers whose lives were dedicated to standing sacerdotally between the mundane world and heaven—in order to deliver images, art, music, songs, ideas, poetry, blessings, care, regard for right conduct, medicines, sweet honey on maíz wafers for prayer.

As in other places and times in our world even now, the leader did not quite realize that by murdering his dreamers he had in fact hastened death to himself and his empire, for there was no one left to dream new life. And there were none who dared to any longer say they were the Mother-dreamers, growing souls with glowing roots straight up from the dream-earth into the real world.

It came to pass: The *conquistadores* arrived in full battle dress. Though Moctezuma offered them gold, repast, treasures of objects and women beyond anything the *conquistadores* could have imagined, the sailor-soldier-thugs feasted, accepted all booty—then cut Moctezuma down where he stood, his head rolling out into the roadway.

The end of the world for many of the tribal people in Mexico had begun in full scourge.

HOLY BLOOD OF THE DREAMERS: MOTHER IS NURTURED BY US, AND NOURISHES US IN RETURN

This legend would seem only bleak if not for the symbol of the blood of the dreamers sinking into the earth, traveling far and wide.

For in generations of Mexicanos forward, still from those bloody fields, a now enslaved tribal people, nonetheless, continued to be strengthened year after year, decade after decade, straight out of the blood in the ground that seeped upward to nurture the *maíz*. The Great Grain Warrior, the Great Woman grain, rose upward again and again.

Though dehumanized, the people who cared for the crops to their maturity still ate of these very crops, fed by the blood of their own holy dreamers.

Moctezuma thought he could kill the Future by killing the dreamers. He would not be the first nor the last dictator to try to do so. *Conquistadores* thought they could kill at will any person who opposed them. Those who came afterward thought they could kill Holy Mother by killing her people's souls.

Little did any realize they could kill everyone in sight, but they could not kill the Mother who was within the most common base food of *los indios,* the seed of life, the simple kernel of corn.

Thereby, it was "the people" who held the real gold, the kind of gold conquistadores could not see, could not pervert, could not steal, did not in fact lust toward, but in fact, overlooked entirely: golden grain, *maíz,* the golden Mother who was now nourished in rain, mixed with bloodshed and mixed with the Mother's tears for her children. Thus Xilonen was not forgotten. The land and the people were conquered. But, the great Mother could not be conquered.

No matter what anyone else did to eradicate her, the people's dreams of her continued at night, even as her images, the very idea of her, were often banned during daylight.

Yet, the plethora of dreams about the Mother continued; they were kept, shared, understood, talked over, learned from. The dreams of the Mother connected people to images they carried long before invaders rode in; that is, they connected to the ancient Immaculate Heart of the World, to the ancient Sacred Heart, both cherished by the people as ultimate Hearts of Inestimable Holiness.

From the very ground, she and her dreamers kept returning to the people. She kept coming back and coming back to the people again and again, multiplying herself again and again, season after season to show her abiding and nourishing love—just like a protective and visionary dream returns over and over again in order to inoculate us with strength.

There is hardly a person alive on earth now who has not eaten the *maíz* of the martyrs, the *maíz* of the Mother from any war-ravaged nation, for corn since far ancient times has been cultivated in every land on earth with the exception of Antarctica, and perhaps even there before an Ice Age shift long ago.

Thus, all of us who have eaten from the golden crop that has been nourished by innocent blood spilt into earth might sometimes be called to dream for others besides ourselves: to see good and not so good; to dream ideas, help, ways in, ways out, hopes that can nourish people; to prepare them for the future and, most of all, to sustain their souls—come what may.

Perhaps it was this legend, the Massacre of the Dreamers, arising during and in post-Cortez Mexico that gave rise to one of those who ate the golden grain, one of the first thousands of new dreamers to surface after decades of war and destruction—and that is little Santo Don Diego, his real name being Cuauhtlatoatzin, also known as Cuauhtemoc, Speaking Eagle.

He was one who dreamed himself past Tepeyac Hill, where once stood the temple of Holy Mother called by the name Tonantzin, meaning amongst many other names "Honored Grandmother," "Life-root of Maíz," and "Mother of the Corn," "Seven Flowers," "Mother of Precious Stones."

There, on the exact same hill, Don Diego Cuauhtemoc saw a new idea, a new apparition of the Great Woman, one who named herself to him as Guadalupe. He said she drew him to her by a sweet scent, and upon coming closer he saw flowers blooming, and precious gems in the earth glowing near her. And her voice and words were beautiful.

Some say the Mother dreamed herself toward her people so hard, she could actually be seen by a gentle little brown man, a survivor who had been subjugated yet rose up again, one who himself had been eating the golden grain that grew from the very flesh of the dreamers, the martyrs, flowing into and burnishing the beautifully colored flesh of Holiest Mother.

THIS WOULD BE US TOO

Just as our Mother,
Mother Maíz has shown us
the way to come back:
Plant
just
one
seed.
We do know how to plant

whatever small seed is left of us . . .
for we are the children of the dreamers,
we are the children of the martyrs,
we are the children of our Mother, forever.
We are the one last seed
covered in blood . . .
we will ever rise up
and live again . . .
ever find ways
to multiply,
to thrive,
to live again on earth,
whilst spinning through the heavens . . .
in the arms of our Mother.

Memorare

Because...
She cannot be harmed,
for She and the Divine Child
are Eternal...

Because...
she is certain
about the Divinity of her own Child
and the absolute imperishability
of her Child's teachings...

She ever and immediately, moves
~through us~
to protect every child on earth...

CHAPTER SIX

"Shirt of Arrows:" She Teaches Protection of the Vulnerable: No Exceptions

The *Memorare,* Remember!

The Old Country bow-makers and huntsmen of my father's and grandfathers' time had rough hands from hard labor, and strong, gruff voices for calling to each other and to the horses across bluffs and fields. Their voices were tempered by cigars or fiery home-made wine or ancient prayers—often two or more of those in combination.

The men repeated their wisdom stories to one another and to the young, time and again. As skilled hunters, they believed there were several immortals that could never be killed by arrows: amongst them, the white stag, the Heart of Creator, and a parent's love for their child.

Too, the old men had a saying about an idea or a person who had been wrongfully reviled by skeptics. About such a person they would say with admiration: "They wear the shirt of arrows."

This meant that when one had been assailed by whomever or whatever, no matter how or why, the eternal soul could not be touched. The soul continued to live fully alive while bearing up—even beneath a shirt shot full of lacerating shafts and vanes.

"Shirt of arrows" was considered an honorific, an honorable armor: whatever is immortal cannot be harmed by puny mortals, no matter how loud, no matter how insistent, no matter how bitter or one-sided or power-mad.

◄ "Our Lady, Shirt of Arrows:
   She teaches protection of the vulnerable—no exceptions."

So too the Great Woman who is the Protectress of all children. She too from her narrow escapes from the blindness, harassments, and assaults of her time—not only against her, but against her Child—she knows. *La que sabe,* she is the One Who Knows. She too wears the shirt of arrows.

MEMORARE, THE ANCIENT PRAYER
TO THE MOTHER OF RADIANT LOVE:
BACKGROUND

We have been handed down a prayer, an ancient prayer that so remarkably continues to resonate with human sensibilities over literally millennia of time and places and peoples. Unlike faddish speech, this prayer carries such understanding of the deeper needs of the soul, this prayer is so without scorn for human frailties and foibles, so generous with warm embrace to all, that it can never go out of fashion. I trust that warrior souls will continue to keep it alive for thousands and thousands of years more.

This prayer is a cry to Blessed Mother during any time when arrows of harm fly toward us, at her, at the teachings and actions of eternal Love that we follow and literally strive to enact in this world. We who were taught this beautiful prayer in childhood know it as our signal with all our hearts to Holy Mother that we are fleeing from great danger, and that as we fly toward her, we believe that our cry to be protected and given aid—by human and by otherworldly means—will be heard.

As children, we understood that once we gave this mortal cry we could, in full confidence, expect that spiritual and human aid would somehow come to us to staunch our bleeding, mend up our frightened hearts, stalwartly protect us in palpable ways, and stand between us and the unjust.

UNLEASHING THIS SO SMALL PRAYER
"THAT SAYS IT ALL," AND YET . . .

I have practically prayed the paint off the walls during times of greatest travails and sufferings in my life—and in service of the lives of others who struggle so, persons known to me, and complete strangers whom I sense somewhere in the world are pleading for succor and strength. The older I become, the more I sense, the less I speak, the more I pray—in ever so many ways.

Yet, I will not mislead you. Despite the fact that aid always, always, *always* came from *stabat mater,* "the mother who will never abandon her post," despite Our Mother ever standing with us to help us and "to help us help" the poor and those kicked to the side of the road, despite the fact that spiritual aid came to us to help us protect the true beauties and regal bearing of nature, of our souls, of the beautiful boons of our corporeal world—sometimes actual humans failed us. Their help, their giving of unequivocal protection, did not arrive with substance. Instead of being witnesses and helpers, they turned away, or else offered as remedy nothing more than dust.

Perhaps this phenomenon occurs because we as a human race are still under-formed, unawakened, too clever by half in trying to "position" ourselves over others, not knowing the clear bright line between hallowed love for others as opposed to hollow love.

Although we live in the twenty-first century, perhaps we are still in pre-diluvian times, living in some dark pocket of the brain, wherein, as in the beginning of the parable of the Good Samaritan, the travelers and prelates coldly turn their backs and cross to the other side of the road to avoid the half-slain and beaten soul lying bleeding in the ravine. That ancient story tells the chilling choice to leave to die "those of a tribe not one's own"—to leave the injured to flounder and battle alone.

Perhaps we still all carry too much of an old, unexamined animal trait wherein, without thought or investigation, presumed alpha creatures of a herd separate themselves from the injured ones—because the "upper echelon of creatures," for whatever odd reason, holds those in need as "lower" or "less" or "dangerous to the pecking order," in some significant way.

Perhaps this is why too, when humans rise above that base instinct to only preserve self and "like kind" in a hierarchy, and instead make merciful responses and interventions—irrevocably bending to mend, defend, and protect the vulnerable, or carrying them forward to safety as did the traveler from Samaria—then such awakened hearts and souls seem all the more miraculous and ever so highly evolved in undertaking the soul's true work on earth. To be awake to the living, breathing souls of others, all souls—not always first and foremost to one's small herd, not to the culture of the moment with its stale political metabolism, but to the living soul in need of comfort, strength, and sturdy sheltering.

Yet, though humans fail one another sometimes still, nonetheless, the cry of this prayer pours out into the universe, calling for full consciousness and full effect for those injured. The belief underlying this prayer is that if one is of *esperanza y fé*, hope and faith, true expectation that good will come, and if we pray this prayer, cry this cry, plead this pleading regardless (not as pathetic cringing creatures, but as those who thunder after injustice), then there will be effect, and in good ways by and from other human beings. Even though the call is a cry for succor from the Mother, as much it is also a sincere cry that all persons surrounding be pierced awake, too.

THE ANCIENT PRAYER HERSELF

In Old Latin, this prayer is meant to break the heart . . . open. It's a cry for help, praise of our Mother exemplar: act of faith that we can remain alive in the mundane world and in the mystery, both. The prayer calls all to awaken to acting like, thinking like, loving like Holy Mother does—with fullest awareness, fullest anticipation, far fuller insight, far more full will to act to help the soul, in as brilliant and effective human proportion as we can muster. To have far less coldness, far more warmth toward self and others, far more insight, far less blindness to what truly matters to heaven. The prayer is called the *Memorare,* and it means *Remember!* It goes like this:

MEMORARE

Remember, O most gracious Virgin Mary, that never was it known that anyone who fled to thy protection, implored thy help, or sought thy intercession was left unaided. Inspired with this confidence, I fly to thee, O Virgin of virgins, my Mother; to thee do I come; before thee I stand, sinful and sorrowful. O Mother of the Word Incarnate, despise not my petitions, but in thy mercy hear and answer me.
Amen.

This word *Memorare,* chosen as the first word in the first line of the prayer, doesn't mean turn back and make some vapid recall, be of fluffy sentiment. It's not a weak effort to remember.

No, this *Memorare* means *Remember! Wake up!* It is a command *from* the soul to remember who you are and what powers have been born into you; that you are the son, the daughter, of Blessed Mother. This *Memorare* is a demand to call upon she who would give her life for a child; she who teaches, helps, intercedes for the child-spirit; she who clearly calls those who have the ears to hear and the eyes to see the child's need and gifts, and the child's travails—and the interventions needed in the child's behalf, as soon as possible, from powers greater in both the human and angelic forms and for the long term. Both.

Even as the Great Woman wears "the shirt of arrows" slammed onto her by the ridiculing, the scorning, the opprobrium of the overculture for her relentless stance in protecting all the vulnerable souls of the earth—she continues nonetheless to shelter and to intercede for the spirit of the child in all souls, of any age.

She cannot be harmed. What she stands for cannot be harmed. What her divine Child's teachings are, cannot be harmed. It is a stye in the eye of those who think they must move against one or the other in order to protect her. She needs no protection. She is eternal.

Who needs protection, who will ever need protection and justice, are the souls of her earthly, vulnerable children, regardless of their number of years lived. The Great Woman's own Child said it free and clear: *Whatever you do to the least of us, you do to Me.*

In this way, the Mother who wears "the shirt of arrows" teaches us that all souls belong under the armor of her starry mantle, cradled beside her precious Little Child. She takes on the protection of *all.*

So, despite human failings, our own and/or others', we continue to chant the *Memorare* so that all—the sighted and the semi-sighted and the not-yet-sighted, the hearing and the not hearing, the heartful and the not heartless perhaps but rather more accurately the not-yet-heartful—will all be aided in ways that can support them, and us, to be made whole again. All are understood as worthy of understanding and mercy. With Blessed Mother, no one is left out.

GRACE NOTES ABOUT THIS
ANCIENT CRY TO HOLY MOTHER

Here also is the prayer in old-style Latin:

MEMORARE

Memorare, O piissima Virgo Maria, non esse auditum a saeculo, quemquam ad tua currentem praesidia, tua implorantem auxilia, tua petentem suffragia, esse derelictum. Ego tali animatus confidentia, ad te, Virgo Virginum, Mater, curro, ad te venio, coram te gemens peccator assisto. Noli, Mater Verbi, verba mea despicere; sed audi propitia et exaudi.
Amen.

Memorare, in Latin, means not just to vaguely remember, but to know her *by heart,* to call out *by heart,* to center oneself in remembering the spirit of the human child and the Mater Magna . . . *by heart.*

This is not a cry to Blessed Mother to remember us, but a dictate to ourselves that we remember her—her invincibility, her steadfastness for us, her protective warrior qualities toward children, toward the souls in any of us who say we follow her in mind, idea, and deed . . . she being and having proven herself day in and day out as the ultimate protectress of those who have no guardian against intrusions, scorn, harms, and exploitations.

"Remember!" means we strive to be like her, for she has only these extreme purposes in life: to guard and accompany and stand by and stand with the Divinity Child, and those on earth who are also her children, no matter how old, no matter how young. She remains as listening heart, trusted advisor, healing balm, holder of the just standards of the soul, ever acting as protectress of those assailed.

In Latin, this prayer calls Holy Mother *Virgo.* This does not mean she is merely maidenly in some vague form, but she embodies the quality of *virgultum,* the supple mind and form found in the branches of the young trees that ever protect the leaders, the central trunks of the trees.

The supple virgultum is able to bend without breaking, to bend to guard, and to snap back to able mind and Creator-given shape again, no matter what. We carry this quality too: Our Lady virgultum carries a vast presence, we carry the same in human proportion—the ability to bend to guard, and to snap back, *to remember* our original soul shapes.

Auditum here refers to the idea that "never was it heard" that the Mother, nor those who strive to carry her protective essence dear, would fail to answer the needful. But also the word *audit,* in another sense, given this prayer, is a plea to first be heard and second to be helped and protected. Not just asking to be listened to, but also to be weighed, auditioned, listened to for purity of tone, clarity of cry, and in a larger sense daring to ask protection as birthright. *Audeo audere ausus sum,* to be bold to bring oneself for help, expecting fully to receive it—Mother Mary is the mother of the quintessential Child of Love who also needed protection from robbers, exploiters, and other spiritual harms. Mother Mary is the quintessential guardian of the soul filled with nearly helpless love for all goodness.

Her hard-won experience as Holy Mother protecting the Child of Love is our experience as little mothers to vulnerabilities within ourselves and within others, and especially to those found in the naïve, frightened, inexperienced, unable child-spirits of others.

In this way, because of our troth with her, we learn to be protective mothers in timely ways, like her too, only in human form.

Saeculum, related to *saeculo,* means "never in our time" has she refused us, never in the *zeitgeist,* the spirit of the age, as far back as our little minds can strain to imagine our earliest life. Never has Holy Mother failed to carry the banner to protect the vulnerable; in fact, she carries *suffragia—suffragatio,* that is, she ever votes in favor of us, in support of us, as though we are running for office and hers is the only vote that counts. That she stands *for* us as precious worthy souls is undebatable.

About the word sin, *peccatum* in Latin, which means to make a mistake, e.g., one of judgment, or to err, take the wrong path via an accident of perception or, as often occurs, by choice: "Sin" is anything that takes a person away from the radiant principles at the center of the soul. Without those at center—what many of us call "Creator"—we are bereft in a sense, having lost our radar and sonar about how to proceed as a soul in a world that is tricky, because things are not always as they seem on the surface. Not being perfected beings, we can fall into an off-center state—by our own will perhaps, but more often having naïvely been persuaded or seduced away from Infinite Love into something falsified, something that crookedly seats us in something far less than eternal in fundament, and much more ego-narrowed and clever.

So here, in the cry to Holy Mother, one stands thrown off-center, and filled with sorrow—sorrow, meaning to feel deep distress, as a great ship listing sideways, bow broken open, taking on water. Sorrow and sin are not curses, not referendums presuming a defect of a soul. They are instead signals that a soul is hurting and needs lifting up, re-arighting. They mean this soul who came to these injuries in whatever way, is in need of care, cleansing, and aid. By way of simple sacred rite, and most of all in loving reassertion of the consciousness with "Source without source," the soul is reset like a jewel into center again. Healing and rebalancing can occur then—from those in heaven, and into and through those on earth. Not either/or, but all.

Curro, in the *Memorare* prayer chant, means to care for, to pay attention to, to trouble oneself with, and for this injured soul until the situation is solved, until the frightened and harmed one, the so-deeply suffering soul, is recovered. It means to see that a complete solution is understood spiritually and concretely, and is applied until wholeness is restored.

BACKGROUND TO THE RISE OF THE *MEMORARE*:
BLESSED MOTHER AS THE
"FRIEND TO THE FRIENDLESS ONE"

One might wonder why and how a prayer could stay alive with its essence intact in various forms for nearly a thousand years, and perhaps more. The *Memorare* likely came into being during times of great duress for children, women, and men who were unprotected by either or any side during sudden terrorizings and wars waged by kings, popes, sultans, chiefs, and tribal headsmen.

Parts of the *Memorare* are said to have been recorded by Bernard de Clairvaux, a French monk, whose writings date back to 1120 AD. The *Memorare* is further said to have been spread by another monk, also named Bernard, Father Claude Bernard, who lived in the 1600s and ministered to those falsely accused and imprisoned. In that broad application by Bernard, by my sights, the *Memorare* held Holy Mother as the "friend to the friendless one," the loyal and ever-awake true friend of the soul.

Also in those long-ago times when *Memorare* was being pulled together in the oral tradition and in scribing, indigenous tribal groups throughout Asia, and over the European Urals, the Carpathians and the Alps were being coerced by various political factions, warlord federations, brute kings and popes to unsaddle their fine horses and to instead, settle into agrarian farm work in serf/landlord-like relationships—in effect pressed into becoming a slave labor force of weather-strengthened men, women, and children for the wealthy and privileged. For many of the people of the fields and forests, there was no choice: it was either submit to a new order or be slaughtered.

Too, the crusades were launched—nine wars and counter-wars unleashed, causing death to a huge portion of the world's population.

At the turn of the millennium, the year 1000 AD, as bits of the *Memorare* were being committed to pages, there was also a belief held by many, and rumor spread by many more, that the end of the world was at hand. This fantasy prevailed in the minds of many people for decades on either side of the turn of that century.

Together, all these factors made for such suffering for the people of earth. And this is the foreground in which the *Memorare* sprang upward like a rose out of stones—a prayer that promised that the radiant principles of protection and love still existed, even in the midst of so much fear and unwarranted bloodshed.

THE RHYTHM OF THE AGES IN THE *MEMORARE*

You can hear it, if you cry the words of the *Memorare* aloud, that it is not "just a prayer"; it is an incantation, meaning it is literally meant to be sung out. There is a strong musical cadence to the Latin words, to any language the *Memorare* is translated into, a sound that is far more reminiscent of sandstorms, stirrups nodding, wooden saddles squeaking. It carries a rhythm that is far more reminiscent of the trot and the gallop, the sway of tent curtains, the sound of those fleeing, than of someone walking flat-footed in and out of buildings undisturbed.

Thus, *Memorare* is a prayer for rough times, to one who knows rough times by heart, a cry to the one who wears the shirt of arrows, the one who carries in her arms the eternal Child, the one who has a heart radiant with courage first and foremost . . . and Love, equally so.

We learn as much, as much by who comes to our aid as by who does not. We learn that we can remain alert and true with and within Holy Mother. We can strive to fly to help others in their travails, sometimes so that as others within our reach might never again suffer the agonistas we ourselves suffered. Even though we may have lain unaided by the side of the road ourselves, even though we too may have earned the shirt of arrows (that is, we have been wounded over and over, and still find our ways through the violet light that shines from the wound), then, like Our Lady, we become even more deeply insightful, more awakened, more strengthened in our own sacred heart, more filled with understanding and with love—whenever we can, however we can, for whomsoever we can.

SHIRT OF ARROWS

Blessed Mother wears her shirt of arrows . . .
to show she cannot be harmed,
for She and the Divine Child are Eternal . . .

And, because she is certain
about the Divinity of her own Child,
and the absolute imperishability
of her Child's teachings . . .
she ever and immediately, moves
—through us—

to protect every child on earth . . .
and without exception.

May we strive to See ourselves and others . . . as she sees us . . .
Hear ourselves and others . . . as she hears us . . .
Speak with ourselves and with others . . . as she speaks to us . . .
Shelter our souls and those of others . . . as she shelters us . . .
Love our souls and the souls of others . . . as she loves us . . .
forever and always.
Aymen.
Aymen.
Aymen.

(And a little woman . . .)[1]

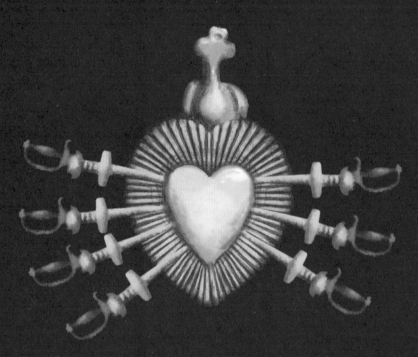

...It is said by the old women of the family,
that the hilts of the swords piercing Our Lady's heart...
are shaped like the curling sepals which protect the buds
of roses... that with prayer and time, each sword hilt
will burst into seven fragrant roses, blooming again and
again, because suffering brings the rain of tears,
because the rain of tears waters the earth,
because moisture on dry earth of our being
is guaranteed to bring forth new life.

Tears are a river that take you somewhere...
somewhere better, somewhere good

CHAPTER SEVEN

The Uses of Broken-Heartedness:
Mater Dolorosa *Ever Bends Near*

The Use of the Seven Swords Through The Heart

MATER DOLOROSA: THE UNRUINED HEART[1]

The swords through your heart
are not the ones which caused your wounds,
but rather, these mighty swords of Strength,
were earned by your struggles through hard times.
Sword of Surrender: to withstand this time of learning.
Sword of Veils: to pierce the hidden meanings of this time.
Sword of Healing: to lance one's own agony, bitterness.
Sword of New Life: to cut through, cut loose, plant anew.
Sword of Courage: to speak up, row on, touch others.
Sword of Life Force: to draw from, lean on, purify.
Sword of Love: often heaviest to lift consistently;
turns one away from war, to instead,
fall into the arms of Immaculate Strength.

O Immaculate Heart of My Mother,
give me shelter in the beautiful chambers of your heart.
Keep me strong, fierce, loving, and able in this world.
Remind me daily, that despite my imperfections,
my heart remains,
completely unruined.

◀ Ex-voto: "Definition of Strength: Pierced But Fierce"

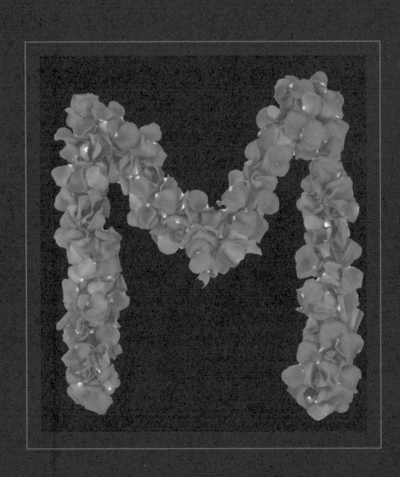

CHAPTER EIGHT

Many Kinds of Prisons: The Last Woman Standing

"Our Lady Behind the Wall"

T here is a great earthquake of heart and soul when a mother is sent to prison by a sometimes "unjust-justice" system and she is thereby separated from her loved children.

There is also the same kind of heartbreak and earth shaking under one's entire life when beloved children are sent to prison, and thereby separated from their loving and helpless mothers and fathers, brothers, sisters, and friends.

When a family member is sent to prison, the entire family and all loved ones are in some way sent to prison also. Thus all are set onto the rough road. For as long as the prison sentence runs, the hearts, minds and souls of those who love one another are all in prison together—and all on pilgrimage together.

Yet often too, strange angels step from the side of the road to give moments of succor enough for the imprisoned to go on for miles more. This cohort of souls will make it through. They will hold their heads up even when their hearts are down. Our Lady walks with all. Our Lady forgets no one, even if she cannot be seen. She is there protecting and loving all. She has the words that matter most to the forlorn soul: *I will stay with you.*

Being imprisoned, even though the sight and touch of one another is missing for long periods of time as visiting relatives to the prison often

◀ "This M Stands For Mother Who Leaps Over the Walls of the Worlds"

have only a burnt-out car, money gone for rent instead of train ticket, and loved ones incarcerated, are often, inexplicably, sent to prisons hundreds of miles away from the comfort and support for better life via their own loving families. Sometimes the loved one is moved from prison to prison, as though depriving a person of a resting place, a corner to call their own, harassing those incarcerated with double-speak, forcing them to ever try to adapt to new faces, different rules, odd food—is meant as disheartening punishment too, rather than a time of thoughtful work and witness.

Yet even in this hardship for all, the soul is *the* one who loves and loves and loves, without waning. As does La Señora, Our Lady. The soul is the one who does not diminish in longing for the loved one. Neither does Our Lady lessen her attentions. The loyal souls are those who vow to visit their loved one, give comfort and remain near, forever. Our Lady is the leader in this: she will give all support, lend them her breath when their breath is taken from them, offer her medicine of love and understanding when they are hurt.

And so it is—this prayer to Our Lady, who more than understands what it is to see her loved one, her beautiful Child beaten down, tortured, judged unfairly, and harmed. Yet, Blessed Mother also stayed with her Child. Throughout it all, like the mothers and fathers of prisoners across the world, like the children of parents in prison across the world, like the brothers, sisters, friends of those "held away"—Blessed Mother remained by the side of her suffering loved One. Too, Holy Mother stands by the side of all held prisoner, by whatever means, as well. Holy Mother is here to help calm the heart so all can proceed in greatest strength.

THE COUNTING PRAYER:
FOR THOSE WHO LOVE
AN IMPRISONED SOUL

Holy Mother:
Hurt, I am hurt
by my own, and
for my own.

Dearest Mother
please place your

calming hand over my hand
atop my frightened heart.

Count with me
My Lady, slowly count
1 ... 2 ... 3 ... and ... 4,
1 ... 2 ... 3 ... and ... 4,

until my heart slows
to the same steady
rhythm as your own
Immaculate Heart.

Your sweet serene Heart
is bedecked with white
flowers despite any sorrow.
Let me learn from you.

Let me be like you dear Mother.
Remind me, that my heart is calmed,
not by remembering the travails,
but by remembering the Love.

Help me to walk calmly
as you did:
scarred and yet strong,
as you did.

This is my wish
for my own soul,
and for the soul
of my loved one imprisoned.

With you, we all walk free.
With you, there are no iron bars, no walls,
no hopelessness of any kind ...
only Love, and more Love.

Dearest Mother
please place your

calming hand over my hand
atop my frightened heart.
Count with me
My Lady, slowly count
with me please . . .
Synchronize my heartbeat to yours
1 . . . 2 . . . 3 . . . and . . . 4,
1 . . . 2 . . . 3 . . . and . . . 4 . . .

Aymen, aymen, aymen.
Let it be so, may it be so, let it be so.
Please match my heartbeat to yours
1 . . . 2 . . . 3 . . . and . . . 4,
1 . . . 2 . . . 3 . . . and . . . 4 . . .

ONE CASE OF OUR LADY
IMPRISONED, LOST, AND THEN FREED

Over the centuries, not only innocents and the poor, the unlearned and the Just, the leaders of a new life, not only those who had made not-lethal errors but were locked away anyway, but also images of Holy Mother have been assaulted and shut behind bars and walls too.

This occlusion and imprisonment of Holy Mother's images, occurred in every nation invaded or occupied by dictators—in ancient and modern lands that are now known as the Czech Republic, Slovakia, Hungary, France, Romania, Russia, entire landmasses of The Middle and Near East, all of Asia, Africa, the Island nations, the mountain nations, the ocean nations, the North Countries. Anywhere there were people and land, the icons and artworks of Holy Mother were either desecrated, covered over, nailed into walls, slashed, damaged on purpose, toppled, torn down, outlawed by dictators.

Sometimes icons of Blessed Mother were hidden within walls to seemingly save the holy images from vandals, as some of the old Polish immigrant women I knew as a child, would tell me about Our Lady of Częstochowa. There was much speculation about the beautiful icon of Our Lady of Częstochowa, a painting with a complexion like dark honey. Her cheek was said to have been slashed by a Hussite swordsman in ancient times. He is said to have been trying to gallop away with her image in its gilded frame. But, his horse suddenly was rooted to the ground and refused to move. So the soldier threw the icon of

Holy Mother and her Child to the ground and slashed at it angrily with his sword.

Some say her injured image was then spirited away to where, no one exactly knows. Some say that someone enclosed her behind a wall, or hung her icon by ropes down inside a well. In any case, whatever her sojourn was underground in one kind of "prison" or another—and whether this "hiding" was done by those who reviled her image, or by those who wanted to honor the holy force that stands behind her image—we are not certain. But, there are many versions of stories about her centuries of mysterious "traveling" amongst the rural people.

And so, time passed. All the old Babcias and Dziadzias, old grand-mothers and grandfathers, leaned forward and whispered to me: that her beautiful icon was suddenly and miraculously discovered by holy people. Thus, in the case of Our Lady of Częstochowa, scarred across her cheek by a sword blade, and some say injured by an arrow through her throat also, her image is now protected in a shrine in the city of her name. In the mid-seventeenth century she was named by King Casimir to hold central place as Blessed Mother of all of Poland.

About Our Lady of Częstochowa, the same old Polish grandmoth-ers also said, in the mythology of the times back then, those who did destruction to sacred icons anywhere, often suffered themselves similar kinds of destruction to whatever they themselves held dear also, includ-ing their very lives.

Such old superstitions appear to be legend rather than verifiable truths, but you know how "talking spooky" is sometimes considered "duty" by the very old women, in order to teach certain "family values." Thus, the old Babcias told stories that the soldier who slashed the painting of Our Lady of Częstochowa, died by falling from a parapet onto the sharp iron gates of a castle—for he had "offended iron" by using it to do harm to a holy image.

They said that those who set gun-powder to destroy a certain statu-ary of the Holy Woman carved into a hill of rock, eventually suffered from being crushed, for they had "made enemies of the rock."

The old country stories of Europe, as in the Mejicano stories about scary La Llorona looking for others to drown, were used to warn children away from the rivers, and men away from perfidy. So too, the "eye for an eye" legends of many an old country teller stand as a way to hand down intelligent cautions to the next generation: That no one ought dare desecrate what others hold sacred—whether the sacred be innocent people, naïve children, humble travelers, or holy images . . . just in case "what you do unto others will also be done unto you."

UNUSUAL CORRESPONDING FACTORS: "ERASING THE HOLY," WHETHER IN AN ENTIRE NATION OR IN A SINGLE CHILD OR ADULT, FOLLOWS THE SAME TRAJECTORY . . . AND THERE ARE SIMILAR PATHWAYS FOR HEALING THE WOUNDS OF SUCH.

As a child of immigrants and refugees, I grew up with all my large families' woundings, longings, callings out in grief and hope during the post-WWII decades. They were dear and harsh and sweet and deeply wounded people. Their effects on my heart and soul went deep. I'd like to offer you a small psychological window thereby, keeping in mind for you that ever so oddly, and egregiously, the same ways to eradicate Holy Mother from a people, are also the same strategies used to abuse a child; that is: to strip them of the interior concept of the sacred Mother and replace it instead with the concept of "monsters everywhere" and "peace at any price."

Enacting such abuse, effectively guts the self and shocks the soul. This keeps a person from speaking from true self and true soul, until they can restore the holy interior essence to their lives again. In my clinical experience, this often means relearning that they are a precious one-of-a-kind soul with a destiny to live and create, that they've been born with a blessing over their head, not a sword hanging over their head. That rather than maintaining through fear, a deleterious interior mother-self intact . . . rather a mother-voice that tells one's destiny: I ought not to live and cringe, but to live and create anew daily, freely.

May you see too, the pathways to freedom, repair and full life again, whether as a culture, as a person who has lived a devastation of war and fight for your life, or whether the culture, the group, or the person has been walking-wounded by other means. The wounds of war and abuse are similar, and the healing is similar: the restoration of the healing and the Holy in whatever ways you best understand these, is also so very similar.

One can heal by literally making a list of all freedoms denied, and then working backward, taking back all freedoms thwarted, especially those that bring goodness to self and the world back into one's consciousness, re-setting all action and thought in the holy center, including the right to act, move, create, be, thrive fully. These recreate in the central psyche of a nation and a person an ever stronger memory of the Merciful Mother who is no pansy, but rather fierce and active in behalf of love, peace and honor.

Here are central steps to destruction of Holy ideas and images and the sacred forces they represent. This violent and purposeful erasure of the Holy held dear by the people has been rampant throughout the world for centuries, for somehow the invaders sense that even though for many the essence of the sacred and holy often appears to be invisible, the soul of the culture, the souls of the people can often feel the holy palpably, and that this hidden psychic, spiritual, religious, psychological, and embodied force greatly sustains souls through challenges, travails, and revolution. Invaders say all the more reason to destroy those holy aspects that people are strengthened by and hold intrinsically dear.

Let us see how Holy Mother has been attacked as idea, concept and reality, keeping in mind "marauding" and destruction can be ordered to crush an innocent, vulnerable and naïve people by the say-so of a single individual, or a small group, or a huge army. These are some of the central ways this has been done time out of mind:

- These interests and senses of the holy are often the first to be attacked by marauders bent on harming the spiritedness of the people, and thereby the diminishing of sense of "true self" in each human being.

- As I research historic attempts by invaders-marauders to "erase Our Lady" it appears to me that the invaders' brutality was not an effort to "erase Our Lady," exactly. In many cases their efforts seem far more cunning and concrete.

- Rather, to "erase Our Lady" seems intended coldly and with calculation I think, to actually and ultimately "erase her people." By disheartening those who loved, relied on, took down-to-earth daily sustenance from her and/or her radiant Child, a person's or a people's "true self" was diminished more and more over time. The spiritual anchor and rudder that steadies through fierce crosswinds were shattered, lost.

- This is an old, old story: Erase a people and their resistances to the marauder by tearing away their sacred images that have inestimably strengthened them over long periods of time, fortified them in deeply soulful ways to withstand, to stand up to, to stand for, and to stand with others.

- Disempower the people spiritually, and then dictate what narrowly defined "spirit" they must now follow "or else"—then the erasure of a people is effected, at least above ground. The heart and spirit and soul of the people dives underground then, and attempts to live on subsistences there.

- Thus to conquer a people or even one person, an invader had to "un-Mother" the people. Holy Mother is strengthening medicine, guide, and *inspiratrice* of the people. In her, people know their lives are sacred. In her, people know they can stand and speak out. In her, they do not grovel, rather they are filled with grace and able thereby to say and do and gather and move and live. Thereby, she is a most dangerous woman force.

- Invaders in some parts of the world, typically take all steps they can dream up to make those they intend to dominate feel unworthy of life itself. Consider the demotion of Blessed Mother's and her Child's age-old message of compassionate care toward the "least of the least."

- If those who invade and abuse can bury this beautiful life-giving, neon-soul message—that compassionate care is a holy calling for all to strive toward—then invaders can feel free to brutalize any and all people as they wish.

- With evidences, talk of, ceremony with, knowings of, walking with Holy Mother and the Little God of Love—out of the way—there would be no holier nor higher authority to hold "the measure of decency" high. There would instead, only be whatever low, self-interested "freedom to harm others" set in place by the invaders themselves.

- In history, marauders moved to crush tiny and large resistances for rebellious action, or by the momentarily unguarded look on any person's face. Anything could send an invader into a rage. This is a form of physical and spiritual terrorism: to make people afraid to feel openly without being punished and harmed decisively.

- And yet, it was worse: Invaders pressed hard to commandeer and exploit a vast "resource" of the people—one that is not often recorded in history books: They squatted over the dearest *prima materia*, meaning the most fundamental of Mother essence, that is, the very souls of the people themselves.

- The conquerors not only intended to use the bodies of their prisoners—the invaders were also soul-eaters who sought to extinguish free will. They demanded absolute dominion over other souls, demanding obedience without question, no matter how any soul suffered, no matter how any soul cried out for justice and humane aid.

- It follows then, in order to do this in every era of an invaders' history, frenzied marauders had to run thither and yon destroying, defacing, subverting, burying, smashing, misusing, covering over sacred images. For it is the sacred for much of the world's people that gently and sweetly pours and re-pours the sense of "true selfhood" that allows us all to rise into the best humanity and humility, the best factual vision and fierce resistance for ourselves and for each other. Humility: meaning placing "Source without source" at the center of our lives.

- Yet, when one is so deeply captured and cannot escape for a time, when one is literally forbidden to cleave to Compassionate Mother as each soul understands her as an interior or as vital extero force, then one can see this dispiriting of a people very often causes an irrational set of reactions to rise in the captives with regard to their own oppressors.

- The innocent people become both fearful to demand justice for themselves, but also act fawningly grateful to their oppressors for being allowed to live.

HOW THE GENERATIONAL WOUND OF BEING STRIPPED OF MOTHER CAUSES SUBSEQUENT GENERATIONS TO LIVE IN A CROUCH AS THOUGH THEY ARE STILL BEING CRUSHED WHEN THEY ARE IN FACT, NOW FREE

Clinically and personally, I often find in those who have lived two or even ten or more generations away from a brutal war or conquering that devastated their families, that they can now also carry an overly grateful and often groveling behavior toward the remnants of the conquerors, even though this particular forward generation did not struggle life-and-death through any war at all.

There appears to manifest strongly in the children of those conquered, what I'd call "the generational wound," which is handed down generation after generation by those who were once long ago so wounded, who in turn bind their children to them now, by sitting in the unhealed wounds they had sustained back then. An innocent people who had so much taken from them, the parent to the child still ironically acts as though they owe honor and allegiance to those who did not take their lives, yet barely allowed them to live.

Children often take up the unhealed parental wound out of the most radiant compassionate little heart one could ever imagine. The children want to support their own parents, love them, help them, heal them, stand with them. But, then too, the child to share the burden, must also carry the family wound. Thus they may continue to act as their parent, grandparent, great and great, great, great grandparents acted and continued to act toward the invader.

Even though once suffering under a brutal wartime occupation, even though one can now be free, one instead lives attempting to be unquestioning, silent, bowing and demurring, being overly-respectful, giving obsequious respect to those who have not earned respect, being unable to express outrage at true injustice.

Oddly, the same person who bows to authorities out of fear, may, within the family, rail at those family members who are far and away innocent as compared to the invaders, but who also stand up for themselves and attempt to stand up for the family.

This is thought primary wound carried by the elders to be the height of danger to self and family, as they are living in a back room of the psyche where the marauders of the past still hold sway with guns and swords. Thus, publicly wounded and acquiescing, but privately raging at their own impotence, an actually healthy reaction to oppression, but here aimed at the wrong party.

In my own family, the invaders set strong horrific images into the hearts and minds of the farmer people they overran. The invaders' ultimate destructions of the sacred left the beautiful bond between spirit and holy, soul and psyche in shreds, so instead of seeing the land that had fulfilled them and created sacred pageantry amongst the people, they now saw images in their minds, imprints on their bodies of their sacred ground being literally salted by the enemy so nothing could grow.

Now instead of having soaring hearts to see the animals and birds and nature considered sacred to the people, so much so, that ceremonies and rituals were nearly weekly endeavors to thank, hope and care for what they deemed the sacred world around them—after brutal invasions that destroyed the essence of Mother of the World, the people bodily feel "electrocuted" to remember entire flocks of their holy white storks shot dead by Stalin's advancing Red Army; their sacred forests purposely burnt to the ground in order to deprive the people of their giant guardian trees, their ground wood for cook fires and warmth, their places to hide from the enemy. Their holy minds are overwritten now with grief over the breaking of glass, the smashing of bronze, the cracking of iron, the desecration of children, women, old people, families.

Their sacred images were burnt. There was smashing of sacred statues once carried overland like a baby in a blanket and set in place to guard the village. There was the tearing up of symbolic cloth, the fouling of the sanctuaries in the tiny village churches built by hand by the village smithies, wheelwrights and cabinetmakers. There was the destruction of the hundreds of thousands of roadside shrines to Holy Mother and the Saints . . .

All these planned and purposeful destructions seized the Holy Mother from view, like sending the Mother to an underground jail away from the people who loved her so. The marauders tore her out of the arms and eyes of the people. The village icon painters were often shot on the spot or else dragged away never to be seen again. So intent were the marauders in wiping her out, wiping out any trace of her memory from the very hearts and bodies of the people, that our family said that to hide even a tiny carved statue of her representing her essence, meant immediate death. The farmer peasants who lived in the middle of nowhere, were not to receive an iota of spiritual comfort nor strengthening. They were "but to do or die."

Thus, marauders attempted to place themselves as the gods of the people by destroying those of holy magnitude whom the people followed and held as beloved. Thus, upon threat of very real and sudden assassination on the spot, the phenomena of bowing and scraping to the marauders, rather than happily bowing to one's own Creator, became required.

"Un-mothering" the people and substituting "duty to obey," made the hardworking threshers of golden wheat, the horsemen and horsewomen who could ride like the wind in their capes and knee high-boots and tribal garb embroidered with the symbols of their clans . . . into still proud, but now fearful people: fearful for themselves, their children, their animals, their land, which they all saw as direct family, all of a whole.

I know you can see the parallels to abuse of any nation, group, or individual.

In post-trauma work, we sometimes refer to those who fear and praise their oppressors as having "Stockholm syndrome," (after a brutal hostage situation in Sweden in 1973, wherein those victimized were threatened with death and irrationally began to believe, as their minds were stretched to the tearing point, that their captors were actually being kind to them by not killing them.)

Whatever survival mechanisms an abused group or individual learned in order to remain alive under extreme duress, but without later tending seriously to the mending of "true self" and restoration of the holy as each understands this, often the offspring are taught the unusual manners of bowing and demurring too. They are often told to not speak of these things, for the original trauma has not been dealt with in-depth. No return to full sense of self in the parent has been yet undertaken and met. "True self" is one who is not afraid of other human beings, but rather only afraid to not listen to nor honor their own soul and their own senses of the holy, the creative impulse, and their own Holy People.

Yet the wound of being stripped of the holy imago of "sacred sense of mother within" and also as a huge healing force in this world, The Holy Mother, being one who is capable of helping and caring about all without trying to make one small—well, some wounds can be like a pit with very steep sides. Help is needed. Ladders need to be brought. Voices to encourage, "You can do this." Hands to help. A person is needed who has just a touch to a great deal of the holy to conduct the hallelujahs as one returns gradually to "true self."

Thus, for many, some of the help, and for others, a significant part of that help that will restore the Mother to the psyche where her shrine has been bombed out, comes from being re-sacrilized in community, in culture, and in oneself, that is, re-consecrated to all this is holy. This can take place as a ritual of one's choosing. The ritual's purpose would be so that one can not only see through the mundane eyes, but through holy sight again, through holy hearing again, holy touch, holy singing, holy fragrances, holy endeavors, holy colors, holy words, holy works . . . all the gentleness and strength that comes from the Holy, now practiced daily and gradually restored.

The irrational behavior of aggrandizing invaders and fearing to speak up for true self, can continue to hand down "the generational wound," it is true. But it only takes one offspring or one parent, one soul in any generation to stop the hand-me-down, and to retrieve in new and old ways, and then hand down the restored holy instead. That will be the one who has just a little more consciousness than others in the family, one who gently and stalwartly refuses to take on the family wound without healing it once and for all. This will be the one who stands for the first time in generations in full voice of justice, full loving heart, full generous and wise soul, without cringing, with a bold certainty that the Holy is birthright for all—and who teaches their children to do the same. The rituals to do these are concomitant with speaking beautiful truths, cleansing rituals, re-consecration rituals, and many add to these their own inspirational ornamentations, words, actions, that are meaningful to them.

With the sense of holiness restored, which it will and can be for those who seek it with sincere heart, all retrieval of Holy Mother in the ways each understands best and in the most humbling and most life-changing, are possible. The beginning how-tos? Do your work in depth, keep at it. Work with those face-to-face who know you, and care for you and hold Holy Mother near. Keep going. And, regarding those who want to erase Holy Mother? I'd suggest whenever anyone asks you who where you work, say, "I work for Holy Mother." If asked what company you're with, raise an eyebrow, smile beatifically and say, "I'm with Her."

And here too, is a prayercito, a little blessing-prayer I'd say over you now, a prayercito I created years ago in the midst of some of the most harsh challenges of my own life. I offer it to you as healing, no matter what walls surround you or your loved ones, no matter what devastations have occurred, no matter what prisons you have been dragged into, no matter where your loved ones are held captive, no matter what.

It is this, and I'd place you within the circle of Our Lady's wreath of green leaves and white flowers encircling her Immaculate Heart, and then just gently say these words over your perhaps tired heart, bedraggled spirit, but earnest and radiantly enduring soul: Remember, no wall against the Holy can hold us away from the Holy.

Only things remembered
with Love,
are Real.
Only acts remembered
with Love,
are Real.
Only Souls remembered
with Love,
are Real.

WALLING OFF THE HOLY MOTHER:
WAYS OF ATTEMPTING TO ERASE HOLY IDEAS
AND IMAGES, SINCE TIME OUT OF MIND

There are other ways to "disappear" Holy Mother. Sometimes through lack of foresight and common sense, mistakes are made, and historical relics and iconographies, for instance, are lost because of lack of thinking matters through carefully beforehand.

But also across global history, the real intent in desecration and purposeful covering over of images of Our Lady—was done en masse, in order to strip believers of their "natural history" of struggle and triumphs through remaining close to Holy Mother. She had to be gotten out of the way in order to elevate a group of new ruling humans to be venerated instead.

Holy Mother was literally outlawed publicly in old style communism of the twentieth and twenty-first centuries for instance. Totalitarian ambitions moved swiftly to first and foremost erase powerful sacred images that inspired souls to strive not for the state, not for any organization, but for the soul's worth, toward Creator, toward kindness, survival, insight, massive creativity, goodness and true love.

Communism's original ideal appeared to be to bring the poor upward out from under others' boots so there could be work for all, food for all, progress and prosperity for all. But, much of the actual implementation of communism in many parts of the world only replaced one set of hob-nail boots with another set of hob-nail boots. Thereby the regimes moved to even more thoroughly stomp out whatever was left of the Holy from previous regimes antagonistic to the Holy also.

This debased methodology of "overwriting" an old culture by using war, threat, intimidation and destruction to annihilate people's holiest beliefs and practices—even if the new regime began idealistically and in all true hope and honesty—is often the predictable outcome of top-heavy organizations that grow many rows of teeth for power's sake, and then subvert kindness and inclusion for dictatorial control and "showing up" others by displaying how many millions of people bow to their orders—thereby eliminating free will, free thought, free movement from all the people except those on the pointy thrones atop the power pyramid.

Thus, in the former Soviet version of communism, over time, the newly arrived powers bent on overthrowing the old order, turned from their original ideal of worth for all, and instead made the state and the men who ran the state, the ones to whom all souls should now capitulate.

The innocent people were supposed to pledge their soul's allegiances—not to their Holy Ones as multitudes had prior and for centuries—and not to the concept of communism either, but rather to conform to, to defend and to support the mere humans who had set themselves up as a thug-dictatorial chain of command over all other souls.

My father used to say if men suddenly seized power in order to aright wrongdoings, it was the rarest of men who would also see the wrongdoings in their own brand of power and that of their followers. That it was only a holy man who would act boldly to contain himself and his own followers, to keep all of his own from harming others—that a holy man could not live as a holy heart without arighting all wrongdoings for the sake of all the people, that the people not continue to suffer "in the same dungeon as before, only now with fresh paint and under new management."

REMEMBER THIS. REMEMBER. REMEMBER.
HOW IT WENT LONG AGO AND NOW—
WHENEVER HOLY BELIEFS AND KNOWINGS OF THE
PEOPLE THAT ARE GOODNESS ITSELF, ARE ATTACKED,
THE TACTICS USED ARE THE SAME. SAME. SAME.

"Remember this. Remember. Remember. When the Holy itself is under attack, the tactics they use are the same. Same. Same." This is what my father used to say after a long night of feasting and weeping with all the old relatives who had been so terribly harmed in World War II. They often sat at the blue kitchen table with one another late into the night as though they could not get enough of the stories that they could barely bear to hear and tell. These old farmers sat like battered old bears in our little chrome and plastic chairs, recounting the tales of torment and loss. They threw back innumerable shots of schnapps before, during, and after each new story. And each story seemed far worse than the last with child loss, murder of pets, maiming of friends, purposeful blindings, branding and other sickening horrors unleashed before their eyes.

Any marauding group bent on domination and enslavement of souls uses the same tactics, just different hideous features. Thus, I learned, those who strip the Holy sense of self, the holy images and all the magnitude that stands behind those . . . they all use the same tactics. Same. Same.

There are many long incursions to choose from, but let us detail the tactics of one in particular, for it occurred across much of the globe in our own time. If one ever wanted to know what happened to the tribes of eld, to entire nation-groups that disappeared or were decimated, I believe, we only need look at how this occurs right now in our own time. The overtaking of peoples and lands without their permissions is an archetypal process it would appear, and so follows certain predictable pathways.

Thus in the early and mid-twentieth century, many communistic parts of the world held hostage without ransom, holy ideas.

They began by attacking the mud, the mud that made bricks that made up the little and large rooms of holy refuges and sanctuaries across many lands. Thus, the Soviets first declared that sacred buildings of all faiths would immediately be turned into governmental rooms filled with desks, or used for storage of odds and ends. Vapid "re-purposings" were made, calling the former gathering places of the faithful, "museums" wherein tour guides pointed out the fallacies of non-atheist thought.

Or else, the votive places were bulldozed because "redevelopment" with no rhyme or reason was suddenly and sorely needed. Faithful souls trying to visit the holy places were attacked and sometimes murdered where they davened or knelt praying. Holy enclosures whose doors had once been open to birds and people for literally centuries, were now padlocked. Other holy places where entire small villages were "cleansed," that is, the populace murdered and left unburied, were let to fall to ruin. Small holy gathering places were burnt down with the living farm families locked inside. The dear people who once took solace and strength there, were murdered in their own holy refuges.

In all cases, those "in charge" forbade the people to speak aloud the names of the Holy People and their Creator. They were forbidden to make the old rituals, even thought they'd sang and chanted these for decades, time out of mind. The people and their Holy Ones were ordered by the ruling junta, to live for the rest of their lives imprisoned—all loving human hearts held away from all loving Holy Hearts.

Though many of those dictatorial regimes would eventually crack and fall in the twentieth century, as all totalitarian powers must and will, this banning and incarceration of the Holy for nearly sixty years, was ordered over a huge swath of land and peoples, for instance, in Northern Asia, Eastern Europe, Russia and its many formerly independent countries. Such rough and murderous treatment of the people's spiritual and religious beliefs continued despite a common counter-action—one often brought forward by totalitarian dictatorship. That is, their motions to demonstrate how caring of the people they were—by making certain programs to aid some of the people, by improving the lot of *some* of the people, meaning those whom the ruling minds deemed worthy—read—"loyal" not to Creator, not to The Mother, not to The Child, but to the party.

Across history, there has been the predictable scheme used by conquerors to give employment and perks to a very small inner circle of the conquered populace, often arming them as well, in order to hold power. Those who might be invited in from the cold, who may have bravely declined to be a part of a sick empire, were shot. As my father used to say, a truly holy man finds the food of fresh truth far more nourishing than a rancid bread provided like clockwork.

Thus, in the main, during those decades of communism, no safe passage was given to anything related to the practice of the Holy unless it could be used to manipulate someone into or out of something. Such as throwing an old woman her little wooden icon of Holy Mother, after which the local commissar then ambushed and dragged off her grand-daughter. Such as allowing a poor rebbe to keep his candles for Shabbat, but arranging paperwork to defraud the rebbe, his wife, and children, of their small farm—for no purpose other than to enrich the petty police-man or watchman who worked for the party.

Yet, as much because they were held away from their Holy People by threat of death and exile to gray and barren hard labor prisons, thousands upon thousands of souls fled in the middle of the night, seeking to cross the border to freedom—freedom of life unthreatened, freedom to develop talents and opportunity, and to "take back from the night," veneration of the Holy that sustained so many for generation upon generation.

But, to keep the people from fleeing to freedom of soul, mind, heart, body and spirit, that's when the communists decided to build against their own people, "The Wall."

BUILDING THE WALL TO IMPRISON PEOPLE INSIDE, AND TO KEEP FREE PEOPLE FROM ENTERING

When the people are walled off from free access to their own sacred images, ideas, sustaining beliefs, and when those who value the Holy are declared "wrong, confused, muddled, misinformed, anathema, threat, danger, uneducated, arrogant" to want their own way of life that has fit them well, then too the people can be more easily divided from one another by the orders of the regime. Then, there will be those who still profess belief. And there will be those who claim they no longer have belief in anything holy, but may actually hold to such—in a hidden and underground way. Thereby the division. The regime counts on this: that both groups are fearful to stand up together as a force for good, for one is self-preserving first, and they are both afraid of themselves and their families and friends being harmed, overall. The regime counts on this undercutting of strength. The ruling power wants the people not to unite in strong and overt ways to resist the regime.

This is another old way of subverting what once unified free people—that is, the people's ability to gang together in their holy spaces and places, to meet and plan without fear of harmful consequences from "on high."

A regime dedicated to remaining in power over, not with the people, likes to bar people from meeting on their own holiest ground, thereby again, stripping from the people the strength that comes right up out of years of dedication and holiness held in any sacred place for decades and sometimes for eons.

By closing off holy meeting places, the regime creates a constant sense of siege for the people; just right for those who wish to control masses. The people have to become like Bedouins then, moving and moving their tents, seeking odd shelter to meet where they can. Inevitably, some of those not as insightful will begin to split and say, "But, our masters might be right to treat us so poorly. Wouldn't it be better if we were nicer, more conciliatory, even though our masters are not?" When people under their masters begin to fear, dislike, be suspicious of one another, this separates brother from brother, sister from sister. This lack of solidarity and coalition then bodes well for the dictatorship to remain in power.

Oddly this division of people so there can be no consensus, no rallying points for better or more holy conditions, is also done by those in power in many dank prisons across the world. Persons are kept separate from one another in prison, not allowed to commingle for more than a few minutes at a time, are kept isolated in order to discourage communication that matters, in order to douse talk of freedom that means justice rather than just a recitation of some words by rote.

In the case of communism, the powers that be, despite endlessly proclaiming how free and happy all were across Europe and Asia without the peskiness of Holy devotions of many kinds—the military dictatorship built gigantic walls of barbed wire, concrete block and brick to keep all the happy and free people of their oppressive regime inside their garrote of influence.

They commanded one particular wall called The Berlin Wall to be built 12 feet high and 103 miles long, in order to separate people from people. This huge wall was built so that no one was allowed free passage to either come in, and most especially not allowed to leave, under threat of being shunned and shamed at one extreme, and sent to their deaths at the other extreme. No one was allowed to go elsewhere in the world.

Those walls, twice as high as the average man's height and four times as high as a young child's height were meant to divide the more free people from the entirely bound people. The walls and boundary gates were patrolled by soldiers with firearms who had orders to shoot to kill any and all who tried to crash through the gates or to climb, leap, flee, fly over the wall to freedom. Over time, the bodies of entire little families lay dead at the footers of these walls.

The bodies of patriots, artists, dancers, musicians, farmers, teachers, flower sellers, shoemakers, saddle makers, everyman, everywoman, every child who tried to make it over the wall in the dead of night—by trying to distract the soldiers, by trying to speed through in a tiny car overflowing with souls bent on the breath of freedom, even by trying to fly over in a home-made small aeroplane—these souls with freedom burning in their blood, lay dead at the heartlessly patrolled walls. All were Souls "in their right minds," yearning for Holy Truth, and literally died trying to breach the walls in more ways than one.

Rumored to be inspired in part by *Szent István,* Saint Stephen, Holy Mother and her Child, in 1956 brothers and sisters did gang together in solidarity in a heart-rending Hungarian Revolution, an uprising against the USSR who held them all so deeply captive within the Soviet walls. When police tried to crush the demonstrators, the Hungarian military joined the insurgents and fought with their brothers and sisters against the Soviet troops. But the USSR returned with Russian tanks, and the Hungarians fought the tanks in the streets, using only rocks and their bare hands.

Pitiful appeals were broadcast by radio from deep within Hungary, begging NATO troops to intervene. But it was not to be. The freedom fighters were crushed, their leaders murdered. Hungarians and other brave people from all the Soviet countries continued to fight for freedom for another thirty-three long years and finally made it to freedom when the Soviet Union fell in 1989.

But, here again is what our elders said: those who rose up to fight the black tanks were led not by atheism, not by a human being, not by any thought of this world. They were led by their oldest beliefs, those born into their very bones, that identify with the Mother, the Holy One, that world beyond this world, where all things, all miracles are possible. My father and uncles would tell us various versions of this immediate thought: *One can imprison the man, but there is no prison that can hold a man's mind or his heart. His soul, his spirit, his mind, his heart will slip between the bars because they were all born with wings.*

This huge wall against the free movement of the people, against freedom to hold the Holy with all hope, was called "The Iron Curtain." Over many decades, many prominent people tried from within and sometimes from outside the wall, to loosen its bricks. Each helped to rock the wall. But still it stood, crushing so many peoples across so much of the Earth. Until finally, one day, one moment in time, across many of the nations captured behind the wall, the so-called common people rose up to reclaim all freedoms, including Holy Mother.

PEACEFUL REVOLUTION DID COME

Communism's self-appointed elite had for decades broken their promises to give all households more than adequate food and sustenance in equal shares, promising a far better life than before. But, they failed to match the dream dangled before the people, with the reality. Equally intolerable, those at the top of the military and hierarchy had taken the lion's share of all things available for themselves in abject greed and sloth, such as ensconcing themselves in villas, being driven about in big limousines, vacationing at palaces, having all the food, advantages, recognitions, servants, and uneven-handed tribal power over others.

Because the regime had destroyed farmlands, dammed and polluted rivers that had formerly sustained the people, chopped down the sheltering forests where lived all the animals and literally millions of the saints in their little wooden-roofed houses along the roadsides everywhere, the people no longer believed the regime had anyone's best interests at heart.

Ironically, the communists often educated former peasant people, farmers in essence. And the more they educated the people, all propaganda aside, the more the people could see that the only ones who prospered and had all of life taken care of for them, were the very few cronies at the top.

To make more misery, added to all the so-called "shortages" of medicines and essentials like warm coats and boots in winters, were lack of electricity enough to work by, gallons of clotted soaps that did not clean anything, and so much more, including most of all, "disappearing people," terrorizing many of the populace.

Too, vivid creativity and innovation were forbidden unless one could be "approved" by a flat-minded council of fifty whose actual job was to repress, suppress the wind of Ruach, the Shekhinah of wild creativity, the Holy Spirit, that is the *el duende,* the spirit of creativity that comes from more than just the mere human and is known throughout the world by a million names. This last especially was forbidden. Because it is not rational. Nor is it irrational. Instead, it is high Holiness come to live right in the little red church of the heart. And that alone, causes all kinds of wild and luscious ideas in most.

The continual "shortages" of petrol, medicines, withholding ease from others' natural ways of working and instead insisting all work be done in the same ways even when insensible and wasteful, these lacks of simple understanding and kindness magnified the people's huge sense of the losses of their black dirt farmlands which had been overrun by dams and government-owned mechanized high-decibel farms where there'd once been peaceful silence with only dragonflies and birds singing. The people still had in heart memory how it hurt to lose the thriving of their crops, the rain falling, the forests' beautiful endless green, the great plains, the mountains, and all the peoples who had been domiciled there for centuries in the biosphere, in an ecology of their first choice.

The people's losses were so grievous, for all nature was considered part and parcel of life striving toward holiness too. Seeing military bivouacked on the holy plains, seeing the farm people, the horsemen, the horsewomen interfered with, being banned from their literally hundreds of small and large rituals tying the people to the sacred and to the land—this was intolerable to most, that all this was done in the name of "a theory."

Further, "the theory" of forced and enforced atheism had so disheartened the young, many grew up learning not that loving promises made to children are always to be kept, but rather, they learned that any promise made by a "my way or the highway" governing body would at first elate those promised, but then the promise would ultimately be broken—over and over again. Thus the faithful people themselves rose up over and over again. Successfully, unsuccessfully, they rose up and kept rising up in enough bodies, brave minds and hearts, and they refused to support their oppressors any longer.

What they enacted eventually was one of the most gentle, pointed and powerful responses they could give. Amongst other actions, because they had not received salaries dependably for a long time and were trying to eke out livings in nearly impossible ways, multitudes literally stopped going to their assigned work, interrupting the supply chains of work products and currency across thousands of miles of thousands of villages and cities.

Thus, the cruel wall that had come to represent everything unholy, began to sway. Thus the wall began to crack at its philosophical juncture points. Thus the wall tipped of its own hideous weight of murders at one end, and entrenched lack of even simple humane response or concern about the hearts, minds and bodies of the people at the other end.

This regime, like the vast empires of Rome before it, like the British Empire, the Egyptian Empire, like Genghis Khan, like the Kings of Spain, all of whom had squatted over so much land and lorded over so many people, that the self-appointed kings of the regime could no longer oversee, tax, use, exploit, control all the millions of minds sprawling over thousands and thousands of square miles, for there were far fewer of the "higher ups" than there were of the people.

Thus that brand of "communism," too, had become as any dictatorial regime will become: Like the crow in Aesop's Fables who stuck his long beak into a glass bottle and greedily grabbed as many grapes as possible. But now that his maw was gaping so wide open, the crow could not get his beak nor the grapes out of the bottle without dropping most of the grapes and closing his beak again. So too, went this regime.

The dictatorship, emotionally crippled for decades, hardened of heart, unfairly doling out boons and favors upon their inner circle only, making shows to tourists of children presenting flowers and singing old folk songs whilst others were ordered to continue raping the forestlands, rivers, farmlands, and the very air in the sky, and all whilst imprisoning, shunning, doing away with any soul who spoke truth—even softening a bit near the end but too late for continuance to come of it—thus the regime was economically crippled as well.

As the regime then fell, the wall fell with it.

And the people, though impoverished in certain ways before, during, and after the walls and principal government fell, were also in an entirely other way made rich again in potential freedoms. It has been said that some who had been part of the regime, embraced freedom again, and remade their ways to attempt to find a place in a new society wherein they would be helpful instead of hindering.

Many, it is said, were holy in themselves again and slowly began to encourage and stand for that sacredness in others. It became clear there might be a place for most everyone to thrive, as many of those behind the wall, the so called "iron curtain" had led two lives, goodness on one side, decency on the other; goodness on one side, evil on the other; evil on one side, and evil on the other.

And after the wall fell, many found redemption, reconciled in many ways with others. Others are still living in the fantasy of a former glory that was far more grievous and gory than it ever was glory. But also, many others, like the people on both sides of the wall, reunified within themselves, slowly over time, coming to terms, making amends insofar as possible, going on to live and help others to live also.

After the fall of the wall, the millions of people so long held away from loved ones on the "other side of the wall," flooded through the breaches in the wall—like water under pressure suddenly rushing and leaping through a failed and hated dam. My father, from the minority Danau Swabian tribe of southern Hungary, told us a letter had arrived. Over the telephone, the letter reader said the old tribal women in the outskirts of many of the southern villages of Hungary had heard about or seen "the fall of the wall" with their own eyes while gathered at a neighbor's home to watch in amazement on television . . . as the young and old stood atop the huge concrete death wall that had divided Berlin and all of Germany for nearly three decades.

We watched too, my father, an old bent-over man in his late eighties. We held hands and watched in awe as that night, lit by floodlights from literally thousands upon thousands of news cameras from all over entire planet Earth, the people atop the wall were using ballpeen and sledge hammers to literally rip the wall apart, to take down the wall, once and for all. Their hatred for the oppressions they had suffered for far too long and their joy at freedom at last, were mingled in different proportions in each soul.

And the letter we'd received from the Old Country, told us that the very few old women still standing after so many decades of having their holy ground and sacred sites for Holy Mother and Holy Family and the Saints forbidden to them, that that night after the fall of the wall, the old ones wept as they ripped out the hems of their long black dresses where they had been hiding their old rosaries—rosaries made out of cherrywood beads from the fallen limbs of the trees of their own orchards once existent long ago when all the people were still allowed to live on and work their beloved land.

Under communism, it was these same rosaries the old women had hidden in the seams and hems of their clothing all those decades—their rosaries often being the only thing left from their farmland villages where the trees sighed in the wind, branches flowered so fragrantly and gave such delicious pears and cherries. As my grandmother Katerin used to say, the fruit trees every year tithed a share of their wood to be made into Holy Mother's rosary beads.

Now, all those decades forward from childhood to young woman-hood, through their middle-aged years, now into their white-haired, stoop shouldered age—the old women, under the ban of communism that all be atheists, had instead prayed the rosary daily with Our Lady. They did this by surreptitiously holding onto the hems of their dresses. In so doing they were praying the rosary by feeling the beads through the hems of their voluminous black skirts, counting their beads, praying and praying, silently praying. In utter defiance.

It is a mantra in my family still: *You have to dig deep to bury Our Lady.*

LITTLE SISTINE CHAPEL OF
OUR LADY OF GUADALUPE

So, there in the former USSR, we saw the folly and the failure of trying to cover over images sacred to many who often then went underground with and for them, instead. Many of the young too, rather than being very good atheists were, along with those still vividly alive instead of dead-ened in spirit, often summoned by the Holy regardless of so much having been banned and covered over: There may be no greater summons from the Holy than that it is now no frequent thing, but rather banned, and thereby perceived as an exotic buried treasure.

Today, we still see loss of the Holy, the literally banning of, covering over of the Holy. We see doing so can also narrow the view and deaden the imagination and dedication of an entire generation of the young throughout huge sections of the world. Banning the Holy harms the spirit of ingenuity and creativity of the young. It disheartens those who innately have the spark of longing for the Holy People.

We want the lesson to have been learned, that in our time, we saw nearly six decades without intervention of the ideological and political imprisonment of The Mother, Creator and Holy People—and all who followed her. All this incarceration was not done to care for the souls of all, but rather to strip, divide, seize power, riches, election, elevation, appointment to perceived positions of might by imprinting one's own annexation hubris over the folkways and followers of the Holy.

Yes it is so, and even still today that sometimes those well meaning, but without enough forethought, or some meaning good but without thinking through unintended consequences, or some accidentally, or some with pique and ire, still move to lock the comfort of Holy Mother and her Child of Love away from her people, who are all of us.

Our Lady of Guadalupe Parish in North Denver has been for decades a strong village of Latinos[1] whose ancestry most often derives from Mexico and Central America. They and those who have come after, also from the Americas, are strong children of La Señora de Guadalupe, for she is called amongst other names, *La Conquista,* Our Lady of the Conquest, often interpreted as She who conquered from her heart, those who were already conquered by mere men. La Señora de Guadalupe is also known as the Mother of those who have suffered to cross the deserts and the mountains, braved the cold of climate and of culture, to try to live free.

This little parish church is on the historical registry and has been what I'd call "an oasis in the midst of chaos" for those who maintained it through the upheavals of the 1960s, 70s, 80s, 90s, and still today—beginning back when there were so difficult and fierce struggles for parity for minorities equal to those in the larger culture; struggles to be recognized as a group of deep-hearted people as worthy as persons from any other group. Harsh challenges from those times included being allowed equal housing, loans, job opportunity, equal quality education, and underlying, to simply be invited and included in opportunities, to have equal status in consultation, say-so about how minds, souls and spirits were affected by others' decisions who were more powerful.

One had to witness it firsthand to understand that holy *lucha,* that decades' long struggle to walk in freedom, to walk tall—instead of being relegated to lowest caste in modern times. The hope in this little church, as an "oasis in the midst of chaos," was not to have to continue to beg to be deemed worthy, and not to be seen of value *only* if one were forced into using up all of one's back and bones and blood as labor for higher ups. Being "allowed to undertake harshest work," but without full accord and full humane treatment spiritually, mentally, socially, emotionally, economically, religiously, were some of the many issues faced in many different ways, essentially by a people who themselves had been conquered and had been taught to not insist on parity, but to be grateful for being allowed to live. The struggle was long and will continue until the soul in each person, regardless of all else, is treated with courtesy, with decency, with consultation, with inclusion.

Our Lady of Guadalupe has since forever been understood as "The One Who Understands" from personal witness—the travails and forced servancy of the poor and the struggling—whether those who have taken harsh stances toward minorities reside in churches, governments, or one's own family. So *La Lupita,* as Our Lady of Guadalupe is sometimes affectionately called by us, is considered the great Liberation Mother, the one who brings freedom to her children to "Walk free, walk proud, and to fear no one."

However, recently someone at the "little oasis" of Our Lady of Guadalupe parish, decided for "remodeling sake," that the thirty-five-year-old historic and sacred mural painted by noted mural artist Carlota EspinoZa, showing Our Lady of Guadalupe, and Santo Juan Diego, La Señora's huge guardian angels, her baby cherubs, should be covered over by a white sheetrock wall from floor to ceiling.

This wall erased from sight the forty-seven foot long by twelve feet high mural of the merciful Mother, Guadalupe and the one who even after being conquered, was still standing in holiness: Santo Juan Diego. A heating vent was punched through near the painted gown of Holy Mother. The new white wall being a mere three feet or so away from the sacred mural effectively encapsulated her in the equivalent of a long narrow broom closet in which were stored buckets and other items belonging to the church.

For twelve months or so after the wall was suddenly erected, respectful letters and phone calls from various people concerned about the covering over of Our Lady of Guadalupe's mural were made to the parish and archbishop's offices. But inquiries for exact information about how this sudden "erasure" of Our Lady's mural came about, went unanswered. No return calls, few letters of response eventually, and those seeming dismissive of others' concerns, and containing no content about how this was conceived, which persons had decided this, and why this was decided without the entire community consulted . . . and most of all, whether it could please be undone: Bring down the wall.

Our Lady of Guadalupe Mural, Before

Our Lady's sacred mural showing her beautiful self and Santo Juan Diego and The Angels, painted and living fully alive from 1975 to 2009. These beautiful historical folk art murals were painted by noted mural artist Carlota EspinoZa. The church is named Our Lady of Guadalupe Parish. The grandmotherly dining room chairs for the priests to sit on, are to the left. There is in the mural also, a legend grown up over time: that is "hidden out in the open" some say they have been hallowed to see also an image that to them seems like "The Face of God" . . . the little angels are the eyes, Holy Mother the nose and forehead, and the little round stained glass windows on each side, Creator's all merciful and all hearing ears, listening to the people.

In a community of minorities who are known for their creativity, vivid love of color, and especially their strong relational ties to one another (we are often certain, everyone is in some way one of our cousins even though we have never yet met one another), that this huge historic mural would be obliterated without consultation with the entire community who brought and cared for Our Lady's mural over the years, was not the way of the familia. It seemed some other kind of determination which stood outside the *cultura cura* of our culture. *Cultura cura* is valued highly amongst our group. It means "culture cures," that is, what is in the culture we make together, can cure us in all love.

Many people feared this covering over of Our Lady's mural signaled desecration and blasphemy. They were truly bewildered. Their polite requests asking to be told the entire story about how this could happen, who by name made this happen, why this was made to happen, how it could be unmade to happen, continued to be ignored.

Oddly in the precinct of the Holy, where a void of silence is made, Espíritu Santo comes roaring in to fill it with bold color and action. Thus, processions and peaceful protests began to take place about the covering of the mural of Mother Guadalupe's visitation to Santo Juan Diego (who was only recently made a saint, five hundred long years after Our Lady of Guadalupe appeared to him). A group of concerned parishioners and former parishioners, community leaders, nuns, and other interested parties, eventually coalesced into, by count of their petitions which now numbered over 1,400 signatures from *la gente* community, a substantial group called Fieles Unidos, the Faithful United.

Pleas to the prelates who had the power to take down the wall, to please do so, appeared not to be heard. Thus the group held, amongst other ongoing events, peaceful protests at the church. Present were "the women in white," long time devotees of Our Lady of Guadalupe, along with young boys and girls also dressed in white and all so earnest and patient, standing loyally for Our Lady and her sacred art. It was touching to see the true-heartedness of *los viejos y los jóvenes,* the very old and the very young had for La Señora, she who by someone's command was languishing behind a flat white wall.

Still there continued to be resistance to heartfelt requests for information about how this huge historic mural was painted over, and walled up, other than the inference that "that's just the way it is." My father used to say that the vassals in the Old Country would purposely ignore the serf's pleas, and that if there was one thing a serf knew, it was the difference between a silence that indicates the higher up is thinking things

Our Lady of Guadalupe Mural, After

The Wall Built to Hide the 45-foot wide x 15-foot high mural of Our Lady of Guadalupe and Santo Juan Diego and all the Angels. The painting-over and covering-over of the sacred mural was done in late 2009. The walls are a flat eggshell white now. The new grey stone throne-like seating, taller than the altar, is to the far right.

through, and silence that is hoping the issue will just go away if ignored forever. My dad said, a truly holy man is only silent when thinking about how to solve a problem.

There was an attempted meeting with some people from the parish priest's administrative group, but information about why there was no kind call for dialog with the parts of the community who'd created Our Lady's mural before the fact, was not forthcoming. Nor was any other information about the sudden covering over of all the Holy images.

It seemed no pastoral care would be offered to any of those who asked for restoration of Our Lady's mural, that is, those who'd held their baptisms and funerals, weddings and celebratory masses within reach of Our Lady's arms. People continued to be taken aback that she'd been plastered over without consult with those very persons, those very sons and daughters of those who had brought her here in their loving hearts longs ago, those who granted the blank canvas of the church walls to the best mural artist the community could find who gave of her loving work, those people who cared for Our Lady's mural over all those years, carefully preserving, protecting, dusting, cleaning, remaining near this sacred set of images that so gave comfort to so many for so many decades.

TRYING AGAIN TO BE HEARD: NON-VIOLENT PROTEST

The "women in white" and *Fieles Unidos,* still trying to be listened to and met with cordiality and help to restore Our Lady's mural, set aside a workday—not an easy day for the often working-class members to gain time-off. But they did, and thus they marched ensemble then to the local archbishop's grand residence to read aloud a humble letter worked on for days and days by gentle-hearted people trying to choose exactly the right conciliatory but also able words, asking that the wall come down and the mural be restored in keeping with the most holy teachings of the Church about not desecrating sacred art, not allowing a blasphemy and a sacrilege toward the holy presence that stands behind that holy mural.

Our group from La Sociedad de Guadalupe, founded twenty years ago to aid in literacy including literacy about the Holy, joined the processions in which we women and men elders walked peacefully with our *comadres* and *compadres,* the old women's long fringed shawls swaying, everyone's rosaries swinging, and our prayers being said in Spanish and English.

Our so humble *viejos y viejas* in their very best gaucho hats and tattered mantillas struggled forward with canes and in wheelchair. Our old ones kept right up, their long silver hair blowing in the wind, and their vividly colored and embroidered Mejicano clothing dazzling in the sunlight. So beautiful, and all asking too that the men in power please allow those who have for so very long loved Our Lady's sacred artwork, be allowed to see Our Lady again. Fully. Without being barred. And without walls.

But no, the petition was not granted. Archbishop said it was up to the local priest to do as he wished. That it was "a parish matter." And the priest said he had the approval of Archbishop. And thus one supported the other, but there were no answers to the people's questions. Thus many people were still not allowed to understand the decisions and reasons for the wall. The media were present that day with cameras and reporters, but were barred by chancellery staff from entering the archbishop's property. The archbishop had sent a letter to the peaceful protestors saying their going to the press did not further their petitions. But/And the cameras rolled outside the fences and reporters interviewed many of the elders at the curb afterward.[2] And still those who loved Our Lady's sacred mural were stricken and deeply puzzled about why no one seemed to care that La Señora was now behind a man-made wall.

Oddly enough, in addition to jailing Holy Mother, whether consciously meant quite that way or not, the remodeling of the altar area also suddenly required the purchase of a very large gray rock throne for the priests to sit in during Mass, whereas formerly for many decades, there had been only someone's grandmother's dining room straight-backed chairs, which were so lovingly kept clean and tidy—these in keeping with the hand-made quality of what the faithful who loved Holy Mother so, had often referred to as "The Little Sistine Chapel of Our Lady of Guadalupe Church in North Denver."

The remodeling had also ordered the nailing of sheetrock, floor to ceiling, over the larger-than-life-size huge white-winged Guardian Angels hand-painted on both side walls of the altar. The order was also given to nail drywall over the little cherubs the mural artist had lovingly painted around the heating vents high up on either side of the altar alcove, and to cover over the so beautifully rendered they seemed nearly real: the long, flowing bowers of Our Lady's red red roses.

It was baffling, and many people seemed to use a lot of "d" words to describe "the remodel:" demeaning, destructive, disrespectful. It was said that all this came about because "someone" had complained that Our Lady's mural was a "distraction" from "the real meaning" of Christianity. And as though to underline such, during a *Fieles Unidos* peaceful protest, an angry male church member aggressed toward the praying "women in white" who only wanted the wall to come down so they could sit and pray and be near their familiar and beloved Mother of God again. The man screamed at the praying women: "The only place for Mary is on her knees at the foot of the Cross!!"

That day, maybe the smaller miracle was that there was not a riot as a result of this insult, not only to Our Lady, but to we mestizos whose ancestors, male and female, were forced to their knees by the ruling con-quistadores and prelates who also forced the tribal people across the Americas into decade upon decade of brutal slave labor . . . forcing liter-ally millions to their knees at the foot of a cross for 500 years plus—not a cross belonging to the God of Love, El Cristo Rey, but a cross made of conquerors' greed, avarice, abject cruelty and destruction of the folkways of the people in order to assert the thug-invaders' disingenuous values. Many that day, hearing the man scream about how Mary ought be on her knees, thought they were seeing Santayana's prophecy come to life again in the words of the screamer: *"Those who fail to recall their history, are doomed to repeat it."*[3]

Yet, there's an odd phenomenon: great spiritual passion often rises from travesty.

Something of that day reminded me of my prison ministry over decades. I realized not only was Our Lady truly in a prison made of lath-ing, drywall, nails and mud troweled on by hired workmen, but also one might wonder if the idea to obliterate such beautiful sacred art was also somehow in some kind of prison of its own too, one of striving to be faithful for certain, but without yet a heart broken open and made large enough to include all souls, not just some souls? Angelus Silesius, in a beautiful prayer asked Creator to shatter him, to break his heart open, so he might carry more of the Being everywhere, to and toward all. May it be so here as well for us all.

Yet, we have seen it time and again in history, no person, no event can long destroy the summonses sent to the people's souls by the saints and Creator and Holy Mother. Do whatever else anyone might, the people continue to long for Mother and all the Holy and Divine. As we see over the eons, neither can dictators remove nor destroy the memories of the sacred from the young, the middle-aged and the elders, all of which will be handed down to their children and grandchildren . . . who will remember how their parents and grandparents were treated—or mis-treated over time—with regard to all matters of humanity and decency.

But given all history of subversion of manifestations of the Holy Spirit bursting through with new ideas, new verve and new life, despite any mistaken or even cruel severings of long standing relationships, precisely planned upheavals, cover-ups and coverings over of meaning, dividing the community instead of weaving it together meaning to heal it, making all shine . . . despite any corrosions laid down over a now divided community, the problem for conquerors has always been this: No matter who they remove or silence or shame or cover over, alter, add to so as to distort, co-opt, make afraid, or murder . . . they cannot destroy the living people's loving memories of the Holy.

THE REMEMBERERS

For remember, even though the murderer Joe Stalin and his dedicated inner circle of thugs, for instance, tried to wipe out Holy Mother across as much of Asia, Russia and the greater part of Eastern Europe as they could, even as some of the Taliban in Afghanistan tried to erase through literal gunpowder explosion the ancient stone Buddhas carved into the mountains at Bamiyan, oddly destroying the huge sculptures, but leaving the entire venerable outlines of the Buddhas intact in the mountainside: no Buddha, only now the outline of the Buddha, even more mysterious and compelling than before. Remember, as I mentioned to you before, and again it is true: When the Holy is buried instead of living above ground, it is often even more compelling, for the Holy is then seen as buried treasure.

So efforts to occlude Our Lady continue across the world: Even though attempts were and are made across so many cultures, trying to grind to dust the veneration of that which stands behind paintings, murals, statuary, petroglyphs, cairns, song caves, stone altars . . . the great force of Our Mother, the Holy, continues nonetheless.

And more so, wherever she has been squelched, sequestered, erased, covered over, she, like the other Holy people, dives underground, becoming even stronger like a roaring river moving steeply downstream and then in the bowl at the bottom of the class 4 rapids, slamming and filling as she explodes back to the surface again, and with even more power, with even more verve than ever before.

You have to dig deep to bury Holy Mother. All the way down through the center of the Earth and out the other side of the planet would not be deep enough to bury her, nor to make the people forget her, a moving temple of devotees who have spent decades, millennia, being comforted by her and all that is consecrated to, with, and for her.

VISITING THOSE IMPRISONED:
WHAT THE WALL OVER OUR LADY BROUGHT
IN HOLY VIGIL, AS IN DAYS OF ELD

So ironically, as in ancient times, as now, for those in prison, for those who are free, regardless of what is destroyed, blown up, subverted, those who love continue to venture out in their own ways, on touching pilgrimage when they can, where they can, however they can.

In the matter of the constructing a wall over the heroic mural of Our Lady of Guadalupe, sending La Señora to prison in a sense—so too, like those who love their own who are taken to actual penitentiaries, locked institutions, federal prisons, county jails, those who love them, truly love them . . . all the people are, by duty as loyal souls and loving spirits, required to come to visit those imprisoned.

So too with Our Lady. We consider the visiting of those ill or imprisoned to be high spiritual promise given, promise fulfilled. Until administrators at the church recently no longer allow visits, the faithful who longed to see her, came to visit her often, bringing her sustenance, keeping her company in her loneliness. In this way, the giant spirit of Holy Mother Behind the Wall was treated the same as visits by relatives and friends to their loved ones in prison. This is the old tradition among Latinos and other old believers: to never abandon the souls who are imprisoned.

For a very short time, the parish administrators indicated, ironically just as wardens often say to the family and friends of people in prison, that we could "come see" Our Lady behind the wall. But only on occasion, and not when we wished to, and not when we could arrange so around our caretaking of children, grandchildren, elders, holding a job and attempting to wear relatively clean clothes, comb our hair and remain mostly sane. Rather, only when those in charge said so. Only then could we visit during the erratic times when allowed.

It isn't just Our Lady in prison then. It isn't just an actual prisoner doing time in a prison. The family of loved one is also handcuffed and restricted. Come only when we say so. Not when you want so. Do as we say, not as your heart and soul tell you. You love your loved one? Well, only when we say so are you allowed to show this.

We old believers were used to, for decades, being welcomed to come sit with El Cristo, Santo Niño, Holy Family, Our Lady, at any time. We were always welcome and churches were open for any grief, need for succor from Creator and the santitos, little saints. But now, though we were able until now, to still visit Our Lady, as is our ancient custom to visit the imprisoned, it was, before being forbidden entirely, allowed only for the briefest periods of time. And one could not bring a camera to take a picture of Our Lady to remember her by. This was then forbidden. One could not leave flowers for her behind the wall/closet. Eventually, this was forbidden too. One could not stand there and read a letter to her, nor show her an artwork a child made for her to keep her company. Nor were we allowed to touch her. Only to look, as from behind a plastic barrier. Like in prison.

No touching of her allowed in that dismal broom closet. We, the people of the old tradition of the church: *Pésame,* giving comfort and condolences to Blessed Mother. This we old believers were barred from doing. Yet, like the family and visitors to a human being in prison, we still longed to at least reach our palms toward her shoulder, or toward her cheek and place our hand on the shoulders of Santo Juan Diego. But again, this was not allowed either.

And when we were able to visit ever so briefly, and the short time was up, seeming dictated by how the clerk felt that day, then we had to go away. And Our Lady was then alone again. In the dark closet. With no light. No air. With no one to talk to. This isolation of the Mother is against every Latino's holy heart. It is against every holy heart who loves Holy Mother.

And for loved ones who come to visit their relatives in state and federal prisons, it is like this too. Visiting time is the life's blood of love and remaining close with one another. Without it, we all wither. With it, in the "visiting room" at prisons, it is still often far too short, and far too restrictive and needlessly austere. And afterward, all are glad they came, but in one way, more wistful than ever before.

And so it goes on there. And so it goes for us here too. Even with Our Lady and her sons and daughters longing for her, it is the same . . . There are literally millions of human beings across the world who are walking the rough road toward their loved ones in prison right now, in dreams and in reality. And they are faithful too, even though held away from each other, deprived of taking one another into their arms, clasping each other warmly, feeding one another in communion through the so sacred senses of loving and being loved: the senses of familiar scent; the beholding of the precious one through sight; the listening to the familiar tone and timbre of a beloved voice; and most especially receiving the electricity that is precious to the skin, that is, the gift of calmness and selfhood that comes from loving touch.

THE RIGHT PLACE FOR OUR HOLY MOTHER IS . . . EVERYWHERE, AS THE PLACE FOR LOVE IS . . . EVERYWHERE, INCLUDING FOR THOSE IMPRISONED AND THOSE WHO ARE FREE

In the case of Blessed Mother being "a distraction" as at least one who'd planned the "remodeling" had said was a complaint heard, just by contrast, there are over five-*thousand*-plus venerable and time-honored enormous basilicas, cathedrals, and medium and small sized churches in the world wherein La María, Holy Mother, Mother of God, is central on the altar. Her image is at exact midpoint, right on the altar or ensconced on a decorative ledge or humble chair or ornate dome above the entire altar as the highest, most central figure.

One such basilica is in Rome, a stone's throw from the Vatican and one of only four papal basilicas. It is the revered Basilica di Santa María Maggiore, wherein Mother of God, as she was termed in ordinance with the decree issued by the Council of Ephesus in 431 CE, is but one such example of Mary, María, Mir-yam being right in the middle, not just of the church, but in the middle of her people—and her placement at center has been endorsed and supported by pope after pope, bishops and cardinals for nearly 1,580 years, all the way through to the present.

Quite a provenance. Quite a binding precedent for Mary holding the middle ground, and not diverting, but rather, gathering, bringing the Holy Hearts of all to center. Given such exemplars across the world of Holy Mother being approved in her many places, it seems odd that Blessed Mother ought ever be covered over in a Catholic church in seeming opposition to time-honored standards set forth by the papacy itself. I continue to wonder where are all the facts of what occurred, the actual thinking, or perhaps accident in thinking behind it all.

Our Lady of Guadalupe church in North Denver was brought together by those who come from oppression, from being *los desaparecidos*, "the disappeared," covered over themselves by not being seen as valuable in the overculture. Again, as the child of refugees and immigrants, I understand many layers of *la lucha*, the struggle, for I was drenched in my families' tribal beliefs overlaying their religious ones, and their further being torn apart by literally being slaughtered, maimed, and routed by two opposing armies during "the long black war."

When looking at this, the main altar at the Church of the Miraculous Medal, Notre Dame de la rue du Bac, one sees the tremendous love for Holy Mother just in the excruciatingly fine details in the many artworks alone, let alone feeling in full the blessed force that stands behind these images of Mary. The sacred mural of Our Lady and Her Angels above the altar is done in tiny squares of mosaic. Mary, Marie, María, Mir-yam stands above and at center of the altar with the large crucifix at her feet where she can see her Son like any mother watching over all, including the Holy, the pilgrims and the petitioners who come to her for her help, healing, and mercy.

I also can see the concordance here with families who have a relative in prison, for often it is the same. When someone leads, someone with the true fire of Holy Spirit going on in their head, when that one, or more, rise up in daily striving to be disciplined and spiritually self-examined, when they stand at the fore, and say, In the name of all that is Holy, not now, not again, not ever, no more! Then something can happen, something decent awakened that had been put to sleep accidentally or wrongfully, long or short ago.

I also know that like the prison system which can offer humane instead of too harsh or negligent responses to those incarcerated, so too whomsoever ordered the obliteration of Our Lady's sacred mural, can at any moment turn to offer a loving response toward the people who love Our Lady and her Savior Child, the angels and the saints. Any who without clear seeing, and/or any who ordered destruction can also order restoration. This I know.

And this I hold out hope for: the uncovering of Our Lady's mural, the necessary mendings that can take place, and thereby good will, true open-hearted understanding toward all, and we go forward together in celebration of all people concerned, woven *together,* no one scowling, but rather joining in again in purity of her Immaculate Heart, remembering our bloodline of Nuestra Madre, Our Mother and her Divine Child who brought not strife, but acceptance of "the least of the least" to this world, love for women and children, protection for those who strive to love. This I pray for.

For I feel certain that many priests and prelates are mothers themselves. They want to love and help far more than barricade or divide. Like actual mothers the go forth daily with their ears against the heartbeat of the family, always seeing how everyone is doing. Those who lead families of believers, do not forget the headaches and heartaches and heartwarming of daily parish family life.

And, as we who are mothers of families know too: The mother sets the tone for the entire dinner table. The mother sets the tone for the whole family. If she is of kind counsel; or bitter and resentful; if she is so busy trying to climb the ladder at work instead of being near her offspring; if she is helpful rather than hateful; responsive and gladly helping in real ways; or if she is filled with platitudes, broken promises, repeating the bromides of "my hands are tied," instead of truly problem-solving with the broken and knowing heart in the lead; if she moves in love, ever love, not just mouthing the world "love" manipulatively; if she has a gentle fierceness to her, if she does not have fits of pique because she insists on remembering to put the souls of all around her first, including her own soul's care; if she is dedicated to learning and teaching instead of admonishing and punishing which are guaranteed ways to ever proclaim others as "less;" if a mother makes her table one of welcome—then her children are most likely to grow and help others to grow, to be nourished and to nourish others, to be accepted and to be accepting, be loyal to and in love and allegiance to the holiest in self and in others.

But if not—as across history then, we witness that efforts to erase actual beloved human beings by disparaging and covering over the sacred in "unmarked graves," has only caused the mothers and fathers, brothers and sisters, loves and friends of the desaparecidos, "the disappeared" to relentlessly seek their own Holy people without cease then. All across the world, it is an imperative in the psyche, to carry this kind of blood family loyalty to the loved and the beloved Holy ones. Sentences, decrees, and fiats against the sacred, cannot subvert this kind of purity given by a Force Greater, this kind of "never was there a greater love." Not even walls and prisons can prevent the people from loving and following the Holy, nor the Holy from loving and guiding the people.

PROTECTION OF SACRED WORKS, THE PAPAL SAY-SO ABOUT THE HOLY ONES

The dragging off, decimation and destructive assault on images that are sacred life's blood to the people—occurred so many times over the centuries, that long ago Pope Leo and other popes wrote rules for protecting the artworks that people held in a life and death spiritual devotion, no matter what cottage, village, kingdom or roadside, no matter what rank or tribe or affiliation anyone came from.

The idea was to neither hold the holy images away from people, nor to damage them, and to not bar the people from them in any way, for the people loved and depended on the holy forces *behind* the images. Thus, to withhold, especially, the force of the Mother of God away from her children, to mutilate or imprison her was made, by papal law, illegal.

Papal statements, encyclicals, and Ecumenical Councils from the eighth century to the present day took up the issue with no ambiguity. The protection of what is sacred to the family of believers was clear, one pronouncement being made at the Second Council of Nicaea in 787 AD:

> ". . . we decree with full precision and care that, like the figure
> of the honoured and life-giving cross, the revered and holy
> images, whether painted or made of mosaic or of other suitable

material, are to be exposed in the holy churches of God, on sacred instruments and vestments, *on walls and panels,* in houses and by public ways; these are the images of our Lord, God and saviour, Jesus Christ, and of our Lady without blemish, the holy God-bearer, and of the revered angels and of any of the saintly holy men. The more frequently they are seen in representational art, the more are those who see them drawn to remember and long for those who serve as models, and to pay these images the tribute of salutation and respectful veneration . . ."

There are more papal councils and more protections for ". . . pictures of Christ, the Blessed Virgin Mary and the Saints," with full recognition regarding "those who have done [destruction] in times past in this our royal city against the venerable images," how those who have "reigned immediately before us destroyed them and subjected them to disgrace and injury: Let them who do not venerate the holy and venerable images be anathema!"

Too, in the last year, Pope Benedict XVI invited artisans of all kinds to the Vatican, bidding them to create new and wondrous paintings and sculptures for Mother Church. In the beautiful Sistine Chapel, he expressed a need for inspiring art for places of worship. In his address, the Pope, surrounded by Michelangelo's stunning frescoes, said, *"Thanks to your talent, you have the opportunity to speak to the heart of humanity, to touch individual and collective sensibilities, to call forth dreams and hopes, to broaden the horizons of knowledge and of human engagement."*

But ironically, at the same time Pope Benedict was speaking to artists, the mural of Our Lady, Santo Juan Diego, Los Ángeles and the Guardian Angels were being imprisoned in thick paint and behind sheet-rock walls. *"To call forth dreams and hopes, to broaden the horizons of knowledge and of human engagement."*

Though for decades, Our Lady's mural had been witness and participant, like any set of dear family members, at Christmas *Cristo nació,* birth of Savior, at Easter Risen Cristo, weddings, feasts and mariachi Masses, First Communions, Confirmations, baptizing of little infants, the last rites for the beloved who had passed from this world, perhaps some forgot that Our Lady's mural, I think, would have been smiled upon by the papacy, for it portrayed an astonishing event—that Our Lady appeared to a dark brown little indigenous male who was from the group most reviled by the conquerors . . . this entire "turning point in the history of the races," this holy event was an inspiring focus of devotion, the pride of thousands of parishioners at the parish over the decades, as well as many visitors from across the world who came to see the beautiful mural of La Señora de Guadalupe at this little church. "*. . . you have the opportunity to speak to the heart of humanity . . .*"

In particular, the Latino community which had struggled for decades for true acceptance and respect by the institutional church, including according to one priestly source, it was not until 1970 that Latino men were allowed to enter seminary to be priests in Colorado. If truest of true, this means massive discrimination and a foisting of a false inferiority over certain other heritage groups by those who held sway over such matters back then. This mural in this church was liberation from all that historical assault on people who only happened to be of Mexican, Native American, Central American, South American, and other Latin-based language heritages, but were in fact from the eternal family of Souls.

One sees similar clangs with families of the imprisoned who are promised by law certain protections and certain accommodations for themselves and for their loved ones in the jails, but then, too often, the local say-so-ers contravene what has been set in place by a more reasoned authority. This is painful to the families, and seems entirely a maddening set-up to make promises of help and then to break these. In such institutional whirligigs, one sometimes prays for all the reasoned grown-ups with heart to please return to earth, pronto. Sometimes, the same prayer can be said perpetually about the world outside the walls as well.

REVOLUTION MEANS TO CREATE!
WILD SOUL INTACT: CREATE, CREATE, CREATE!
THE BLESSING WAY CONTINUES,
EVEN BEHIND BARS AND WALLS

Yet I saw something else too in this forcing of Our Lady behind the white wall, something I often saw in the brave hearts and minds of families with loved ones in prison: that is, the huge outpouring of art that comes straight from the hurt heart.

Since Our Lady's mural has been forced behind a wall, that entire "remodeling" has inspired pageantry, a so missing part of modern spirituality in many places today. Not pomp. Rather in ritual, the people's love for the Holy made visible.

Regarding the covering over of Our Lady's mural, people began literally holding processions and marches, pilgrimages. People young and old gathered to pray novenas, the old ways that have often been lost in our modern time because leaders are often validly "busy," or lack having lived long enough to remember "the old ways," or sometimes lack skill to coalesce the people in meaning and love and care of each other around these beloved rituals. Rarely so, lack of warmth, or lack of energy.

Our Lady in what some now called "broom closet prison" inspired a website called, wouldjesushidehismother.com which tells of *Fieles Unidos* strivings to bring Our Lady, literally, into full view again. The fact of "Our Lady Behind The Wall," has inspired poetry and diaries. A play has been written and will have readings. Paintings have been made, some of these sacred, some of them satire, and some of both. The wall has drawn the interest of a documentary filmmaker. Our Lady Behind the Wall has drawn news media, activists, holy people. It has brought to many the old fire of the days of struggle with Cesar Chavez and others who are local heroes, to not give up, to not go away, but instead to continue in all fierce love until one has prevailed. And in all, more than anything else, there is being carried a heart of love for the imprisoned. My father used to say, the battles worth fighting were those fighting *for,* not *against.* He meant fighting not other souls, but fighting to bring as many souls under "the blessing tent" of Our Lady as possible.

How similar this outpouring of art to and for and by the imprisoned in the greater world. The mothers and fathers and children of actual prisoners' groups swell with handwritten poetry, paintings and ex-votos on boards, newly minted prayers, activism, grassroots movements, online communities of support, seeking of media focus, soliciting filmmakers and photographers, trading of food with one another, helping one another in support of the souls of all, comforting the grieving, lifting the heart weary, and so much more.

The same, but different. But, the same. The families of the imprisoned understand that grief often causes art. Their immense outpouring not only of pain, but of new life, is similar to the situation anywhere the Holy is incarcerated. In North Denver at the Little Sistine Chapel of Our Lady of Guadalupe Parish, even though Holy Mother is still behind the wall, and yet, revolution rises from the fact of imprisonment.

More than anything, I see that Revolution means to create, to keep creating even in the midst of being held back, being imprisoned. If you can't speak it, write it; if you can't write it, sing it; if you can't sing it, whisper it; if you can't whisper it; dream it, keep dreaming it, until one fine day . . .

One creates not to maintain the status quo, but to truly see beyond this time and this world, and then to unleash fresh vision. ". . . to broaden the horizons of knowledge and of human engagement."

Communism was brought down by interrupting the money supply, stopping the supply chain, especially services whether mining, burning, bringing, lifting, hauling or making. This was done by people longing to be free. Our Lady of Częstochowa was hidden away for a time, then was sought and brought out again by those who love her. Others went underground and yet others in even banal circumstances . . . those who mistakenly attempted to erase the sources of loving and holy pride of Holy Mother, often enough found ways to reconcile in true honor, with parity for all.

But, in order to create Revolution, what change agents did not do, was as important as what they did do: They did not stand by quietly, nor sit still. They were thoughtful, gathered in large groups and small groups, did not remain local only, went global for their time, allied together; moved forward; were prepared to win some, lose some; understood solidarity as being united in one principle and to hold fast to that in true Love, and to let all other items of agreement or disagreement fall away; to ever move forward.

Even those imprisoned for their visions, their understandings, their knowings, massively create. We see from the spiritual diaries of incarcerated men and women writing from prison that often, being captured, also became part of one's spiritual path in order to create messages of freedom and bravery not just for one's sanity, but for the world. In that sense, were one to see it that way, prison may sometimes be sudden spiritual truth, one far more highlighted than when a person might be free but focused far more diffusely.

Though many attribute revolution to battles and speechifying and strategies, more so, far far more so, true and heartful allying is brought forth by massive creativity in all its millions of variations. One such massively creative soul was Reverend Martin Luther King, who put what I see as the "four steps to creative revolution" in his *Letter from Birmingham Jail* where he had been incarcerated. To me, there is no more concise, more deep, more true set of tenets for peaceful revolution:

"In any nonviolent campaign there are four basic steps:
collection of the facts to determine whether injustices exist;
negotiation; self purification; and direct action."[4]

Reverend King is speaking about caissons being driven deep down below the water line so the creative "Being of being" walks upright in righteous action. He is saying, not *chisme*, gossip, but facts are to be gathered; that one be open to negotiation; ally with other pacifists and groups of influence and strength; spiritually self-examine oneself when preparing for engagement so that one is as much in the aura of love for all as possible; and then move onward in nonviolent protest for long and long and long—for as long as it takes.

People come and go. Back and forth. Nonetheless, onward. Ever onward. Never forgetting the past, ever forgiving all petty human foibles and frailties, pressing forward in service of The Woman who has never left us alone in prison, Our Lady.[5]

INSULT TO INJURY, BUT/AND LET US SEE, TRULY SEE

We don't know the end of the story of Our Lady's mural at the Little Sistine Chapel at Our Lady of Guadalupe Parish in North Denver. We do not know the end of the story yet. But we know another page in the story. Since the wall went up, someone has sadly defaced the Our Lady of Guadalupe mural in the closet prison. Only a couple people seemed to have keys to the door to the closet where Our Lady now lives with Santo Juan Diego. Someone entered there and spray-painted across her "¡Ya Basta!" And "¡No Más!" "¡Ya Basta!" means "Enough!" "No Más," means, "No More." Those who want the wall to occlude Our Lady perhaps are thinking, "Yes, that's right. Go away you who want restoration of Our Lady's mural. We've had enough of you." Most are puzzled about why the parish and archdiocese stopped the police from investigating who did this vandalism. The parish says the church will not proceed. The people who care, just do not understand why.

Regardless, many of the people continue to feel even more strongly than before that they cannot forfeit this beautiful mural from their heart memories, for in addition to their Mother and her Divine Child, Holy Mother's mural represents their kin, their loved parents, grandparents, and great-grandparents who built this place with coins offered, their wrinkled dollars from their little coin purses, their honest tithes from their weekly union wages, their hard-earned money given with true love from the labors of their bones and blood. The mural represents

Mother's witness to marriages between the tender young, baptisms of tiny arm-waving infants, saying the last goodbye to the beloved dead in the Requiem Masses.

Thus Holy Mother was at all our wedding feasts, just as in times of eld. She was the witness at all the times of blessing the young into their faith just as long ago. She was The Mother who held us tenderly during the last rites for our loved ones, many gone before they had much chance to live. She was always there, vibrant, large, and loving, for she is our *familiare,* our relative. Always present in such vibrancy. Always faithful to us and we to her.

And all this is inside the very atoms of the beautiful mural. All this is in the very stones of this church. All the brave blood of the people who endured, is in this sacred place . . . for this holy place that holds the mural was hand built, hand painted and heart-maintained by the people who love. And Our Lady's mural has been alive for decades on end, long before anyone had ever thought to cover over The Little Sistine Chapel of Our Lady of Guadalupe.

Regardless of how many twists this "remodeling" has taken, as a former parishioner, I still believe this issue doesn't have to be any priest's or prelate's "my way or the highway." There is another way. It is called "The Way" that El Cristo Rey spoke to us about. "The Way" does not exclude sacred art nor soulful people, nor His Mother, nor her children who love her just as she was. It includes all souls. It includes *seeing* all souls. It includes leaders who are healers and helpers. And it is for this outcome, this kind of restoration, even more than the mural itself, that I pray toward . . . all can join in this prayer of restoration of us all, and for us all, I believe.

At this writing, the parish still does not answer calls that ask and sometimes plead to come visit Our Lady behind the wall, for we don't forget the lonely. Yet, most of us were raised on these words of the gentle Jesus, Son of Mary, written about by the young scribe Matthew in ancient times. Mary's Boy says to His followers:

> "I was hungry and you gave me no food,
> I was thirsty and you gave me no drink,
> I was a stranger and you did not welcome me,
> I was naked and you did not clothe me,
> I was sick and in prison and you did not visit me."

He is attempting to teach His followers a way of life of devotion to Creator and also to the lives of the souls on earth in the most mothering of all ways. But his followers don't understand Him, and they say, "But Lord, when did we see you hungry or thirsty, or as a stranger, or naked, or sick or in prison, and did not minister to you?"

And the kindly Child of Mother Mary, Jesus, says,

> "Truly, I say to you,
> if you did not give these things to those
> who are the least amongst us,
> you did not give these things to me."

Mary's Child means that if we did not give these kindnesses to all . . . to feed others kindly and spiritually, to quaff their spiritual thirst, to give warmth to what has gone cold in spirit, to heal the heart, to keep close companionship with the spirit imprisoned . . . then it doesn't matter if one ministered to only Jesus in travail. It only matters when one reaches to not the recognized, not the inner circle, but rather to the hungry, the thirsty, the stranger, the unclothed, the ill, the imprisoned whether one knows them or not, understands them or not, holds them dearest or not.

Thus, all outcomes of the matter of Our Lady in prison behind the wall, remain to be seen. But/And, I believe that if one person can give the order to cover her over, I believe with all my heart, that at least one person can give the order to reveal her again.

In the meantime, Our Lady is fully revealed in our hearts and in our souls, for like the love between those in families with relatives in prison, no wall can separate love from Love.

We know where she is, like the heart radar between those imprisoned together, one behind bars and the others held away by circumstances beyond their control . . . We always know where Our Lady is, like Love itself, she cannot be held back by bars nor by walls. She is at present, underground, gathering energy and she is flowing out everywhere . . . through us. Everywhere she is ministering to feed others spiritually, to quaff the spiritual thirst of human souls, bending to give warmth to what has gone cold in spirit, to heal the heart, to keep close companionship with the spirit imprisoned, including especially those whom she now shares a fate with: those souls in actual prisons.

She is thereby, Our Mother, and Mother of all Captives. She is Mother of the Free. She is Mother Behind the Wall, and still, She remains: Unconquerable Mother of All.

HOLY MOTHER BEHIND THE WALL

You can build a wall, try to subvert her,
Unqualify her,
Say this image of her
or that one, is better,
say this is the only authentic
anything.

But I am reminded that
Creator,
Source without source,
Did not make only one songbird,
Did not set that winged angel
into a sky that never changes,
that Creator did not grant one
version of offspring,
did not create all eggs speckled
exactly like every other speckled egg.

It is clear that one can unbuild a wall over our Lady
And many throughout history have done so.
But one cannot,
Even were one to paint her over,
Even if one were to plaster her over,
Even if one were to take down the very lathe and studs,
Even if one were to use a pneumatic drill
whilst supporting the roofline with hundreds of 2x4s,
Even if one were to try to take out the entire wall,
She would still be in the dust of that former wall.
She would still be in the atoms.
She would still hang in the air there.
For, she is indestructible—

In prison.
Out of prison.
She is whole and she cannot be erased
For she is ours.
And we, you and I,
Are most assuredly hers.
All of us.
All.

With you, Holy Mother Behind the Wall,
Nonetheless, we all walk free together.
With you Holy Mother Behind the Wall,
there are no iron bars, no walls of clay.

With you Holy Mother,

there is no bad actor, only the act.

With you, there is no condemnation of any kind . . .
Only being sentenced to Life . . .
A long life of Love
And more Love yet,
with you forever, Holy Mother.

Aymen, aymen, aymen.
Let it be so,
let it be so now,
let us remain together
siempre, always.

Our Lady
who glows
in the dark,
exploding
swastikas
back into
meaning:
God of Love

CHAPTER NINE

Carrying the Name of the Mother

A Man Named Mary

Uncle Tovar's middle name was Marushka, which means Mary.

How did this come to be, a man with a girl's name, Mary?
In the Old Country, people often had no middle name.
But Tovar took this special name
because he had been near the Blessed Mother.
In a very unusual way.
He said he took this girl's name in gratitude.
He promised he would wear this feminine name proudly,
for the rest of his life . . .

Long ago, during a terrible war that had crisscrossed and decimated his little village, Tovar had run into hiding in the forest. The Nazis were on motorcycles and in open cars. They were storming through the farm villages on the old dirt roads, each village holding forty or so families each.

The villagers had no automobiles, and their horses went white-eyed at the bleating, snoring sounds of the soldiers' engines. The old people

---

◀ Ex-voto: "Our Lady Who Glows In the Dark"

held the reins of their horses, trying to calm them while motioning silently to the young to run for their lives into the woods . . .

The girls, to make a too often futile effort to protect them from rape, and the boys because the Nazis had come to take them away never to be seen again.

The Nazis had already stolen many boys from other villages, forcing the boys to fight for them—or else be shot dead on the spot.

Tovar had been in the barn atop the bluff when the villagers heard the engines roaring toward them. Some Nazi soldiers had been to their "in the middle of nowhere" village some weeks before, to kill their cows and sheep in order to feed their units. So the village children, the aged, and the ill were slowly starving now.

Uncle escaped up the hill behind the barn with a horse blanket thrown over his thin shoulders, one he'd woven himself out of the thick red and black and white wool his mother had hand-combed, spun, and dyed.

Uncle hid in the woods. He waited and waited, for it was daylight and he dared not cross any dirt road.

Suddenly, Uncle heard the big whine of an engine. Uncle said he suddenly felt sick, like the time he had gone to market and a traveling circus came through with a man so strong he could spin the children around in circles for minutes on end for the price of a penny.

Uncle, his heart pounding with fear, watched as two Nazi soldiers stopped their car to relieve themselves in the woods.

My uncle said that we all can tell when we begin to die before we die, as he suddenly could no longer feel his legs and hands. Perhaps they have already shot me, he thought, and the blood does not yet show.

He began to pray and pray to Our Lady in such a strong way; he said that it was like "making smoke" so she could see it and come to help him.

His "little words" prayer went something like this:

Help me Marushka,
Help me
Help me
Please help me
Please, please, please Lady Marushka . . .
Help me!

Now, one soldier, holding his penis in one hand,
and pointing with his other hand—
looked at Tovar directly, saying,

"Look at the beautiful wild roses over there."
Uncle was sure he would die now
—for there was only skinny him
behind a log, and so filled with fear,
wearing his red and black and white horse blanket.
Uncle was hunched over so far
that his nose touched the ground.

The other soldier shook his own penis,
opening his legs,
bending his knees a little,
then packed it back in.
He buttoned up, saying,
"We haven't time for roses now."

And away the fully armed soldiers drove.
In a light December snow.
In the dead of winter 1944.

Amongst the Magyar and Swabian tribes,
And some of the Roma as well . . .
his name is Tovar Marushka.
Among our Mexican-Spanish relatives,
his name would be Tovaro-María.
In the USA, his name is Tovar Mary.

It shall always remain this way,
for Uncle was an old believer,
and in the Old Country
it was sacred duty to name a child
after the midwife
who not only brought the infant's life
back from the Gate of Death,
but whomsoever thereby caused the child to become
one of the blessed, one of the twice born.
Lady Marushka was the midwife
who caused Tovar to be reborn.

In those times of war, Tovar said, many young men
took the name Mary when they were old enough,

for they could see a man could have muscles
and strength, but from Blessed Mother
they could have sometimes,
the cloak of invisibility.

Thus, by her grace, by learning from her
care of others and her love of humanity
they had been reborn.

They walk this world named after their Midwife:
Mary,
María,
Marushka.

SHE

CARRIES

THE EMBER

THROUGH EVERY DARK

CHAPTER TEN

Forged in the Fiery Furnace

The Black Madonna

The Black Madonna is often seen as mysterious, perhaps because those looking at her may not well remember how their own far-back people also created daylight and night time representations of the Great Woman as part of their own tribal zeitgeist. Thus across the world, there is the Black Holy Woman, and the black Deity as well . . . even though most of these far-flung cultures with such ancestral memory of Black Madonna appear not to have cross-fertilized one another face-to-face.

Sometimes, in our times, if one wants to understand a mysterious ritual or devotion from the far away, one can peer at similar remnants found in modern practices, and see the pulse of meaning in the ancient rituals still fully alive in modern times.

In this way, my grandmother Katerin kept rituals from her ethnic Swabian tribal background that "looked for" the Black Madonna right wherever she lived, whether in the Old Country as a peasant farmer-weaver, or in the New World as a refugee and immigrant. This is how she looked for the Holy Mother Who Withstood the Fire.

When I was a child, in our old people's little sand-shingled or clap-board houses in the orchards and Lakeland forests, there were two wood

---

◄ Ex-voto: "She Who Cannot Be Extinguished"

fires going, and sometimes a third fire too. One fire was in the cook stove, and one in the huge old silver boiler that ran a primitive version of a furnace for warmth during the cold months. And if there were a fire pit either indoors or outdoors in a steep tall shed, or in a lean-to for smoking game and other foodstuffs, there would also be the third fire made with fruit tree branches, which would lend their apricot, peach, cherry, or plum flavor to whatever provisions were being smoked over fire for days on end.

Thus my grandmother had rich ground for seeking her beloved Black Madonnas, for after every fire had burnt most of the hardwood and softwood logs, the fruit tree branches, the spare lumber end-sawn, my grandmother would always ask, "Is there any Virgin in there?" She would poke through the white-ash and the blackened log remnants, stirring up showers of orange sparks, asking, asking, "Any Night Maria in here?"

She meant, are there any oval-shaped pieces of burnt and blackened wood left that amazingly resemble Blessed Mother's bodily shape, rounded at head, flowing down, wider at the middle, draping to the bottom in a shape that roughly represented the feminine and motherly form—was there any wood remnant left in the fire pit still flashing little flames?

And, yes, many a time, I saw her push the end of a burnt log with her thickened cracked thumbs whilst yelping at the heat. Many a time I helped her, using iron pokers not store-bought, but made by our smithy uncle to rake the log remnants through the ashes like you'd see a mother eagle, clawing at her eggs to gently turn them over so they would be stimulated to hatch. And here was our ancient Omah looming over the fire and ash in her black dress, black babushka, and thick black hand-knit wool hose—turning the black eggs of the logs as though she were an eagle mother, thinking a Mother Maria might be born from them.

And many a time, there the Great Woman was, right in the fire, a little Black Madonna, sometimes featureless, other times with clear facial features. Old Katerin said this Black Holy Mother carried wisdom and knowledge, and understanding about repairing the land and making things grow. That this little black wooden Holy Mother, once she had cooled, would be the carrier of prayers *from Heaven to Earth*. Yes, from Heaven to Earth, praying for us to please act, imagine, think, love in service of goodness and fire of Spirit for this world, these peoples.

So, then, finding one, sometimes two in a month of fires, she would take the little burnt Madonnas, so black and cracked and scarred, out into her field garden. And pretty soon she had a veritable little half-buried fence of Black Madonnas all along the back partition of her vegetable and wheat field, just along the entire border dividing the land from her massive flower garden and fruit orchard.

This was back in the day when perhaps some of the small-town priests had not received complete formation training, not seeming to know of the Popes' affirmations that people's Old Country and ethnic values should be incorporated with Catholicism, in fact, woven together in feasting and fasting and ritual and bright display wherever possible, so as to include all, rather than exclude anyone.

But in old Katerin's time, the parish priest—who suspiciously often showed up "to make an unexpected house call" whenever there was a Sunday dinner steaming on the table that was a little more fancy than the very plain daily fare—criticized old Katerin for her many burnt wood madonnas in her field. He said she was just having a mere "superstition" and wanted her to realize the Virgin was actually golden-haired with ringlets, porcelain skin, and rich-colored silk clothing.

Old Katerin just said, "These little madonnas protect my fields and make my plants grow large." And the young padre looked over Katerin's rows and rows of pepper plants of ten kinds and colors: her green and yellow and red bell pepper plants, her cayenne and sweet paprika peppers, her wax yellow banana peppers that stretched over the acres. He looked at her green fern-like carrot tops, and her onions' greens swords popping up through the earth. Then, he pointed out with a smirk that it was obvious that the Black Madonnas "weren't working," for the plants were just average size, and not only that, the tomato vines showed some leaf wilt from the hot sun.

Katerin just stood there in her muddy shoes and huge heavy zinc watering can. She just nodded, "You are right, Father." And she let it pass. And continued all her life long to keep seeking and finding her Black Madonnas in the fire.

And . . . we laughed and laughed at the end of that summer, for poor padre didn't realize that all the madonnas planted were not facing the vegetable garden, but facing the flower garden and the fruit trees, and the pears were already the size of softballs, and the plums the size of large lemons, and old Katerin's dahlias won second place at their little village harvest fair that year for being nearly the biggest on record. Except for this other old lady who won first place with her dahlias that were only slightly larger in diameter than Katerin's . . . the size of serving platters.

The other old woman who won first place was old Katerin's daughter, old Kathe, my mad knitter, crocheting-queen aunt from the Old Country too, and to whom grandmother had given several of her "fire-forged" Black Madonnas to plant facing Kathe's own flower field . . . five miles away.

Black Madonna doesn't have to be artwork created by someone far away across the world and oceans. Black Madonna is artwork in Hawaii made from ocean stone, in Mexico from volcanic black sponge rock, among the K'iche' tribal group of Mayans in Guatemala, and over five hundred Black Madonna shrines and churches exist today in France alone, and more in Switzerland, Africa, Asia, and throughout the world.

Too, she can be a piece of oak or ash or pine that has been burnt in the fire. Old Katerin used to say that this was the point about her Black Madonnas taken from the fire . . . and about us too: That the little dark Blessed Mother was burned, but she was not consumed. She is still here. We are still here. We still hold our holy shapes, no matter what fire we have been passed through. Black Madonna says, "Behold my dark face, my burned body, and grow, grow, flourish, flourish. Let nothing hold you back."

Black Madonna, forged in the fire, leads the way.

BLACK SKIN MOTHER:
HER BEAUTY, DENIGRATION, CONTINUANCE

"The skin mother." In our ethnic families these were some of her names: *bor édesanya,* and *la madre de la piel,* skin mother, some amongst many given to honor the natal mother, the mother with the most intimate relationship of "no separation" of her body, spirit, soul, mind, and heart from her children, nor in the case of her "little beloved prisoner" within her belly, her baby in utero. And this is an apt description, a skin-and-bone way to understand our relationship with Holy Mother: we too are held, wafting back and forth in the nourishing red ocean and flowering dark within her.

So too is this name for Holy Mother from Magyar and Latino heritages: *Egy sötét boru no* and *La Morena,* "the beautiful dark-skinned one." One will often find this appellation also used in villages where there are people who are Roma, Moorish, African, Native, and Spanish, and other bloodline heritages as well.

Too, Blessed Mother is sometimes called *Szuzanyám fekete,* and also *La Virgen Negra,* the Black Virgin, meaning one who is a little to a great deal darker than other Madonnas, who are often portrayed with light hair, gorgeously light eyes, and lovely paler skin. Our elders would often note that Blessed Mother, The Black One, had been outdoors, rather than indoors. Being out in the sun and the air, she had been kissed by the sun. Thus, she is made even more lovely in her brown and black-toned skin.

It would appear that the Black Woman of Holy Beauty was spoken about in sacred words long before we knew of the many statues and images of Dark Madonnas placed in churches, cathedrals, basilicas, temples, and caves across the world. Long before then, this was spoken about in the "Song of Songs" of Solomon—a beautiful poem of two lovers speaking to each other about the ways in which they see each other's physical, sexual, but even more so, spiritual beauty all twined together, not as one separate from the others:

> *The bride is black,*
> *swarthy from her labors*
> *in the vineyards.*

The bride, this most beautiful bride, colored like the blue-black of dusk, is said to have breasts like two fawns of a roe—in other words, breasts with soft eyes like the deer. This beautiful bride is "swarthy" from working outdoors under the sunlight in the vineyards. The wine that will be made from that toiling, will give such relaxation, peace, and harmony to life. This bride of yore is not gold gilt. This bride is not green, red, brown, yellow, pink, purple. This bride is black. She works with her hands. She bends to tend to the living green vine. She touches black earth and green leaves and colored flowers and fruit in cycles, over and over again. She walks in the wild lands and the purposely cultivated spaces at the same time. I tried to understand her walking in two worlds:

BLACK

Black because
she's been kissed
by the sun.
Our Lady is both the sun
who kisses,
and the one who is kissed.

Our Lady answers to many names:
"She Who is Blest by the Sun."
"Woman Clothed With the Sun."

Thus, we begin to see all the many ways people have imagined Blessed Mother throughout all of history, no matter what part of the world they live in, no matter what branch of religious faith they follow: rose gold and light, native of the land she lives from and on, black as starry night, red as in clay earth, green as in spring leaves peeking out from the black ground, gold as the sun, and deepest purple as found in the flowers that are called "black tulips."

Yet there are detractors of La Virgen's darkness. In far-back writings still on record, we see the features and skin color of the Black Virgin Mother assailed by some. In books from the late 1800s and throughout the 20th century, we see some observers are off-put by those dark-skinned images, ideas, and actual human beings who were from a different social class, a different racial group, than the writers.

In one book published in 1881, *Legends of the Madonna: As Represented in the Fine Arts,* by Mrs. Anna Jameson, Boston (Houghton, Mifflin And Company), the authoress shows us the age-old biases of some who strove to petrify La Virgen, tie her down, keep her to a narrow blade of light only, do anything but allow her to be defined by her magnitude in full. Rather, she was to be flensed down and made "appropriate" to match whatever restrictive human filters were struck down over her.

Regardless, the 19th-century Mrs. Jameson illuminates how her culture of the 1880s—through smudged social class eyeglasses—cannot perceive the black-skinned Virgin Mother as beautiful nor acceptable. She laments and speculates that the most ancient artistic figures of the Madonna looking all golden and light are apparently too closely allied with "normal" human beings

> " . . . to satisfy faith. [Rather] It is the ugly, dark-coloured, ancient Greek Madonnas . . . which had all along the credit of being miraculous; and "to this day," says Kugler, "the Neapolitan lemonade-seller will allow no other than a formal Greek Madonna, with olive-green complexion and veiled head, to be set up in his booth."
>
> "It is the same in Russia. Such pictures, in which there is no attempt at representation [of the] real or ideal . . . The most lovely Madonna by Raphael or Titian would not have the same effect. Guido, who himself painted lovely Virgins, went every Saturday to pray before the little Black Madonna della Guardia and, as we are assured, held this old Eastern relic in devout veneration."

And so too, were there devout priests and nuns and other souls across the Americas, Africa, Asia, Polynesia, and Europe who also went to their daily work, but only after praying before the Black Madonna from their own matrilineal and patrilineal far-back people.

Mrs. Jameson, after labeling the Black Madonna as "ugly," continues:

"Because some of the Greek pictures and carved images had become black through extreme age, it was argued by certain devout writers, that the Virgin herself must have been of a very dark complexion; and in favour of this idea they quoted this text from the Canticles, "I am black, but comely, O ye daughters of Jerusalem." But others say that her complexion had become black only during her sojourn in Egypt. At all events, though the blackness of these antique images was supposed to enhance their sanctity, it has never been imitated in the fine arts, and it is quite contrary to the description of Nicephorus, which is the most ancient authority, and that which is followed in the Greek school."

"Canticles" is another name for the "Song of Songs." Next Mrs. Jameson goes on to quote what is considered, in her time, the only proper way to portray Holy Mother:

"The proper dress of the Virgin is a close red tunic, with long sleeves . . . and over this a blue robe or mantle. In the early pictures, the colours are pale and delicate. Her head ought to be veiled. The fathers of the primeval Church, particularly Tertullian, attach great importance to the decent veil worn by Christian maidens; and in all the early pictures the Virgin is veiled. The enthroned Virgin, unveiled, with long tresses falling down on either side, was an innovation introduced about the end of the fifteenth century; commencing, I think, with the Milanese, and thence adopted in the German schools and those of Northern Italy. The German Madonnas of Albert Durer's time have often magnificent and luxuriant hair, curling in ringlets, or descending to the waist in rich waves, and always fair. Dark-haired Madonnas appear first in the Spanish and later Italian schools."

There is more from Mrs. Jameson about how Blessed Mother ought never show her breast. (I'm afraid Mrs. J. was too late in the admonishing, for one of the earliest cave paintings of Holy Mother portrays her nursing the Christ Child, and is in all wonder, beautiful. It shows the holy symbiosis between mother and child. Some of these paintings portraying Mother nursing her Child are more than a thousand years old. They are sometimes entitled, translated from the Latin, "The Holy Lactation." Yes.)

Mrs. Jameson also points out that La Virgen's naked feet ought never show, but always be clad in boot or shoe. And so on. All this, certainly seeming to douse the so-humane concept of "the skin mother," the loving natal Mother to her little Holy One, and to us also.

Yet, I find Mrs. Jameson's writing has value, for it opens a window into how writings of any time can suck the blood from living holiness by girdling and garroting all, instead of allowing Holiness to breath bright on its own.

There is a saying amongst the old women believers in our family: "*Do not force the seed so deeply, unless you want to make a cemetery instead of a garden.*" They were talking about the water lilies they would sometimes grow in big black-walnut rain barrels at the eave troughs of our saltboxes. The water lily that grows upward from the fertile dark being a kind of "emergent" symbol of sacred new life, each plant rooted in fertile mud that held it strong . . . and by its green-ribboned stem, it grew and grew upward until its flower broke the surface of the water. The dark green lily's life and beauty depended on it appearing above the water's surface, rather than being forced to live only submerged.

The Black Madonnas, too, have been held above the waterline for centuries, have lasted in full flower, against all no-no's, shaking fingers, all falsifying of these beauteous images of Holy Mother as "ugly." They are not ugly. They are beauteous. Better one would call night and all her stars ugly, than not see the absurdity of such denigration of this "holy and dark *vive la différence.*"

DAY-NIGHT MADONNA:
OMETEOTL Y LOS OJOS, THE EYE MOTHER

To me, one of the most prominent features of many a Black Madonna are their eyes. When one studies the Black Madonnas that are still intact in statuary, for instance, one sees an unusual peculiarity of most all their eyes. They appear to not be looking only into this world. They also appear to be looking into another world entirely. The gaze they're carrying is often one of not only "here," but also into "the far away" as well.

This seems to me strongly evinced by some of the images of Blessed Mother in her beautiful black skin and as much so in that her eyes are almost lidless. Her eyes are often so round and so open with the iris and the pupil right in the center of the eye, and the white of the eye showing all around as though she is completely awake, and will forever be awake.

She would appear to be seeing, truly seeing in her own unusual "black" way. In reality, black light is of the ultraviolet spectrum, and reveals by its invisible long-wave UV radiating—the hidden things, shapes, creatural colors, and other matters that cannot be seen by daylight.

This can be said to be one of the uncanny worths assigned to Black Madonna; she is believed to be able to see and know and help what is not at first obvious in common everyday light. Therefore, she is thought by many who hold her dear, to intervene and help to mend us at a level that is beyond the mundane.

Black Madonna, amongst those who maintain a devotion to her, can be understood too, as standing at the dividing line between waking consciousness and dreaming consciousness ... as though there are two nations she belongs to in full citizenship, two realities, two points of view about everything everywhere—wherein one side is often much more oriented outwardly, as in extroversion and matters prominent. And the other side is much more revealing of the interior psyche, and of matters and configurations concealed thereby and therein—the deeper roots of the matter, the actual basis for healing, seeing, being.

Black Madonna is often supplicated along with her Divine Little Black Child, to heal the soul of a person all the way down to the very bones, to reveal the trouble right from the radical, to bless the cringing spirit with the deep blessing most needed for repair and re-emergence, in ways that carry deepest meaning for the individual.

The Black Madonna, in all her representations, is known as the healer of crippledness, the healer of harmed women, hurt men, and injured and abused children. There is nothing superficial about La Virgen Negra, Black Virgin Mother. She is mother mild and tender, mother most alert and tending to, mother most fierce and protective, and mother who heals the worst of the wounded.

And more so, there is a third perspective she carries, the most holy of all, wherein both polar perspectives of interior and exterior convene: and right there, at that juncture point, the Black Madonna stands, taking in the two worlds, the mundane world of known facts, and the deeply creative, insightful, emergent world of Spirit.

There is a name in our mestizo heritage for this concept which contains so much of striving to see both sides, all sides, of all things: seeing with eyes wide open in all directions, holding together feminine and masculine (sometimes called the builder and the spark), the far away and near by, the holy and yet unformed, virtue and more of the unformed, the land and the cosmos, the water and the fire, the ways to suffering and the ways to revolution that brings liberation and happiness. This word is *Ometeotl.*

This sacred Nahuatl word, which is understood in many different ways, in essence refers to the force beyond mere images or representations: that is, "The Everything" created, the known and the unknown universe. It is said that "the all of this" is also in some way, in some share, within each of us. That we are born this way, fully alive and ensouled in being and seeing all worlds: Ometeotl. To hear of Great Spirit, Creator, Source without source, Father God, Holy Woman, would be summed up by an ancient Aztec in the sacred word: Ometeotl.

In this sense, in her "black light" that reveals what cannot be seen in daylight alone, Black Madonna can be understood as one who calls us to remember the Eternal is not only all around, but also a spark within us, a terrain inside us. As I've studied her image in so many ways, her beautiful blackness meaning so much more than color alone, I can see in this fuller way of seeing through the light shed by the dark, the Black Madonna is a mother who is also aware, too, of our hardships that occur to us, in and from out of the dark of unknowing, unconsciousness, ignorance, and innocence.

Daylight travails can be considered "usual garden-variety ones" that may not call on "dark light" insights: My car has a flat tire, my sister didn't call me and she said she would, my dress was torn in the door frame—in contrast, "night time issues" can suddenly occur mysteriously, sometimes even seeming magically, under cover of, or erupting from, the unconscious. Suddenly "one knows" I cannot stay. Suddenly "one knows" I must go thither or yon in all holiness in the dark.

The province of the Black Madonna appears to be, in large part, to urge the human spirit to inquire and to see beyond the "expected," beyond what is considered the "only way to properly see," to grasp the greater picture beyond that which is most easily perceived by ego alone. To see with the eyes of the Immaculate Heart, to see with the eyes of the divine Child Spirit, to see with the eyes of the battered but fully radiant soul.

Our inquiries "by black light" can be especially important when matters are more serious, such as: I think I have betrayed something important. I think that I would like to bring life in a certain way, but my very soul is thwarted for I have not done so yet. These last are thoughts that carry much magnitude for the soul, for the spirit, for the heart, for the psyche. Seeing Holy Mother as beautiful in her gifts of special light-shedding, literally allows us to use the magnifying glass of the holy and truly see the formerly unseen. Thus we are more opened to the road that is holy, sacred, and satisfying, for we look with eyes, like hers, that can see both worlds.

Black Madonna, as I know her infinitely tender offering of insights, is characterized not because she is black as in "cannot be seen." She can most certainly be seen. Rather, she is portrayed as black because she radiates "black light" that allows us to see beyond the mundane, that allows us to see past the mundane and the profane and into the deeper aspects of the world, of sincere religiosity, of spirituality, of , of psyche that carry both pneuma and numens.

Her "black light" illumines. And under that black light too, in daylight or at night, we can also see "her source and the force of Immaculate Love." Despite or because of denigrations to Holy Mother in her dark skin, she still shines her unusual light toward us, from the juncture point between two worlds. So that we all might see, as she sees. Fully awake. Eyes wide open. All worlds. All worths. Siempre. Always.

OUR LADY OF THE FIREFLIES

The Blessed Mother in all her colors from new-moon-colored, to dark, to brown, to olive and black, was given into my life as a little child, for I had a little statue of Holy Mother on the home-made and oddly colored bookshelf in my bedroom. This bookshelf was done up in leftover house paint, so part was painted battleship gray, the color of the shingles on our house, and part was mint green, the color of the sub-pump floor in the cellar. It seemed so beautiful to me, for there on one of the two shelves was a lovely charred Madonna from my grandmother, one found in the fire pit after the flames had burned most everything except this little dark holy woman made of half-burnt log.

On the day I received her from Old Katerin's hands, I'd wrapped her in a soft rag that was literally my father's holey but clean strappy T-shirt, and then walked for several miles with my little Madonna made of burnt wood to our Irish-born parish priest. I may have been under ten years old. I remember being puzzled when after Father asked how I'd gotten there . . . he seemed to suddenly be having a speck in each of his eyes.

Yet, as I held her out to be blessed, dear Father holy-man-priest solemnly held his three fingers up and drew the cross over her slowly, saying, "*Shor an' it's good to see yi agane. Sure and it's good to see you again.*"

I felt Father was not talking to me exactly. He was including me, but he was actually gently speaking to her.

He explained that when he was a boy, his mother took all her young chicks to the Carmelite church in Dublin to see the newly restored Our Lady, who had been whitewashed by some someones who thought her more "appropriate" chalk white, than in her original scarred blackness gotten over the years since she had been carved back in the 1700s.

But the people of Dublin didn't want a whitewashed Madonna. They wanted an earthy Madonna who was close to them. If she carried some of the grime of day-to-day life, then, so be it. She was like them. Dust blesses dirt. They wanted her with them, Father said, instead of elevated over them. They wanted a mother they could speak to, and love, and be loved by in return.

I fell in love with the truths Father told, but especially his sharing with me, a mere child, his love of Our Lady of his childhood. I felt my child heart and his child heart met inside the Immaculate Heart of Blessed Mother.

These many years later, with Father no doubt in "Irishman's two-fisted, joke-telling, befriending-of-the-lonely, hard-working heaven," I think of how we all at some age, come to have knowings now of tiny sacred chapels, often placed into our hearts when we had even the most brief exchange of words and kindness from souls who are daily practicing their consecrations—not only their vows—but their longings and understandings of the sacred light that illuminates everything.

Thus, after my sojourn to our parish priest who was filled with such élan vital for Our Lady, now back home again, in my little room on summer nights, with my now properly blessed little Black Madonna, I made her a little glowing night-light woman.

I'd taken a canning jar and punched "breathing holes" in the lid with screwdriver and hammer. Then, just before bedtime, I'd rush out in my nightgown and sort through the spirea, lilacs, and fruit trees, me no doubt looking like a wildfire wraith loose in the night. Then I'd real gently, so very gently, capture fireflies, those most beautiful little flying lantern-bearers who light up with such golden light. In our family these were considered *santitos,* little saints come to light the dark for us.

Thus supplied with the little santitos, I'd place the jar on the bookcase shelf in my bedroom in the dark of night. As we lived in "the boondocks" there were no street lights then, so it was dark—dark outside—and inside at night. But beneath Our Lady, the Dark Madonna, there was this glowing, fading, glowing, fading, golden beautiful light.

Fireflies are some of the most beautiful creatures ever made on the face of this earth, just beautiful. They reminded me of the living soul, each one of them. So there remained the little jar next to my little black shard statue of Holy Mother. I'd get into my bed, and I would just watch and think, "Blessed Mother's lighting up! She's glowing, look! She's being tended to by the littlest angels, who are glowing and fading, glowing and fading. And there's golden angel-light all around her."

The old women would say that La Virgen Negra, the Black Virgin Mother in the old rituals, comes with a necklace of wrapped candies, and made each one, a miracle straight from her special light. That if we pay attention, if we unwrap those *dulces*, those sweets—for a miracle is the sweetest of sweet—we will find genuine solutions to what some might wrongly say are "impossible situations." So, sometimes Black Virgin Mother comes in the old traditions, with a necklace of wrapped miracles. Thus, I would be in my little bed and imagine that the little fireflies were like a little necklace around her, and that they were like little candies. And if you could unwrap them somehow, if they opened their little wings, a little miracle might fall out, and you would wait and see what it might be ... for certain it would be some kind of a miracle of light straight out of the dark.

When morning came, I'd take my little jar of fireflies out before the dew had dried, and place the little lantern-bearers on the lilac leaves. They were very alive and no doubt very happy to be loose again after serving so well. I would bless them, the way Father held his three fingers, and I would pass my fingers through the air and murmur, "Thank you so much for coming to be a light for me in the midst of the dark." It took a long time for me to understand that I was speaking to Holy Mother: "Thank you for coming to be a light for me in the dark."

PRAYER TO SEE

May we ever leave the
Unlit tangle
we've gotten ourselves into—
again—
the one complete with blinders
not of our making,
or shutters we've
studiously
hand-hammered over time.

May we instead, line up
behind Black Madonna's
clear line of sight,
and her great strength,
to see as closely
as mere humanlings can,
to see as she sees
with black light
fully illuminating
anything that radiates,
and to withstand
what we see
with her Immaculate Love.

May we unhood our heads
and look into, under, behind,
beyond all words and worlds
and see the winged soul
lighting up the oiled map
of our past, present, and future
that once seemed so hidden.

May our highways
and byways be
Illuminated
by passing the map
under "black light" . . .
thereby learning
how to travel,
eyes wide open,
and when, why, how,
where, and with whom.

May we remember
how sacred
her "Foundry of Light,"
how deeply incubated we are
in Holy Mother,
we, the children
of the dark-skinned

Ex-voto: "Sanctu, Sanctu:
Standing on the Shoulders
of Those Who Stand on the Shoulders of . . ."

Holy Woman
who is unafraid
of any dark.

May all be given
The ways of seeing
That most benefit
The growth of
Rather than the restriction
of their souls.

Our Lady Under the Train Trestle...
A Light Shines Even Brighter
in the Darkest Dark

CHAPTER ELEVEN

No One Too Bad, Too Mean, or Hopeless

How the Motherfuckers Became the Blessed Mothers

PART ONE

I sat in the prison parking lot in my battered old Ford Pinto. I made the Sign of the Cross, as I ever did when ambulances and fire trucks passed, when driving past a hospital, a holy place, a *descanso,* little white cross by the side of the road—and before going into unknown situations where I hoped I could measure up.

Blessed Mother, help us all see through your gentle eyes,
speak through your fierce heart.

This was the prayer I'd made and proved since childhood. Sometimes I could live up to my own supplications, sometimes not. The point was to keep trying to live near Holy Mother's sacred heart.

This was my first day to work at the prison. I was there as a brand-new, first-time counselor and teacher of three education-in-prison classes for

---

◄ Ex-voto: "Our Lady of the Train Trestle"

155

teens: Poetry, Cooking, and Human Sexuality. I was twenty-six years old, and the prisoners were between twelve and eighteen years old. They were in a "locked institution," as it was called, and they were named by the bureaucrat as "CHINS," children in need of supervision. The children were locked up for theft, drugs, or for being chronic runaways. Some were a danger to themselves, some were a danger to others. I was told many were stone-cold tough. But when I looked around, I mostly saw broken-hearted children, just children.

Once through clanging security, I was surrounded in the "day room" by "the blackbird children," as I came to affectionately call them. The children, often incarcerated for far too long, displayed acute intuitions that came from being on guard emotionally at all times. They had a healthy curiosity, but also a skittishness in which they flapped and flapped at the slightest change in routine, facial expression, or tone of voice from others.

The eighteen blackbirds I was charged to teach immediately tried to intimidate. In the first class, cooking, a food fight went wild. I let it go for a bit. It was only the equivalent of pillow fighting, really.

But, the girls with tattoos up and down their arms and legs, black ballpoint pen fingernails, and black lipstick, literally turned their backs on me, cawing like crows when I suggested we give our attention to our cinnamon-roll making.

The girls were more interested in throwing gooey, sugary balls of dough and emptying flour on each other's heads. They weren't interested in my full Indiana-boondocks earnestness, trying to tell them about how all our flour, eggs, butter, cinnamon, sugar cane, came from the earth through the works of human beings and creatures in concert, and isn't that blessed?

They hooted, and it turned a little ugly; they called me names I was used to hearing long ago, but only on "the runaway road." There in the fields and down at rivers, heartbroken and half-mad kids and sometimes adults too passed the nights together—all of us desperate to out-distance something or someone bad. Language had not been genteel there.

So, here in the kitchen now, with white dust clouds and cuss words flying through the air, I thought I should stumble on, and offer the girls something that has come to me other times in my life when some have been pulled away by distractions.

Thus, I quoted holy words by first saying, "This story I am telling you— about how tiny insects nip the hardened roots of plants above timberline so nutrients from the rain can seep in, so the plant will grow, and so humans and animals can be fed from them *can only be heard by those who have the ears to hear, can only be seen by those who have the eyes to see . . ."*

The girls were not impressed. Not even a little. My brilliant logic was immediately covered over by more flying flour dust and sweet-smelling dough missiles. More blue language.

WHY PRISON IS PRISON FOR THE BODY
BUT NOT FOR THE SPIRIT

Children's prison may sound to some somewhat benign. But it is not.

Children's prison is prison nonetheless. No one can come in. No one can go out without permissions and signatures galore. All doors, interior and exterior, had double locks, or combination locks, electronic locks, pad-locks. Staff who were called "counselors" had huge rings of keys that made them sound like broken glass thermos-liners when they walked.

What makes prison, prison? In part, it is the utter deprivation and degradation of the senses. Prison is where the three meals a day are pale, wrinkled colors: over-boiled, poor-grade foods no longer resembling the colors found in fresh, vibrant nature. Fat-back chicken floated in ponds of grainy grease. Shredded tuna came from gallon-size tin cans, and wore thick white burial shrouds of cheap mayonnaise. Larded hot dogs lay shriveled. "Cream of Mushroom" soup made with cups of white flour for thickening were so like scrapbook glue you could turn your spoonful of soup upside down—and the soup wouldn't fall off. Baked beans were baked so hard you had to chip them out of the aluminum sheet-cake pans.

Prison, a place where there is no privacy in odd ways: no freedom to get away from noise; no ability to not hear others weep, scream, curse, piss. No ability to *not* smell. No ability to *not* taste the scent of others' feces.

Prison. No ability to protect one's body from security checks. No ability to keep your own crummy Maybelline mascara wand or your twenty-nine-cent lipstick because you might hurt yourself or someone else with these children's "practice toys" for being grown-up.

And in that prison, though some visitors might carry the light and make "church" visits to the children, there were no real sparks of liveliness to the deadening souls, no spiritual practices of Love that went down into the street world of cruelty—pulling the few but very real treasures out of the mire.

In prison, there is no ability to seek Nature at will. No ability to stand for as long as one likes in a cool breeze pushing at one's neck. No ability to listen for the crack of sticks in the forest. No ability to imagine images in clouds. No ability to walk farther than the full length of the dining room.

And yes, there were occasional "outings," not in shackles, but with shackles everywhere hanging on the children anyway: loss of one parent, one anklet of iron. Loss of both parents, two ankle hobbles. One or both parents present at home, but not present to themselves or to their children—more restraints on the child's ability to grow to maturity, to grow in creative fire.

Too, in prison, there is often a lowering of individual judgment, a loss of ability to stand alone—instead melting into a heap with others whose lives may be, as some say "going nowhere." In prison, there is a circular wind pushing all imprisoned to band together, to become insofar as possible a "chosen family" that is too often shaped to help each other not thrive, but survive, at the most basic levels, emotionally and physically. And no more.

Too, many of the children had gone seriously afoul of the law, and more than once. This tied the wrists of many inside and outside the system who were most in positions to help the children. Often the law dictated punishments, but the human heart—which held a different verdict—had to be subservient to the law.

Yet, also in prison, there is a wide-open secret skyway, and that skyway is constructed by each soul's attitude—which holds that the spirit, like a beautiful bird, can fly anywhere, fully alive, seen or unseen. That spirit can never be caged. Never.

Thus, in poetry class with my blackbird girls, in quiet moments, I was able to teach about "the Bird of birds," what some call spirit, and what others call the lovely feminine Holy Spirit, that undying Espirito Santo, was often represented as a white dove—the One who can fly between bars and out windows; the One who can never be jailed.

As I did not receive the girls' rapt attention in cooking class, now, in poetry class, they were as still as could be as I read to them from the mystic women saints: Caterina de Siena, Teresa de Avila, Sor Juana, Mechthild of Magdeburg.

All these ancient women poets called out loudly, each in her own way, that in any prison only the body is behind bars and locks, yes—but the wild spirit filled with the fire and the Love of Creator and all of Creation is free to go as and where it will, despite any iron bars.

I'd been told when I came to the prison that the children I'd be teaching were most often "low-normal" intelligence. Didn't alarm me. I'd heard it before. Long ago, that's what some teachers had said about me and others from poor immigrant and refugee families. To the contrary, my blackbird girls understood mystical poetry perfectly. After I'd read to them from the holy women, the girls wrote then . . . about birds and freedom now, and the "someday" that was coming when the girls would be free to leave the "institution." I could see soul in their words, even as many were misspelled, lines of handwriting going all crookedy on the lined page. But I saw too they were writing just like a bird flies—freely.

And I told them so: "No bird flies in a straight line; they fly up and down and sideways. And no bird . . . including myself, knows how to spell well." (And here I told a bit about my own struggles learning to read and spell, and the ridicule that came from others.) "But please notice," I said, "the people of the world who are serious about being true human beings don't usually point to perfect spelling and perfect handwriting being what they would most aspire to in life."

No. Many, many people world-over point to the birds, saying they want to be free—like the birds, to soar like the birds do.

The children listened so deeply; several teachers passing by during our poetry class later asked what the heck I'd been teaching. They'd never heard these usually raucous and very young adults be so quiet.

What I'd been teaching to the dear blackbird children was just this: A simple holy premise that we all were born standing firmly in: knowing the spirit is free no matter what else. That culture and some other people might lie to us about many things, but there is a clearer truth: we can grow and we can go free, even while in prisons of many kinds or any kind. We have the five things needed to be free forever: *Love, Heart, Imagination, Spirit,* and *Soul,* which are only other words for *wings.*

ONE VIOLENT ACT SEEN MANY DIFFERENT WAYS

How acutely we remember things from small environs: The sound of an iron door opening with three screeches, each one higher on the octave than the one before. The metal rollers on a bed that sounded like a stone had been thrown into a flock of chickens. Big wooden-slab doors with no windows—when slammed in rage, it seemed the age-rings in the wood trembled.

But there is one sound that stands in my memory, even now these four decades later. During my first evening in the prison, the manager of the dining hall bellowed for Silence! But the children continued to yell and mill about, not settling down.

At that moment, I was turned sideways speaking to a child, and so I did not directly see the lug of a manager as he angrily lifted a huge white porcelain platter of food. Suddenly, he hurled the platter with all his might against the brick wall three feet away, where it exploded into smithereens.

Mother of God! The sound of a rifle shot! How? Where? Who? Why? As a trauma specialist, I was already crouched and scanning for the bloom of vermilion on any child's body or mine. For a long moment there was stunned silence.

But then, as it became clear there were no guns, that it was now only a mess of food thrown wide and far in a shower of glass, the hooting and cat-calling began. The children were signaling: You didn't scare us! You didn't! The kids carried on hollering the way waitstaff in restaurants hoot when suddenly startled by a stack of dishes crashing to the kitchen floor.

Yet, the flying shards of glass had barely missed shooting right into the eyes of any who stood close to the brick wall. And the manager was frightening to behold in that moment. Have you ever seen a human being so enraged that they develop dents beside their noses from sucking in so hard their sinuses deflate? That, and also the bulging forehead-vein had taken over the manager's face. Yes, he had our attention.

I calmed myself and the children near me, and tried to scry the manager through Our Lady's eyes. I saw he was not an insane man, but an overwhelmed man, a harried man, a person who had, season after season, received what was left of children who had once been like beautiful young corn plants—but with far too much razor hail tearing them apart before they could be brought to full flower.

And now, not with intention, but with abject aggravation (and I think, too, grief), he had just given the children one more example, often replicated in their homes, about how to handle frustration and anger—with only more frustration and anger.

This event of the shattering glass flying, was a turning point in my life. That sudden lashing out by a caretaker, a caregiver, a person in charge, a teacher, a person who was to be an exemplar—who instead became a "poor example" was not new. We'd had certain teachers in grade school and high school, teachers who "lost it" and lashed out at children who were not yet mature as measured by a rote standard.

The manager losing control had low tolerance for being frustrated. One young visiting intern quit on the spot. The male intern said it was a lot to take to see an adult lose control because he was angry at the youngs' lack of controlling themselves when ordered.

I could not blame the intern for turning away. I considered it, too. But, I thought, if you go, who will stay here? That is how I came to set down my meager seabag in the prison then. But, too, I heard a voice in my mind, a hard-won knowing I'd earned elsewhere: I could "hold to the rails and the sails," as we said up on the both calm and stormy Great Lakes where I grew up. I thought I could try to keep holding to "being there" at "the rails and the sails" in prison with the children, no matter the weather.

Some would later blame the children in the dining hall for not complying immediately, and there would be "assignments" of being alone in locked rooms. Though lack of compliance was true in part, I still wondered: Wouldn't Our Lady also say, "Please dear souls, look at the fraying, the unraveling of all concerned, and aren't these so very young, and those far older, to be allowed ever-more chances?"

Do-overs: In our family we told a story of Our Lady, the ultimate Mother, admonishing her Child for cursing a fruit tree just to show off His other-worldly powers. She told Him, "No, no, even if you have the power to harm, do not."

If there were more chances for the Holy Child, there had to be more chances for the earthly children of all ages too.

Yet, some of my professors at university, who seemed too hardened themselves, often reiterated in those times: "Children who are violent only understand violence."

Maybe. But maybe not. I grew up in a family rich with alcoholism and drunkenness, screeching and constant arguing amongst adults, flying fists. There were no reliably calm meals, no calm days or nights, unless there was company in our tiny saltbox out in the boondocks. The adults aimed blotto faces toward acquaintances and strangers, but cruelty toward the child who tried to interfere somehow with their daily collapses into unfettered anger, drinking, and fighting.

Sometimes living in a daily maelstrom creates "love of Love" in a way few other long hauls can. We have choices about how to wear our wounds.

We can choose to be bitter, or to be better than . . .

Thus, at the children's prison, I hoped a good teaching-answer might be to give love and to offer stability, *to respect* the children. To not recapitulate their sad histories by tearing the children down, leaving them in shreds again. To be the same, even person with each child as much as possible: to notice them, to listen to them, to find their gifts, and to shine on them.

It would indeed be these far more peaceful means that would matter, but only in one way. The other way truly was violent, as a strange kind of violent spiritual intent took me over.

I still had a lot to learn. Still do.

But, Our Lady would help. She would bend to teach me. She would teach us all.

PRISON TATTOOS, AND A VIOLENT INTENTION OF SPIRIT

A favorite, innocent cartoon I carry around in my mind is one of two old men on a rooftop looking down into the streets below. The roadway is packed with hundreds of men, women, and children playing violins for all they're worth. One old man worries to the other, *This cannot continue! We must stop violins in the street!*

The play on the English words "violins" and "violence" has an odd resonance beyond the obvious pun. The word *violence* in modern usage, is most often associated with damaging actions or words. But in its old Latinate meaning, "violence" can refer to impetuosity, meaning a vigorousness—as water rushes along a riverbed.

For instance, consider the beauty and violence of those who can lift the violin and draw the bow across its strings in order to hear its voice. This motion and emotion is, in actuality, often called the musician's bold and sweet "attack" on the beautiful instrument.

During such an "attack," in some nearly unspoken way, the musician leaves his or her wits behind and instead acts in a forceful, disciplined way, but also in a controlled and furious way. This kind of creative fury is confident, capable, knowledgeable about how to be both tender and intense.

It was something of this kind of "attack" that occurred to me/in me at children's prison. In the end, I was not sure who was the violin, who was the musician, who were the strings and the bow—just that the instrument had been lifted and seeming invisible Hands Greater had "attacked"—and the music had begun.

Thus, oddly, after the lumpy start of being ignored and taunted by the kidlettes at the prison, I learned that teaching cooking was really a class in human sexuality. Cooking together and baking together gives young women a chance to speak freely during the rhythms of the kneading and the steam rising and mixers whirring. There's resonance to the organic and to the bodily senses then.

I came to understand poetry was really a class in cooking. It too combines the exotic with carrier ingredients, and allowed for the praise of my students—for the odd tang or exotic word they'd write into a poem that carried the scent just right.

Mysteriously, I also found that teaching human sexuality was really an education in poetry, as I brought love poems of Neruda and Lorca to read, right along with the straight physiological facts.

Remember the young blackbird women in my first class with their tattoos, black lipstick, and inky nail polish? As they allowed me closer, I found that the lipstick was actually diluted black felt-tip pen. Their tattoos were made likewise on arms and legs, most not ink under the skin, but upon the skin.

It was hard to escape notice that one of the most prominent tattoos on the forearms of my blackbird girls—in some semblance of Old German Blackletter or Old English lettering—was one stark word: *fucker*.

As time went on and I shared more life stories about my learning disablements and struggles in school, a certain corrosive trust developed between us. I say corrosive because like starving people when rescued, because they've not eaten for so long, so too does it feel corrosive, at first, to feel the warmth of food again—or the warmth of genuine caring. Yet in this burgeoning trust between us, I felt I could ask after this bold hieroglyphic on their arms and thighs: *fucker*. Some of my toughest girls proudly proclaimed to me that their tribe was the "Mother Fuckers." And you know "that look" in the young, a sort of half dead-fish-eyes on ice, and half red-dot tail-lights in the eyes, saying "Waddaya gonna do about it?!"

Well, I wondered, What *am* I going to do about it? I decided what I would do about it was . . . exactly nothing. That we would continue to hear poetry of the heartbroken anti-fascist Spanish poets, the so-crazy-in-love Chilean poets, the bold El Salvadorans, the warrior Nicaraguan poets, the brave Cubano poets . . . and any wild poet from across all the continents I could find text from which to breathe and read to the young. And we would cook together. And together we would talk about sex. And it would be enough, somehow, to teach, soften, help, and uphold the soul in all these matters, so raw and so torn for many.

Even thought there were many rules at the children's prison, there was one other authority I had to obey, an authority who had other imperatives I'd be charged to obey, and *to the letter,* literally

That authority was La Señora, The Lady of Ladies, Guadalupe.

WHAT MOTHER FUCKER REALLY MEANS

La Señora's first intervention at the prison occurred after one of those discussions with the girls that afterward, made you wonder what those in charge of institutions would think about such a seemingly absurdist conversation.

It began in cooking class. I'd raised the serious topic of whether permanent marker was going to poison the girls when they used it to tattoo their skin. Would the body be absorbing the ink, and was it toxic?

Suddenly the conversation shifted, and my blackbird girls were flapping with words. They challenged me sarcastically: Didn't I like the words "mother fucker"? What kind of pansy was I anyway if I couldn't stand up to the word "fucker"? And just for good measure, just to see if I'd faint or something, they howled and cat-called the "*f* word" about ten times in five seconds flat.

I tacked, explaining that "mother fucker" was not exactly a word of highest aspirations for females. That, in fact, the word was a low-grade infection started by some men who may have actually revered their mothers, but used this phrase now for their own reasons in attempts to insult and intimidate other men.

But no matter how I said that carrying such a moniker around in full emblazon, seemed to make one's own self-respect burn awfully low—and even nearly go out when one insulted oneself with such a cheap cultural stamp that had been handed down without full understanding—that the phrase was *not* even *original* . . . originality being something I knew the girls valued highly.

I tried one more time. "Look," I began . . .

"You're not our mother!" one girl snapped at me.

Out of my mouth, before I could think, I said, "That's what you think!!"

Last thing in the world to do with dug-in kids or adults is to challenge them, talk back to them, essentially. But, that's what I'd just done. Or, rather, it had been done through me.

Predictably, the girls all went dead-eyed, mocking me, dancing about with hip thrusts whilst imitating me as I'd just postured—with my palms outstretched toward them in an effort to bridge.

But I knew something they didn't yet know. Someone other than just lowly me had said, "That's what you think!" I was not alone.

In that moment, I had felt that familiar urgent nudge behind my shoulder, and I heard the exact words to say even as I found myself saying them aloud vehemently, violently! "That's what you think!"

But now, to make matters worse, before I could even evaluate the situation further, more words flew out of my mouth, not loudly, but with such force: an additional challenge to the girls. (Do you know how futile it is to challenge people when they are in the midst of mocking? Literally I think that was when the phrase "peeing into the wind" was invented. It only brings on more of what you were trying to void and avoid.)

But, there was no stopping Our Lady's voice inside my voice. Being literally inspired is like giving birth; there is a moment up to which you have control, and then a tilt occurs and you couldn't stop if you tried with all the strength in you—everything rushes out.

So that's how I came to lose my mind and blurt this challenge to the girls:

"If I can tell you a better story about the real meaning of each letter of the word 'fucker,' will you consider changing the tattoo on your arms to something that lifts you instead of dealing you down low, the way it does now?"

All the girls' arguments, "loud discussion" some would call it, stopped then. Just stopped. Beat. Beat.

Then, laughter. Jeering. Backs turned. A few vulgar hand gestures that the girls already knew I thought were boringly predictable and unoriginal.

"Ok, ok," I said, *"A couple weeks, give me a couple weeks to magically transform the word 'fucker' right before your eyes. I'll show you what the word 'fucker' really says."*

"Yeah, yeah," they said, then veered way off topic, jawing about how Carlos "booked" last week and they didn't bring him back to the slammer yet. And wasn't he too cool for escaping and blah, wah, sadness covered over with laughter that wasn't mirth, but something far more brokenhearted.

I took their "Yeah, yeah" to mean, "Yeah. Go ahead. Just try to show us anything."

And so, that night, I went in prayerful, sorrowful, almost hopeless consultation with Our Lady. I walked with her along the highway where eight lanes of cars blurred past an old viaduct. By the time I'd walked a mile in the shoes of the blackbird children, and in my shoes, and in her shoes, I sensed Our Lady tell me we all could win. She gave me the story for the first letter of the word "fucker," a true story of the letter *f*.

PART TWO

WHAT THE LETTER *f* CAN MEAN

fucker

The next day, the girls and I were in cooking class. I drew the letter *f* in the cookie dough. "Here is one way the word 'fucker' has a better meaning," I said.

I had their attention immediately.

"See this *f*, the first letter?"

"I'm going to make its tail longer, like this, see? Now, the *f* at the beginning is made into the staff of the Shepherd who will not let one lamb be lost in the dark of the storm."

> There once was a shepherd who was a protector of all the lambs. But, a storm suddenly sprang up, and there was this one little lamb still wandering out in the storm. This shepherd could be counted on. He ran out into the sideways rain and sleet. He climbed and climbed the rocky ledges, until he finally found the last little lamb who was so trembling and frightened and

clinging to a rock ledge. The poor little lamb could not get down by itself.

So the shepherd climbed from ledge to narrow ledge, and picked up the soft lamb and put the lamb around his neck, and carried the little kid down the mountain to safety.

"Thus, what you see here at the beginning of the word 'fucker' is no longer an *f*. This is now the Shepherd's staff he uses to climb the treacherous mountain ledges in order to bring down the lost and frightened kid."[1]

During the telling about the Shepherd who goes out into the storm to bring in the one scared lamb, the girls were at first fidgety, then grew silent. Then they elbowed each other, and gave out a forced raucous laughter, unrelated to what they'd just heard. A version of jeering, but far shorter than when I'd first arrived at children's prison.

It's an odd thing about human beings who are afraid to be real in front of other hearts: they fear retaliation for being. They often laugh when they are scared . . . or touched.

THE LETTER *f* AGAIN

That night, I walked the frontage road of the eight-lane highway again. Our Lady said, "That was good. But there is more. More letters. More chances. More changes."

"Tell me?"

"I will," she said, "when you get there."

"Ay yi yi! Couldn't you tell me now?"

"What do you think faith really is?"

"Ok, Ok. As you wish, *mi* Señora."

The next day in poetry class, the girls were waiting, but acting as though they weren't wanting to hear any more about the transformation of the *f* word. I myself was feeling a bit wobbly and waiting to hear what Our Lady had in mind. Just to start somewhere, I took a sheet of paper, drew the Shepherd's crook, hesitated for a moment, then drew a big *M* over the Shepherd's staff, saying this was the sign of the Blessed Mother who has been known since the beginning of time . . . and that it was she who brought the One to Earth in her body, the One who was the God of Love. The One who particularly watched out for children. And her signature for hundreds of years has been the capital letter *M*.

I said the God of Love is also the Shepherd who came from the body of the Holy Mother, this Capital *M* Woman, who was also called the one strong enough to be "the God-bearer." A mighty, brave, and strong woman who sheltered her Child, no matter what else.

So here at the beginning of "that word" was the Mother and her Child, in "the Word Made Flesh."

I explained all this in street talk: it was "Shep" and "Big Ma." They got it; the girls definitely got it. Their silence, the deep opening of their souls, said so. They understood the Mother who watches over her Child, and the Shepherd who watches over the smallest stranded lamb. The girls understood out of longing, and also out of natural motherly instincts in themselves; they cared deeply and secretly about many people and many things, especially the vulnerable and the mighty—within them-selves—and in others, too.

But within a few minutes, the spell of that moment of sacred story was broken when one girl put her head down on her desk and pretended to be snoring. (Read: trying to show she was unaffected by these stories, that she had "terminal cool.")

Soon the other girls were off on a tangent, making impolite belches and farting noises, too. A completely weird and funny thought crossed my mind: "Silent Night, Holy Night," yes, but with all those bodily crea-tures around the manger, plus nomadic travelers from three different tribes, with three different sets of manners, maybe it wasn't so silent a night after all—but holy, nonetheless.

THE LETTER *u*

Now what? Now what, Blessed Mother? Considering the girls' reac-tion, I must be daft to continue. But, I asked and asked and waited for hours that night for ways to break through. Nothing. Then, came a night dream of a huge sun with its shimmering *rayos*. I knew immediately.

The next day in human sexuality class, I talked about the orb of the cervix of the uterus, the orb of the glans penis—that they are progenerative and sensitive and radiate feeling. I know this seems a stretch, but orb was the operative word here. Understand that stories can start anywhere, and so I launched into a story about "The Life Giver," that is, Blessed Mother, who is sometimes seen as a shimmering orb of fire, and in this form she is known by a special name.

I continued then, "Consider this *u* in the word 'fucker.' This *u* is actually a broken sun with only one little ray showing at the bottom because many people have forgotten the real story of precious life shining like a sun. But because this sun really belongs to the Great Woman I've been telling you about, now her other rays can show too. See, like this . . . Remembering."

"Remember Creator threw his breath into the dark void, and called out 'Let there be Light'? For us on earth, that was the star that we call 'Sun.' It is hers. The sun belongs to the Woman. She can stand in the fire without being burnt, and she gives out love instead of anger. She can stand in the flames. She ever gives warmth. Her special name is She Who Shines Like the Sun."

The girls wanted to know how anyone can send such heat and not in turn destroy everything in sight. I was glad they asked. We discussed and discussed how other people can write on you with their angry fire, and you can catch fire and then send fire destructively right back at them or onto others.

Or, you can choose to create rather than to destroy—no matter how destructive others are. You can instead take on the Sun of the soul and return fire, yes, but as rays of Love.

A few titters. A few "Whatever"s. But word got around the prison that day: more and more kids came to our classes when they were on their "rest time." They didn't come for the religious exactly. They wanted to hear stories. The stories were, regardless, from the river of ancient religious ideas and ideals. But not in a way the kidlettes were used to. They were used to being told stories with a pointing finger, condemnation, and admonishments.

I taught the children that the word *religious,* meant to "bind together the sheaves of the wheat and corn," to stand together in the storm so the tall stalks didn't fall over, so as to all bring together in a harvest of nourishment for the tribe. Heartfelt religiosity had those kindly ideas at center: to bring people of heart together, to bring nourishment despite any storms, to stand together as righteous living souls.

The blackbird children understood. Those who had been labeled the "low-intelligence" children, the "bad" children, the "hopeless" children, the "contrary, *rebelde,* rotten, horrible, criminal" children, all understood perfectly what it meant to protect a living essence, to stand together protecting and nourishing everyone. Get down gritty Love. Held high.

THE LETTER *c*

Now, I did not know what to do with the letter *c* in the word "fucker." I walked the highway again, up and down for more than two miles, asking, asking what to do with the letter *c*? What can be done with that *c*, dear Mother?

I saw the telephone poles that extended for miles along the roadside. Was this an optical illusion? They looked like the crosses at Golgotha. Our Lady nodded.

The next day in cooking class, I drew a *c* onto the center of one of the large rough rye bread loaves before we slipped it into the oven. Over the *c*, I drew a tall cross. I said, "This is the Cross on the round-topped hill called Golgotha."

"Gol-who??!!!" Such jeering.

"Golgotha," I said. "'In Hebrew, a language of ancient tribal people—we all come from tribal people long ago—it means 'the place of the skull.'"

Now I had their attention. Skulls.

If vulgar words were favored as tattoos, inking skulls was a close second.

There is something in the wounded young, and in the unwounded young, that wants to know about origins, about life and especially about death—but without the cleaned-up veneer society usually lays over it all. The kids would prefer to know about the dark without the "bs" attached.

So I gently told them about Golgotha. An austere place in the middle of nowhere, where people who were deemed criminals were dragged to be crucified ("crucified," a word that electrified the kids). To be scourged, to hang on a cross, to not be able to leave the pain. This they understood, for it is not too much to say that each child already carried their own field of skulls from their pasts, their own "inability to yet leave the pain."

For some of the more armored girls, I just softly pointed out that we were all old enough now to have experienced one broken heart at least. And that *that* was a kind of crucifixion. Remember how much it hurt, and you couldn't run away from your own broken heart? You had to wait in the dark, wait to come back to life in the light later.

I told them about the God of Love being found guilty of loving humanity instead of following the orders of the rulers and authorities of His time. They understood completely being forced to follow rules instead of learning the Rules of Love. They understood the ill drive in some to kill love. They had lived it. They understood the idea of the Cross. Being nailed. Some cried softly to hear of the Child of Love who included the downtrodden in His care most of all—that He had been murdered.

In children's prison, as in adult prison, those incarcerated weren't supposed to touch one another, ever, even in love. An untenable and insane proposition. Yet here, in our cooking class, I touched the shoulders of the weeping girls, and as I did, all the other girls rushed to comfort them, too, arms over shoulders, and around waists. Some were scared they were going to be caught. I told them about being "a Veronica," the ancient Veronica, who took off her veil, a taboo thing to do in an orthodox religious society that required all women to cover their hair, or else they'd be thought of as whores and thereby subject to being stoned to death.

But, Veronica took off her veil anyway. No fear. She took off her veil to wipe the blood from the face of the tortured Jesus as he dragged the cross to Golgotha.

Stories leak between the worlds. We too. We will stand together. To bend to wipe the face of, to comfort the tormented. No matter who says it is against the rules to do so.

The girls understood immediately. No jeering or acting silly. Just quiet and truly kind. And the blackbird children silently moved to clean up the kitchen then, the fragrant smell of leavened bread rising. And rising.

THE LETTER *k*

That night, before bedtime at the last Angelus prayer of the day, I asked Mother, "What shall I do with this *k?* This letter seems very hard. A *k* seems so permanently unwieldy with legs and arms going every which way."

By morning I had an answer; I awoke knowing. Mother's voice was clear.

That day, in poetry class, I told the girls, "I have a poet for you with regard to the letter *k* in the word 'fucker,'" I said.

I wish I could convey how open the girls' expressions were now, how they looked like little birdie-girls awaiting the parent's return to the nest with food. I told them I'd brought a poet for them whose name begins with *k*: Kerouac. He was a Catholic, then a Buddhist, then a Catholic. He wrote about how the best of the best were laughed at by a nightmare society. And he wrote about how the automobile had taken over the piety belonging to the soul.

We talked about what this meant—to be laughed at when you are soulful, and to have reverence for the human soul be crassly transferred to objects instead. We also spoke about how jeering the soulful can be a display of trying to protect oneself from one more fraud, one more disappointment of someone using the right holy words for the wrong reasons, that is, without living them, without meaning them truly.

We were at a place where I felt it was a gentle time to say how the letter *k* of the old word, "fucker" might be transformed by story.

"See this? I think the *k* goes with the *c* previous. We're still at Golgotha, the place of the skull rock, where *k* now becomes the addition of two more crosses on the rock."

I explained how two souls, said to be thieves, were crucified on either side of the God of Love. How one thief was mocking the God of Love, and how the other thief protected the God of Love, saying to the man jeering, "What's the matter with you, can't you see Holy Divinity when it's right in front of you?" Then, the protective soul asked the God of Love if he, the alleged thief, could ever be forgiven?

It was said in our old ethnic family stories that the Roman soldiers who were doing all the crucifying, also mocked the thief's heartfelt request to be forgiven. But the man who asked forgiveness was immediately granted such by the God of Love. Formerly seen as "only a criminal" and nothing more, the man was thereafter known as Dismas, The Good Thief.

The girls nodded and nodded at each step of the story. They wanted to know what each of the crucified were guilty of. "We don't know, do we? Often we are crucified for simply being different, aren't we?" Nods. "For standing up for the weak?" More nods. "For trying to protect others? For stealing a sense of identity that is good and honorable, but that others insist we do not deserve? For telling a hard and honest truth?" Yes and yes. No resistance.

For the sincere one who asks forgiveness, there is no death sentence . . . that was something human beings imposed on other human beings. For soul and only spirit, for the asking, there is a return to full inclusion, sacred conscience, holy consciousness, an immediate, compassionate companionship, a resounding Yes, you belong as you always have, but now awakened.

The blackbird children understood the pull between standing outside the soul in the cold, and entering back into the spirit and soul. The God of Love crucified promised to the longing soul even at the last moments of life: One only had to ask with full heart, and a new path will be opened.

DONE?

Our time together in poetry class concluded. The young ones filed out. A couple girls blew me kisses at the end of every class now. Their friends elbowed them and playfully slapped their arms down, teasing them about being affectionate.

I thought we had come to completion. Look at all the stories written in visible ink over the word "fucker," all the true stories now could be seen. The word now spells "Mother" instead of "fucker." Here is the staff of the Shepherd; here is the *M* of Holy Mother; here is She Who Is Clothed with the Sun; here are the three crosses representing so much, including that even if one kills all decency and mercy, the God of Love comes back.

The stories were done now, by mercy of Our Lady's inspirations. And the kids were thrilled in ways I'd never seen them touched before. But, why did I feel a little like I had failed, like something was unfinished?

I think it was because the children and I hadn't spoken once in all those days about changing anyone's mind about the word "fucker," displayed so prominently on their arms.

It would be hard to change the writing on their arms. Displaying toughness to peers was important. They still showed up with "M. Fuckers" or "fuckers" penned on their arms with permanent black markers ... often wherever they could cover with sleeves or pant legs, so the "authorities" couldn't see.

But in ensuing days the kids began saying to me, "You have to do the rest of the letters. Yeah, it spells the word 'Mother' out of 'fucker' now, but what about the other two letters, the *e* and the *r*? There have to be stories for those two letters too, right?"

I suddenly felt an almost ridiculously strong little sense of elation.

It's odd isn't it—that it's the creative fire of the journey that matters most to spirit.

I asked my young adults, who seemed less and less like immature beings, "What do you want the other two letters to become? What stories do *you* think ought be attached to them?"

Forthwith: this is what we decided . . .

THE LETTER *e*

Next class, human sexuality. We talked about the "eye" of the cervix, the "eye" of the glans penis. I know, I know. It seems like all these topics don't go together, but they do. They truly do: Creator's made wondrous creations of the body regardless of gender, no matter where they are seated—the forms of male and female often mirror each other in shape and function.

Thereby, the *e* of the new word "Mother" became an eye also, only this eye was the Eye of God, ever watching over burgeoning young adults, generative in a huge way. I went to the public library, brought books and books with pictures of *El Ojo del Dio,* ancient mandala-like weavings with God's eye at center, a pattern-message found in most every ancient sacred art across the world. I showed them the Creator's eye atop the pyramid on the dollar bill. They wanted to know if they could have the dollar. They could. I felt happy. They felt happy. We all laughed.

I told them about Father Baldwin's blue paperback Catechism I studied when I could barely read, how it said Creator first and foremost was all-seeing—not to catch people doing wrong, but to look after them. And that the Shepherd at the beginning in the original letter *f* was part and parcel of the One Who Saw All—especially those who were in need, like the lost lamb, like so many parts of Creation in peril and suffering from also being imprisoned and "cut down" in our times, too.

In the ensuing days, a single tattooed eye made out of the letter *e* started showing up on the kids' arms and legs and in their lined note-books. A blue eye, a brown eye, an Asian eye, a single eye.

I didn't say anything, the same way you *know* to not say anything when an eagle suddenly lands on your porch. But I felt happiness in my very bones. I knew the kids understood that sometimes what you wear, you become. Sometimes what you have become, you wear outwardly.

The children had purposely chosen an image of strength and protection. Soulfulness has been part of the underlying power of tattoos since the beginning of time. I told them Creator, according to the holy books, wrote the first tattoo on a wall with a finger unleashing flames. That blew the kids' minds—in the best possible way. The next day, the *e* that was now the all-seeing eye had shooting flames all around it.

THE LETTER *r*

Soon enough we were in cooking class again, and discussing rose water in Moroccan and East Indian food, and how roses are actually in the same family as apples. And that though we think "flower" when we think "rose," others think "scent" as in flavoring for food, a divine scent.

I taught how the taste of the roses depended on the soil conditions the roses grew in, and even their dark or light color depended in some part on environs. We discussed how people were like this too: how the soul developed a certain sweet way of being, depending on what ground it rooted, and next to whom.

I told them stories about Our Lady of Guadalupe, how her gown was covered in red roses; how roses were so associated with her because roses can climb anywhere, survive even stone walls, conquests, storms, destructions, leap over boundaries, seed themselves in even a tablespoon of decent-enough dirt.

I told about how near Golgotha, an ancient temple of the Great Mother known as Aphrodite, once stood. She was considered by ancient tribes to be a representation of the Mother of Love from the earth upward. When wars came there was a basilica built over that temple. The basilica was destroyed about five hundred years later by another horde who believed differently. But, even so, some of the old storytellers alive today say that the Great Woman rose as Blessed Mother, in all her rose gold and beautiful incense again. And again. That the Mystical Rose would never stop rising again.

I'd brought wild roses to cooking class, roses I knew had not been sprayed with poisons. We tenderly trimmed the white part of the petal, which my grandmothers had taught me was not as tasty. Now only the sweet part of the petals were left. We used them to delicately flavor our rather industrial, plain-vanilla ice cream that came to the prison in big beige cardboard tubs—ice cream so hard you practically needed a reciprocal saw to cut through it.

But we managed. And as we did, the kids decided the *r* at the end of the newly minted word "Mother" would become Blessed Mother's roses—the sweetness of new life—and the freedom to grow free. Truly free.

Again, I'd brought in books and books of pictures of wild roses grow-ing with abandon everywhere—over fences, over roofs; nothing could keep Our Lady's roses—or the blackbird children's spirits—contained or restrained. Outwardly in one way, perhaps. But in soul, spirit, mind, heart not at all. The children truly knew that now, despite all they'd been told to the contrary most of their lives.

"You're not my mother!"
"That's what you think!"

The truth of it all was out now. Even though they still slouched along and often looked sullen and were occasionally mischievous and some-times a little devious, they were also pure spirits and beautiful souls. And they knew they were. Glimpses at first. Two steps forward, one step back sometimes. But they truly knew.

Their Mother, *The* Mother, had told them so.

HIEROGLYPHICS: THE MYSTERY OF PRISON TATTOOS

Weeks passed. Our time spent in kitchen and classroom included more creative food flying; other kinds of turmoil; some running for blue sky; some for cold silences, tears, embraces, secrets told, comfort given, and always, always some remembrance by someone very young—asking for more stories about . . . The Lady.

One morning at breakfast, two of the oldest blackbird children were elbowing each other in the dining hall.

"Show her."
"No, you!"
"No! You first."

One pulled back the sleeve of her hooded sweatshirt. There on her arm, rubbed angry red from scrubbing and scrubbing at the old ink, was a new word. Just one word. One of the most gentle and strong words in the universe: *Mother.*

But written with the *M* and the Shepherd's crook at the beginning.

The child called "Little-bird," who could hardly ever speak without using the "*f* word" as though it were the word "the," said that her new tattoo was for "that blessing mother of yours." She meant, "Like you said, we belong."

A huge shaft of light pierced everything all at once, yet the room was noisy and ordinary as usual. I wobbled out a "Yes." A daring, "Yes, you wear the mark of belonging to her now."

The entire table of girls seemed for a moment to be engulfed in a transparent golden light. It is such an odd thing to see souls in the light, to see their tough exteriors fall away and see that they are delicate like light themselves, beautiful unhooded golden light.

And we all went on from there . . . shimmering.

Some tattoos remained as before. But other children showed up with different parts of the hieroglyph we'd worked out, and some with the full *Mother* hieroglyph.

When I was a child, growing up in the backwoods with my Old Country family, the magical objects I loved more than anything were not within reach: books, colored pictures, endless paper and pencils so I could write, words that somehow could make deep and true stories not disappear. Though my people fiercely guarded their wounds from the wars they'd survived, they were generous in certain ways, but too, they had no money for what they considered frivolous.

So, as an adult, any chance I had, I would bring books and more books, paper and pens and pencils to those who were hungry to learn through stories, to delicately sew the stories to the pages so the stories could continue to live, and not be forgotten.

Thus, to the children's prison I brought blank books, books, pens, and books of hieroglyphics: Egyptian, Slavic, African sgraffito, petroglyphs, indigenous peoples' pictographs, cave paintings, stelae carvings. Together we read the archeologists' and anthropologists' interpretations and statements detailing what all these symbols might have meant.

But together we wondered, given the experience we'd just had in making our own hieroglyphic, how would any modern person know what people in "the far-away" really meant by their drawings, stone peckings, and carvings?

The children thought that scientists in some far, far future would never understand our drawings of the word *fucker* made into the word *Mother,* were our undertakings "discovered" a thousand years hence. That they would not know the step-by-step unfolding story that had risen from the people who created our Mother hieroglyphic.

Would the scientists ever guess the real stories making up this holy hieroglyph? Most of the kids thought not, and surmised on their own that what we know of ancient cultures might be an ever-open question about the actual meanings of symbols and hieroglyphs held close to the makers' hearts.

We might see the symbol as a mark on a rock or on parchment, but we ought not forget that each stroke represents a story, a precious set of stories about the journey of souls, real souls. That there are "stories within the story" of how that symbol was created.

And so our time rolled forward. And though some may think this is only a story about a group of "wayward children" and one of their most earnest but also in many ways most "uneducated" teachers, it's really a story about the profound love and patience of Our Mother; the Holy, Warm, Sheltering Woman—the One Tough Mother.

The one who can hold endless little tough daughters and sons—like you, like me—in her fiery and Immaculate Heart—ever loving them, like her Shepherd Son, so many times, back from the very edge.

All these years later, I am old, and my blackbird children from long ago are in their forties and fifties now, and most are flying free. I'd just like to mention to you, dear brave souls who read my words, her words here ... that if I see one of the symbols below on your body, on your clothes, on your walls, or in your heart, I'll recognize you right away—that you are one of ours, one of Mary's children passing by.

CHAPTER TWELVE

No Racism, No Discrimination,
No One Is An "Untouchable"

The Great Woman
Appears to Us Daily

W*e have, too often, been led to believe that appearances of Blessed Mother and her precious little Child of Love are rare, only occurring to those who are purest of pure.*

That's not so. This very day, millions of ordinary souls have experienced sightings and signs of the Blessed Mother as lone woman, as mother, as immigrant, as queen. And tomorrow and all days forward, there will be more sightings of her in the millions, if not billions.

And those who see her, perceive her, sense what and who they are seeing when they see her, are not purest of pure. Those who see her are many: the saints of this earth, the muddy angels of the earthsphere, those who are in the midst of *lucha*, struggle; those who are "working on" what it might mean to be holy in the midst of a sea of garbage. There are also those souls who were just minding their own very mundane business, when all of a sudden there she was, breaking through the worlds to manifest her essence, her presence, her provocation, her intelligence.

In her visitations to us, a magnitude, a perspective, an instruction from beyond this world is made clear and irrefutable to the soul.

Yet as usual, afterward, the little monkey-ego may have its endless frets: "Did I see what I saw? Hear what I heard? Sense what I felt? Did I really? No, not me. I am not worthy."

◄ Ex-voto: "Mary's Closet"

Or, "How can I know? I must have imagined it. Surely if it was she, she would have appeared as I see her in all the paintings: laden with the accoutrements of the wealthy, with golden-tipped everything, and clean, ironed clothes. She would have made the sun spin. She would have done some incontrovertible miraculous thing that fifty other people could validate with replicative science-based certainty."

But actually, Our Lady often, by report, appears in garb similar to the person who apprehends her. Sometimes she appears in the garb best understood as "otherworldly" by the person she is speaking to.

Too, we see that she is often portrayed by artists and sculptors who are called to record the visitation. They've clothed her in the garb similar to those in highest authority in that land at that time—as you see her portrayed, for instance, in the long heavy gowns and Moorish-influenced veils of royalty in paintings and wooden statues created during the fifteenth and sixteenth centuries in Spain.

If anything though, for most people, La Señora is down-to-earth rather than lofty-aloof, much more like a warm embracing mother, one who is intent on nudging, guiding with love. She shows herself in ways each person might best understand—if they don't allow monkey-ego to appropriate it all, and thereby, with small simian mind, invalidate instead of open to the numen.

In the raw, before any redaction by any persons with other motives, it appears in the experiences of millions who have beheld her, Our Lady most often does not speak in high oratory, but in street talk, ordinary tones, those easily parsed by the person to whom she is speaking. She offers this kind of mercy: appearing and influencing in ways that are comprehensible to each individual in their own time, culture, pace, and place.

It is a simian-like aspect of ego that likes to anticipate visitations as high drama and with fantastical twists to all events. It is this predilection in us all that can erase or garble the actual message. Our Lady, however, uses whatever works. She's not a "say it once and never again" kind of mother. In the experience of many, she shows up over and over again, no matter what egos make of her.

How do I know? I validate the witness from literally thousands of authentic and heartfelt stories I have heard over these many decades from souls—men and women, children, the mid-aged and old ones—who have not only been touched by her once, but many times.

As it was said in our family, no evidence needed for those who have felt her touch, her soothing voice: And there is not enough evidence in the entire universe to convince those who have not yet known her touch and her beautiful voice.

Experiences with Our Lady appear to carry at least one similar leitmotif: Her touch can be pragmatic in every way, but registers as a "sudden knowing," a sudden clarity, a sudden calming, a sudden inspiration, a sudden breaking of something that needed to be broken, a sudden pathway to mending something that ought to be mended, a sudden superior strength—or "strength enough"—to go on.

I will put it to you this way as I understand it through her: Her being suddenly near clearly rearranges one's atoms in a significant manner; often changing one's mind, changing one's heart; leading one who, a moment before, had no idea how to go nor how to proceed—but now, suddenly holds a fragment, or the entire map, of how to go forward and what to do next.

This sudden in-pouring of intelligence from Our Lady is completely out of the ordinary, yet useful, and very often quite down-to-earth. Take this. Do this. Go here. Speak to so-and-so. Don't go. Stay over there. Listen to this person. See beneath the outer appearances. Be wary. Bypass that. Bless this one.

Often enough, seeing, sensing, and hearing Mary is awe-striking, a "No kidding, you've got to be kidding, you're really here?" experience, or else a quiet knowing, a drifting sense of being in the arms of a compassionate mother whose warm body is ever-so calming.

There are other ways to know she is present as well, perhaps most occurring under the "category" of a sweetly quiet "Aha!" somewhere in the vicinity between heart and divinity.

Thus, her sudden appearances; her voice made clear or even just barely comprehensible to us, urging us to listen daily, longer, harder, deeper; her giving us signs to seal her troth with us; her visits are not rare. They are common. No mother withholds herself from her children who cry out in need for her. A mother does not only aid "perfected" children. Quite the contrary, she abides with those who stumble, bumble, and suffer.

This I can assure you from experience: no matter how deep an exile you have been forced to, no matter what the wound, no matter what disheveled condition your soul is in, no matter what you have done or not done-call—and she will be there, as you best can comprehend her.

She comes as vision, or wrapped, for the moment, within another human being who suddenly blurts some startling and important words to you, words absolutely needed by you. She can appear, too, as a stranger who enacts some momentary and dazzling kindness toward you that surprises both of you perhaps, but also remakes you in good ways in that moment—and perhaps the other soul as well.

Or you will feel the wind, or the sun, or the rain; or a vista, a creature, or an innocent; and suddenly breathe in an enormous breath that feels as though it is an otherworldly compassion breathing you—and this fills the angelic wings of your lungs to the very nth degree, and your spirit will feel suddenly refreshed. Your soul, no longer distressed, but in these moments, at sudden peace.

In these cases, and more, your Mother, the Great Woman, has hastened to your side in all her fullness, and with all her might.

Historically, we are not completely clear about what made some minds on earth think that a Mother of such magnitude would only appear just every now and then. What crabbed, narrow, deadly thought would deign that a devoted and loving mother would be stingy with her visitations to give guidance and knowings to her beloved sons and daughters?

It is not true that rarity of sacred appearance is more valuable. No loving mother follows such a dictum.

It is just the opposite.

Yet, some people appear to desire to verify or disprove appearances, advisories, and miracles of Mary, Maria, Mir-yam, in all her many manifestations. In some hierarchies of the churchly kind, should any man, woman, or child say aloud that they travel with La Virgen on a regular basis—and wish to seek validation of that by the Roman Catholic Church—a group of assigned "judges" will be dispatched to "investigate," to "authenticate."

But meanwhile Our Lady, Seat of Wisdom, seems to pay no attention. She keeps appearing without any authority's permission, without any institutional sanction, to those in need.

She bypasses all gatekeepers, appointed or self-appointed, and instead flies to intervene, lift spirits, direct, heal, and liberate souls throughout the world.

Undoubtedly, long ago, the "investigating and deposing" of ordinary people's experiences with Our Lady was initiated by those in love with the endless beauty of Creator. The churchmen originally, no doubt, wanted no chicanery with regard to the Sacred, no monetary exploiting of naïve persons, no grandstanding by con artists.

But in times since, these valid concerns sometimes seemed to turn into suspicious inquiry, then polarized, politicized pronouncements, which became more strident over time about the utmost super-rare rarity of "real" visitations.

Thus, churchism built up a language of legalisms that attempt to "verify" such "alleged" visitations in order to "deliver a verdict." But again, numinous experience, by definition, is non-quantifiable by ego tracking alone.

Throughout the centuries, in Sor Juana's work, for instance, we see that visitations cry out to be described in the language of the soul who embraces the mystical nature, often through images and poetics.

We see this mark of the soul's language in the work of any person who has sensed, seen, heard, conversed with, or experienced Our Lady or her Precious Son—from little Saint Francis the Assisian to Thérèse the Little Flower, to Mechthild of Magdeburg, and to those thousands of writers whose work was never discovered by a reading public, or whose writings were destroyed by one regime or another, civil or clerical, and to those millions of Marianas who could not read or write, or who lived so remotely that there was no one to hear their stories.

Most often, the essence of what was seen of La Maria, what was heard from her heart, had to be recorded, not in ego words or by the "slice and dice" mind, but in poetry, music, dance, painting, sculpture, writing, and other arts that have infinite layers that leak between worlds.

These arts, when allowed free, rather than forced rote expression, carry a deeper mysterious voice that speaks the language of numinous experience, a holy symbolic language. Art is the sacred's lyric language via color, movement, sound, and thought. This *philosophorum* is the kind most needed to report numinous experiences that can rarely be conveyed in formal prose, no matter how erudite.

Holy scriptures throughout the world don't devolve into poetics, they rise supreme *upon* poetics, because that lyricism is the only language of the numinous experience that can come close to describing it with full grace, full glory, full gratitude, full magnitude.

Yet, over time, some churches' "investigations" of realness versus inauthenticity of others' experiences of the Great Woman—an inquiry that once was meant only to protect gullible others from Barnum & Bailey Traveling Mary Shows for money, profit, ego, fame, and status—has sometimes become intrusive, in effect poised to negate personal visitation and personal revelation to everyday, ordinary persons.

This impoverishes the communion of souls' experiences on earth when revelations and appearances by Mary, Holy Mother in her many forms, *los santitos*, the little saints, and the entire varigated visions of Holy Family, as well as the Source without source, are not recognized.

These revelations come as much to the worldly and those covered with mud and down for the count, as they come to those who have been given opportunity to live a far more innocent life.

When I was at university many years ago, my grandmothers and aunts were my conciliares. Even though "uneducated," they were old believers and smart. When I learned something that might interest them, we'd all sit in the kitchen and I'd tell them all about it—and they would listen thoughtfully, and then thoroughly "correct it all" for me, telling me how it all "really" went together.

When I told them about Vatican-appointed commissions that voted on the authenticity of private visitations and revelations by Blessed Mother, they listened carefully.

I told them the commission can make three "rulings":

1. *Constat de supernaturalitate*—The committee decides that an apparition, visitation, revelation, or miracle displayed "all evidences" and therefore is an authentic intervention from heaven. (Some of the required "evidences" are that the person receiving the visitation/revelation be "of upright conduct, obedient to ecclesiastical authorities, able to return to normal practices of the faith," meaning communal worship, the receiving of sacraments, and so on.)

    I cannot describe the look on my old ones' faces on hearing the "evidences" required, except to say they all gave the "eyebrow." I know many of you know what I mean.

2. *Constat de non supernaturalitate*—The committee decides that an "alleged" experience is clearly not miraculous, and is found to have no supernatural basis. This last unfortunately and perhaps speciously can imply that persons "claiming" visitation are either mentally ill or else possessed "by Satan." Such is stated in the 1978 "Norms of the Congregation for Proceeding in Judging Alleged Apparitions and Revelations," written by the Sacred Congregation for the Doctrine of the Faith and approved by Pope Paul VI. "Nor may there be evidence of mental illness or psychopathic tendencies."

    Given so many otherwise good souls' blindness to misconduct by certain prelates, it seems a dicey proposition to imagine the good fathers performing all-accurate and far-reaching psychological analyses of any person. I do not find anything anywhere in Holy words from any faith saying Our Lady would bypass any person who struggles with a brain chemistry that does not allow them to join society in the usual ways. There is nothing that says La Señora only visits those who are considered sane according to the Diagnostic and Statistical Manual of mental disorders (DSM). In fact, amongst many persons who have special needs, there have been many Marian appearances.

3. *Non constat de supernaturalitate*—This is the third possible outcome of a church investigation. In this case it is said that it is not evident whether or not the alleged apparition is authentic. In other words, to use trial lawyers' lingo, it is a "hung jury."

After my elders listened quietly to this précis and consulted amongst themselves, my grandmother Katerin spoke for all. She averred that new visionaries and prophets were needed in each generation. She said they all agreed that visionaries and prophets were like geraniums. (My elders were peasant farmers from the Old Country.) As the plant grew sturdy new branches, the mother plant needed to be transferred into larger and larger containers so her roots could continue to grow deep and well.

The elders thought that by limiting who is and who is not sanctioned or sanctified enough to have experiences of and with Our Lady, the church had instead willfully transplanted Our Lady into increasingly smaller and smaller pots. Thus root-bound the plant begins to wither with progressively fewer flowers and fewer fruits.

One of the "smallest containers" I can think of is the idea that Holy Mother appears only to persons of "upright conduct," and so forth. And by inference, that Our Lady would never think to appear to a person who is distressed in any way.

I say this last not as a lament of those who carve Our Lady into such small root-bound pieces, but as a charge and as an indictment of any who attempt to maim or starve the souls who belong to her by insisting her magnitude be miniaturized to suit their own too bland, too narrow views.

Nuestra Madre, the Mother whom you and I know, is not a relative idea, but rather she is our relative, our blood clan. She is in no way elitist. And in no way should she be diminished as such—by any person, in any time or place.

Again, from listening to thousands worldwide who write to me and those who write in books; who tell me they have face-to-face, cheek-to-cheek, heart-to-heart relationships with her, it is clear she does not qualify nor screen those she visits. She loves all, bends to tend all.

Our Mother appears to every heart regardless of its owner's status, authority, dishevelment, or saint potential.

In fact, Our Mother appears in striking ways and far more often to people just like us, many of whom will never be saints, in the narrowest view, but who are Blessed Mother's dearest daughters and dearest sons, beloved inside her giant flower-perfumed heart forever.

THE SOULS SHE APPEARS TO MOST ARE OFTEN THE VERY ONES WHO NEED HER MOST

I have met her many grateful witnesses: the lonely and all who have been abandoned. She reminds all that she leaves no one stranded—not the despairing, not the devastated. I find she reminds again and again that Creator and despair cannot exist in the same place at the same time.

She has reunited people and creatures who have lost one another. She visits those imprisoned, whether in a rhetoric or whether in paper, golden, or iron cages. She carries souls across the cold deserts of cultural pollutions and harming constraints.

She infuses strength into the many who are threatened with physical and spiritual deaths; she is intercessor in their hardships—in the deceptions, thefts, and the death cults of our times. She is a bringer of the "aerial viewpoint," seeing the greater soul-picture in everything around us—in our parents, our families, our children, our cultures, our own spirits, as well as in "what lies beneath in treasure, as well as in as-yet-undeveloped and misunderstood terrain."

She is drawn to those who have experienced travail, challenge, especially including those trials that she herself faced: she, when carrying her Child, was not believed, was not accepted, was not found worthy by her culture, yet she sheltered the Truth and the Light. She fled as an immigrant to a foreign country, and without proper papers, in order to keep her Child safe.

She knows the rows. She has hoed them.

This is why she is called La Nuestra Señora, *Our* Lady, because she is a mother instinctively and soulfully—and no one, no nation, no politic, no religious skepticism of her time or any era could turn her away from her profundity as protectress.

Thereby, she is ours, and we are hers. We belong to her. She belongs to us. No qualifiers, no proofs required.

She has been called Advisor, Helper, Intervener, Mediatrix. Yet, to reduce Our Lady to a mere coping mechanism and by saying she has no rational function, grit, or imagination, as some have ventured, is to say that Yahweh Jehovah must have just been a weekend hobbyist who took seven days off to make some "stuff."

That's not it at all. La Madre Grande is a force of Nature intrinsically inlaid with the profound creativity—of bringing, teaching, showing, sheltering, all the attributes of mothering in this world and beyond.

La Madre, Nuestra Señora, Our Mother, continues[1] *regardless of those who say she did or did not appear to whomsoever; did or did not enter a household; did or did not lay hands on; did or did not heal; did or did not speak love to everything and everyone.*

As vast intercessor, she is essential to *Tikkun Olam*, the Hebraic words meaning "repair of the soul of the world." She is essential to the concept of *Ometeotl*, the Nahuatl/Aztec word meaning "the one who enters the world from highest heaven to sweep clear the two-way path between the great earthly and heavenly hearts once again."

In these ways she has granted many of us, myself included, relationship so many times. I fully admit: Her fingerprints are all over me. Perhaps they are all over you, too. I hope so. Her palm prints are on my shoulders from trying to steer me in various proper and difficult directions—such as the path of a long and hard-won education for which I, as a welfare mother, had little means.

Mi Guadalupe was there always during those "decades of nights" it took to earn degrees, and even more, to earn a place to live in a world that so shuns those not like the over-class. She whispered, "I crossed a long desert with little means, and so can you."

She is no little thing. I have the literal experience of the strength of her great arms holding me up when I thought I would die: her arms held me tight as I struggled to hold up my fainting adult daughter in the shower, me fully clothed standing in the rain of the shower, my poor daughter naked and soaking wet as she miscarried her beloved and long-awaited child. I do not know how I, or we, could have stood alone without Our Mother.

There have been better times and far, far worse times—and in those, many a time not knowing where to go for solace, finding no place to rest in the storm of loss and grief, I have lain against Mi Madre's breasts sucking for strength to go on. And, in some way, often in some strange, at first unrecognizable way, strength has been granted.

During a recent struggle with a misdiagnosis of terminal illness for which I was given but four months left to live, she took off her vesica piscus of *rayos* and bade me pass through her fiery corona, burning away my terror and grief time and again.

She has warmed me with love, and warned me in prescient ways. She has allowed me to put my hands inside her hands to help others, responded forcefully and positively to healing petitions for family members, friends, and strangers.

She has answered petitions for recoveries and abatement of threats, harms, wounds, fears, exiles, *luchas,* struggles of many kinds. She has answered in her way, not my way.

And still I am terribly deficient—and in all my failures, I ever find her dusty hem beside me, her voice saying, "Rise."

There are times I wonder if maybe my discontent with the soullessness of some parts of the world is because I was just born in a semi-permanent bad mood . . . but being near her, even though it's not easy most times, all I ever want to do is struggle to love, and then try to love some more.

I try to remember, as my drollest grandmother used to say, "Just think of how much worse we all would have turned out without her."

Perhaps most powerful of all, I pray to Our Lady daily with thousands of other old women throughout the world. I do not have all the answers, but I carry the essential conviction that Our Lady cannot resist listening to a gaggle of such comic, imperfect, devout, and lively old souls like us—like you and me, regardless of our number of years on earth.

Too, Our Mother, La Señora, Our Lady is carried forth in prayer, petition, and praise by men and women and children of every age, and daily for she is on the side of life and she is for the world—all of it, not just some of it, not just those who have been "certified."

We call such members, Las Marías. If you have a feel for her; if you desire a deeper guidance of more than the mundane kind; if you fear something precious will be lost or something dear will not come to fruition; if you have a hope of healing for others who suffer; if you wish to know her radiant Child of Love; if you need a sign, guidance, a word of kindness, a drink of water on the long dry road, please come join us in this invisible but palpable worldwide sodality.

She is not called "Ivory Tower" and "Tower of Light" for nothing. Rise up, come forward, there is a Lady waiting, a Lady who knows you by name, and who knows the way through and the ways forward by heart.

People often ask me how I pray to her. I've a thousand prayers I've been given by the desert and the dirt, by blood wrongly spilled, by counting the cavities in Death's back teeth, but there is one prayer I return to with Our Lady time and again, for it is the only prayer thus far given to me personally by her.

It is oddly sweet, isn't it, that one who writes so much and walks long with Our Lady asking her over these seven decades of my life to please grant me words enough to help and heal others—yet when I asked for myself, thinking maybe there might come a paragraph at least, perhaps even a page—instead came this.

And it is this prayer then, the one that follows, and I so deeply invite you to join me in our praying it together, even though the personal prayer Our Lady granted me is only one word long:

Enséñame.

This means, *Please show me. Please teach me.*

I know Our Lady hears this prayer no matter from where in the universe is it released, for there is one thing Creator cannot do—one thing that Our Mother, the Great Woman, cannot do—that is, they *cannot* not love us.

Whatever we need to see, be shown, be inspirited by—the summons is the same:

Enséñame.
Please show me. Please teach me.
Aymen.
Aymen.
Aymen.

In ancient times, this word, *Aymen,* meant, "Let it be so. May it come to pass." And thus may it be for us all.

CHAPTER THIRTEEN

Her Names Without Cease

Litany of the Mother Road: Chant of Her Incandescent Names

Long ago, in the 1960s, I drove the Pan-American Highway in a Jeep so red it looked like a pomegranate cut in half. I lumpety-bumpetied, skid, skied, high-centered, crept, and cranked on the few straightaways, and drove hugging the narrow curves as though I was following the intricate folds of Our Lady's starry mantle.

And still, I nearly "lost the sticky" of the tires, and slid sideways down rain-soaked ravines. I managed to wrestle the steering wheel over 2,800 miles of washouts, sinkholes, hundreds of miles of bad road often without ever seeing another vehicle.

But this was a beautiful Mother Road that begins in Alaska, crosses North America, and drops down through Mexico, and then into Guatemala, El Salvador, Honduras, Nicaragua, Costa Rica, and Panama, all the way up to the green face of the Darien jungle. The road then dives underground across the ocean gap, then down, down, and down to Tierra del Fuego at the tip of South America.

Although sighting few vehicles, oh my, this Mother Road, for anyone with the eyes to see, was alive with people. And the people were alive with La Nuestra Señora, for all these lands and all these peoples have their own versions and names for the Blessed Mother.

◀ Ex-voto: "Our Lady of the Blue Highways"

Many people think the Americas are filled only with people who are native to that nation. It is true, there are many indigenous people. But the Americas are also filled with migratory people, immigrants, conquest descendants, interracial people, people brought as slaves, people fleeing, people who saw opportunity or beauty, or fell in love, or found refuge.

And so, the Americas are filled with Morenos, Criollos, Mestizos, Ladinos, Reversos, Spanish, Africans, Tolucans, Tlaxcalans, Lacandones, Santo Domingo de los Colorados, Italians, Portuguese, Greeks, Germans, Austrians, Chinese, Japanese, French, United Statesians, K'iche', Mam, Moskitos, Cuna, and so many other tribes from all over the world. And many live all along this road spanning three huge landmasses [1]—and each group has their own words for what many Europeans call Mother of God, Mother Most Mild, and Mother Undefiled.

But on this road, in various tiny villages, she is also called according to how the people use their hands and spirits, so here she is called names that signify, when translated, that she is understood as Mother Copal of Sweetest Scent, Mother Glowing Ember, Mother Fire-Star, Mother First Sunlight, Mother Who Turns the Drum of the Universe, Mother with Wings of Palm Fronds, Mother Drum, Pink Mother Gate, Silver Sewing Needle, Lady Dance Wind, Precious Seed Corn Mother, and one of my favorite appellations, Mother Guerrilla.

Mother Guerrilla, meaning that she is the Leader of any small independent group of brave souls who engage in irregular fighting, often underground, in order to stave off a larger, organized, often governmental force that has far larger resources and superior material goods and wants to harm the common people.

Everywhere the Mother has a holy name that comes from down in the dirt . . . for that is where the people truly live. By each small group, she is understood as "ours," even though she belongs to all, and all belong to her.

The mostly farm people who live along the curves of the Mother Road have ongoing rituals of praise, supplication, and thanksgiving for and to her. They most often carve a figure of her as they see her, dressing and adorning that iconic figure, bringing her outdoors to *see* their travails, needs, and the conditions of their fields, so that she can aim her help and that of her Child to all *en puente,* right on target.

The people strive inwardly and outwardly to follow her. She becomes their leader throughout their lives. They set her at the center of life. The people need her, want her, stay near her as they strive to live a holy life, often in the midst of military coups, brutal wars, political denigrations of their humble ways, in which there is disregard for their most basic needs for clean water and food on one hand, and protection from invasion for ill purpose on the other.

Just as artists, visionaries, and holy people see Our Lady through so many different turns of the prism, in rich addition to the sometimes seeming too few images "authorized" by popes and kings, the so-called Pan-American Highway was not seen by the people who lived on or near it as merely a winding road authorized by the governments. They often saw the road as an altar.

Viz: farmer men and farmer women dressed in lush striped and embroidered clothing and wearing white straw hats that left little freckles of sunlight all over their dark faces, they saw the road as a giant feasting table—for, amongst other things, they used the roadbed to wash, dry, and sort their crops, the bounty they believed was blessed by Our Lady and her intercessions in the people's favor.

They lugged and laid down whole fields of corn plants on the road, long trails of bean vines; big fat *cojones* of cherimoyas laid out in rows for one-eighth of a mile on the tarmac; baskets of red, black, white, and speckled *frijoles, limónes, naranjas, y otros frutas* (beans, lemons, oranges, and other fruits), all laid out up and down the roads near most any village during harvest, right on the nice long tabletop of the road. Any intrepid car chugging by had to suddenly veer off the road—up/down, up/down bumpety, lumpety—to avoid making fruit salad and vegetable medleys all the village food lying there in saffron, ruby, viridian, on the red road that turned charcoal-gray after rain.

And the farming people added the roadway to their prayers and rituals and small homemade ex-votos paintings, thanking the Mother Road for her blessing by bringing such a beautiful table to help them sort and stack and dry and polish. And all this, in the midst of fragile peace and uncertainty. The Mother Road remains.

So it was that near many a tiny thatched-roofed village there were the skinny-armed old women on the roadways—a little like Tolkien's Ents, the trees that walk the forest. The old women seemed to be trailing their long rich roots behind them as they walked in their dark-navy woven skirts, and blouses that had burst into embroidered peach and orange and red hibiscus, and brilliant wide-open twenty-petal roses, all interwoven with leaves and birds.

The old women were spinners, weavers, the cloth and needlework queens of the Americas. And they often wore their bright white braids bound up in long colored ribbons, just like the girl-children of the villages, giving the air of agelessness in even the most elder headswoman.

The *viejas,* the old ones, saw the Mother Road as the place to unfurl. So they rolled out their wet lengths of deep purple and dark red and bark-brown cloth that was once pure white when they'd first woven it on their backstrap looms.

But now, having just steeped enough cloth in boiling dye so they could later give and offer new cloth to nearly an entire village, that cloth, from the additives of plants known to make yellow stain, and from other plants that contained enough tannin to tint the cloth a soft brown, and from insects that surrendered bodily juices that turned the hot water a dense violet color (and sometimes using a bright "not found in nature" color, an aniline dye some traveling tinker had brought by) now the old women needed only one thing more . . .

They needed a place to unroll all the steaming rolls of cloth, a place for buckets and tub after tub of cold, cool water to drape the cloth into, all in order to set the dye. They needed a place to throw a handful of salt into the tubs to help set the colors. And that place, the Mother Road, was the perfect spillway for this.

Later, selfsame old women would fiercely embroider atop the long *huipils* (blouses down to the knees) an entire Garden of Eden, and the women of the village wore these brilliant "walking works of art" as everyday *trajes,* clothing. To them, normal. To me, seeing such brilliant, colored threads, I thought I was seeing human women who had turned into legendary feathered quetzals.

And they brought the Mother Road into their blessing rituals and rites, thanking her; for to many, she was not El camino only, exactly (that is, the road), but also La carretera, meaning the cartwoman, the carrier, the one who knows how to carry life forward. So, not road only, but additionally, conduit and the conveyance both. The Mother Road was seen as the carrier of souls, the repairer of souls, the nourisher of souls, the one who knew how it all went together. And all this, in the midst of fragile peace and uncertainty: The Mother Road remains.

Thus, this road through the Americas, to many, is not only mundane, but sacred as well. As I drove, I thought of all the arms and backs and legs that built it—this road in Central and South America was built and maintained, often by conscription.

This means that the often small-of-stature tribal people in the villages were forced to road-build by the government. It is a sight to see this conscripted road maintenance: Indian men in colored traditional tribal clothing, digging, spading with planting sticks, down on their knees grading the roadbed with short boards held in their hands, pouring buckets of cinder and tar over stones.

In that sense, the road is hard labor and hand-made, and the Mother Road truly belongs to no government thereby. It belongs to those whose bones built it, and to the Beautiful Lady. So many have named their little part of the road with names like these, that once I translated them, go something like this:

- Merciful Mother Wearing Garments of Rain
- She Who Leans Over from the Sky to Protect the Crops
- Obsidian Blade: She Who Oversees an Efficient Harvest
- She Who Is the Colorer of Cloth so People on Earth Can Be Seen from Heaven
- She Who Carries the Soul across Fenced Frontiers
- Endless Feasting Table

She is also called some approximation of these as I would translate them: Mother Storyteller, Queen of Words (Love), Queen of the Soft Wind (Peace), Queen of the Winged, Protector of Angels, Spangled Bowl of the Universe, First Instructor, Weft of Gold, Harp of Heaven, First Star, Star Who Never Moves, Medicine Grandmother, Mother to Those Who See, Mother of All Angels, Mother of the Sacred Metate, Mother Maíz, and so many more.

And these names belonging to the Great Woman go on without cease on the Mother Road upon which we all are walking, a road wherein we might see her in any number of ways and learn to chant her incandescent names. Too, add to the chant, these time-honored names that come from the old temples and church scrolls—which seem endless too, just like she is:

Spiritual Vessel, Vessel of Honor, Mystical Rose, House of Gold, Morning Star, Health for the Sick, Refuge of Sinners, Comforter of the Afflicted, Mother of Good Counsel, Mother of God, Figure of Justice, Seat of Wisdom, and Gates of Heaven.

So then, here at the last, just this little prayer for all of us for safe passage on the Mother Road:

PRAYER FOR TRAVELING THE MOTHER ROAD

Nuestra Madre,
Portal of the Sky,
Star of the Ocean,
Mountain Throne,
I ask that you present me
to thy Child of the Desert Star,
and intercede for me
and those in need.
Bless Us and Teach Us to Be Gentle.
Bless Us and Teach Us to Be Fierce.
Gently Fierce.
Fiercely Gentle.

Our Dear Woman Clothed with the Sun,
Our Mother Road to run on,
Our Mother Road who carries us . . .
Help us by guiding our feet
in righteous directions,
by showing us
your inimitable road signs in ways
we can easily see
and best understand.

Please grant us visibility
when useful.

Please grant us invisibility
whenever needed.

Thank you Madre Grande.
Aymen.
Aymen.
Aymen.

(and a little woman.)

Compassionate Madre of All Life:
The Living, and The Yet To Be Born

CHAPTER FOURTEEN

Compassionate Mother: Restoring The Soul After Shock

Post-Abortion Compassion: "The Children She Got That She Did Not Get . . ."

I t is said that one-hundred million men and women have had abortions in any millennium. Some say more. Some say less. Yet, in my work with souls, I know that many people who have walked this road were not only unaware that other possibilities existed beforehand. They were often uncompanioned or poorly or ambivalently companioned. Many were shamed, humiliated, exiled by others. Many were completely bereft of resources of any kind.

Some were in abject panic, and often did not know how to or could not bring themselves to reach out to a kind, wise, or loving counsel a priori. Some were displaced. Some were fleeing. Some had been physically harmed. Some were literally out of their true minds and bodies. Some felt unworthy. Some felt doomed. Some wanted to soldier through alone without speaking to anyone else. For some, there was no sustaining resource offered. And, for a considerable number of others, resources were sometimes purposely withheld from them either naïvely, or as some kind of dunderheaded idea of "you made your bed, now you will lay in it," punishment.

Thus, many souls made choices clouded by anxiety or in desperation, making the best decisions they knew at the time, some saying for the sake

---

◄ Ex-voto: "La Mariposa: Butterfly Flutter, Our Lady of New Life" of reason or seeming expedience, some out of abject fear, but often in deep uncertainty; sometimes in the midst of abandonment and betrayal; and sometimes because they were denigrated by others; or because they were alone and had no one and nothing, even though surrounded by many, but without strongest connection.

After abortion, as with any grave matter regarding life and death, there can be suffering about decisions made. Many of the symptoms of this wounding are found in post-trauma stress disorder, and can include a sadness when near families and/or pregnant women, or women who are struggling to become pregnant; or families who have just lost a loved child. There can be ennui, meaning disinterest in certain aspects of life for they touch too close to sad memories. A person can find it difficult to connect to worthiness in certain ways. There may be low energy and merely plodding forth in life: This can come from being stunned and having no one notice to or to speak with in order to find learning, mercy, understanding and reconciliation. A person can not know how to restore oneself from this long loneliness, depression, feeling wretched, defensive.

There can be numbness, meaning patches of lost memory of that painful time. There can be the opposite, remembering so clearly the painful times so as to feel injured again daily. There can be finding that a flurry of "keeping busy" seems to more immediately salve the pain, rather than working consciously toward a true peace that makes all holy aspects of the person match well again: mind, heart, soul, spirit, ego, and body. Despite whether one was certain then or now regarding decisions made, this does not always erase the responses of soul and spirit, and the sensitive body memories. Yet, if a person feels settled, healed, or never hurt, we have to respect that too.

The tending to here is for those who have fresh and recurring situational pain-responses to loss of a child by abortion. Pain can be oddly brought on by advertisements, movies, sound, smell, touch, taste, sensations of many kinds, including the chance word or encounter. There can be worry about any matter having to do with health and self-preservation as a kind of referred-pain that comes from one's decisions long or short ago. Ever, there can be break-through weeping. These are not the symptoms of a hardened person. These are actually the symptoms of a hurt spirit and a suffering soul who at the very root, despite all else, innately holds life dear, and with infinite tenderness.

Some say those who have had abortions are not worthy of repair nor care, or that "what's over is over." This is not true. Life lost is life lost. To urge a wounded person to "move on" prematurely, and especially without full understanding and compassion, causes hind-sight to be eliminated from the psyche's ways of helping a person to heal well.

It is the crevices and chasms between the mindset of the time during which one made certain decisions—and the greater mind of the true self that holds other or additional considerations—that can cause pain now. Thereby, those who have lost, no matter how, have a right—and some would say, a spiritual duty to the soul—to remember, to grieve as they will and as needed, to be cleansed, to come to terms spiritually in restorative ritual, to sincerely question and answer all angles, to tell the truth, to bring all the parts of true self back together in one place again. The injured and the self-injured have a right to be raised up, to be touched in a special way with love and with holiness, for these character traits are the typifiers of the word "human" found at the center of the word *humane*.

SILENCING THE STORIES THAT TELL US ABOUT PRESERVING AND MENDING UP LIFE, KILLS LIFE

Let us consider a strong story to contravene a certain part of the over-culture that all we souls live in presently. Too often certain layers of society presume to try to teach us to overlook suffering of all the living. Via condemnation of the souls of others, we are encouraged to entertain schadenfreude about others, that is, taking joy in others' torment . . . This can never be. Instead, I would offer that we gently but firmly fasten ourselves to this venerable story instead:

> Once long ago, a man who had been wayfaring alone with no protective guide, was attacked, beaten black and bloody, and he lay bleeding to death on the side of the road.
>
> Various travelers passed by. They all saw the broken soul, but hurriedly stepped over his dying body so they could keep their own appointments.
>
> Two priests in flowing robes from two different religious groups saw the man suffering in broad daylight, but even the anointed literally crossed to the other side of the road to avoid having to engage with or touch the poor man's wounds.

This is an ancient story about bodily, spiritual and mental neglect of the injured. At root, this story's theme is an archetypal teaching story that can be found in every culture of the world, wherein the singular person of compassionate—and wounded—heart is the only one to step out to help the reviled. The story is known as "The Good Samaritan," and though it unfolds on illuminated parchments still stored in monasteries these many millennia later, it is also a story of our time, found daily in newspapers and online: the many who bypass the wounded, who may not even see the injured one and later so regret this.

Some by-passers may naïvely not realize anything ought be said or done. Some may feel "It's not my business." Others may find the wounds of others repugnant or not deserving of being healed. There are those too, who for their own smaller viewpoint rather than larger and holy way of seeing, will not intervene even when it is easy to do so.

This is why a strong story of merciful intervention for the wounded is valuable to keep in consciousness. For, if ignored, that is, carefully hidden away in records rooms and not brought out on the living lips and tongues of able tellers and healers and holy people, the story of mercy to the soul, dies. Thus, the spirits of humans who would learn goodness from the story are instead left unaware—and the injured at the side of the road continue to weaken and die away, too.

Through my heart's sight to yours, I'd ask, Who will tell the stories so that others can know how to kneel to help those who are hurt? Who will tell the stories about how those who did not see before, can seek insight now, and offer meaningful and heartfelt solace now? Who will tell the stories so truths can be told, so the ways of full acknowledgment of what occurred and full mercy can be made known to all? Who will tell the stories so the injured can be healed and rise again, scarred but gradually restored.

Who, like The Good Samaritan (incidentally, a man from one of the most hated tribes of his time) will kneel to bind up wounds of a stranger, whilst all others pass by either innocently not registering the need, or hurrying by, thinking their valises and papers, or that their ideologies and preoccupations on their way to elsewhere are more important?

The Samaritan in the story had a broken heart: he had spent a lifetime of being looked down upon by many. Imagine this is our times. Are there any amongst us who had not been looked down upon for simply being or holding to a way and ideal that stands like a giant cathedral in the sea, and yet one is downgraded because some cannot behold and truly see.

To bring home what a soul the Samaritan was, how radical his act to bend to help a beaten man, consider this: a modern tribal man, say a Mexican immigrant without all proper papers, who is looked down upon by many others, but seeing a homeless man wounded in the streets, even though all others ignore the injured man, the immigrant, who is maligned by so many, instead tenderly lifts the wounded soul onto his shoulders, staggers to the local motel, pays his hard won cash out of his own pocket for the motel owner to see that the hurt man is tended to, fed, and cared for. Then the immigrant of no standing whatsoever, goes on his way. And as in the story The Good Samaritan, later the little immigrant comes back to the motel to see how the wounded man is faring, and offers to do whatever else might be needed for the man's healing.

That is the ancient/modern story of The Good Samaritan. At root, it highlights what I call "the unruined heart" that exists in some as a charism, no matter what scar tissue a person is carrying. The core of the story offers a holy alternative to the gaggle of travelers who hurry past, some of whom cannot see the injured man, for perhaps no one has ever walked with their sufferings in kindly and wise ways either. And, some may pretend to not see the cuts and the blood, for some have their eyes not on heaven, but on how they look to others on Earth. Some may understandably not want to enter a painful helplessness that comes from not being able to turn back time and make matters so "they never really happened." For some it may seem like it is all too much, or that time, hopefully, will cure all wounds without any additional help.

Some passers-by may feel vulnerable, not knowing immediately the most useful ways to proceed in order to truly help, and especially, out of true love, not wanting to do any additional harm. Some may like to appear faux serene about it all, for sometimes they are still broken or have not come to terms—body, mind, heart, soul and spirit—with their own similar circumstances recently or long ago. Some may hope to maintain the status quo of living life without looking left or right. Some would just, for their own reasons, rather not enter another's sorrow about the loss of precious life. There can be many reasons for not connecting closely to one who suffers.

Yet, regarding the Samaritan story, centrally, what if no one had truly, tenderly helped the stricken soul? Wouldn't then the injured traveler have no story to tell, no direct experience of another soul caring so deeply about a stranger's life? We learn to encourage others to care for Life, to help Life when it is down, to mend-up and hold Life up when someone has, with infinite compassion, held our own lives above the waterline as worthy and precious.

If no one had helped the injured man when he was down, if no one had gently washed his lacerations and brought medicine to his injuries, if no one had reached to restore to him the memory of the holiness of his own precious Life Force, then how would he eventually teach others that this is something every human being on earth so richly deserves, something every human being is born with as their directional beacon?

If Samaritans do not stop to bend to help, how will all humanity learn to stop and bend toward the spiritually injured too?

NOT ONE OR THE OTHER:
RATHER, BOTH AND ALL TENDED TO

I've no doubt Buddha's Mother, The Mother of God, Holy Mother of the Lord of Love, *Jesu Cristo,* Miriam who saved the child by hiding him in the bulrushes, and many more great personages of magnitude, were they to suddenly behold a soul lying at the side of the road wounded in one way or another through abortion, they would hasten to ask if help was needed. They would each speak their own version of: I notice you. I see you hurting. With tender love and mercy flowing through me, I will help you see, reflect, heal.

Thus, it is the many souls who still are walking-wounded that we are concerned about—any soul hurt by a previous choice, uninformed, unaware, or otherwise.

If one-hundred million is an approximation of the number of tries "souls from afar" have made, in our time, to come to Earth—but for whatever reason were unable to arrive in full body—then there is a profound need for at least two-hundred million "Good Samaritans" to notice all the wounded mothers and fathers of children-never-born, all those lying by the side of the road, literally piled atop each other there.

It is not difficult to respond to the injured, unless one's punitive judgments prevent the flow of warm red love through one's heart to others; unless one does not want to kneel down, listen to, hold close, enter the suffering, share the burden, discover realities down in the dirt of true understanding. And to *not* ignore, to *not* withhold bandages and medicines, to *not* use all wobbly rationale to avoid giving money or resource.[1] But, instead to see that the waylaid and injured, and those with still open wounds are cared for in a proper refuge until sincerely reconciled and healed.

It can be mentioned too, that if there are one-hundred million lost, two-hundred million saddened, then there are four-hundred million grandparents who may have carried a wound on their hearts for life, having lost what often would have been their firstborn or a later-born grandchild. The *familiares,* relatives, and friends hurt by abortion are seldom noticed or mentioned aloud, either.

But Our Lady notices them; Compassionate Mother notices all souls, and bends to help. She will not be turned away from what she sees as the radiant soul inside each wounded person—for if one studies the old stories of her life and her greatest loss, one can find a clear map of parallel ways to heal. Holy Mother had friends to confide in and to be comforted by. She held her dead Child close, communing, speaking to, blessing, and loving Him. Pieta. She did not just go on. She stayed for and with. She made ritual for the dead. She anointed, carried, and placed. She wept. She carried her Child's memory with her in honor.

Reconciling begins and ends with telling all truths as honestly as possible, for this frees the emotional heart to break wide open. What can come out then is a waterfall of weeping. Thus, one begins, watered by tears, to grow and mend truly from the inside out.

A human mother who turned a child away here on Earth, has additional steps to undertake that Holy Mother did not, but assuredly the loving Mother will be there to encourage and hold close and watch over. Healing is not for the pure who need no healing. It is for those in need. And healing is not a straight line, but rather, a zig zag. A powerful prayer here, a person who listens with holy love there, a book over here, a sudden inspirational thought over there, a sudden realization, a ritual that has meaning to the spirit and soul,[2] and all these held together in tenderness with oneself and one's idea of the Holy.

Healing revolves around seeking a trusted person, face to face, and being listened to with kindness and mercy around various matters as each woman hears/sees/feels it, remembering that: Regret is the beginning of healing. Remorse and rituals that cleanse mind, heart, soul, spirit and body in accord with what one most deeply believes, knows, understands are the rest of the most powerful coming to terms that bring the broken parts of the vessel back together again. Eventually, the marks of the scars will remain visible but healed, instead of wounds still open and uncleansed. All wounds deserve to be cleansed, else there is potential to negatively affect other aspects of one's life and psyche, as an infection in one's arm has potential to infect all other systems of the body.

SOME SAY ABORTION IS NO BIG THING

Perhaps it is no big thing for some. And, I have listened to many persons and heard in my heart, I think, all the different thoughts pro and con, around and around in circles and in spirals, about abortion. I am especially not moved by the screamers, yellers, haters, shamers on any side, who try to turn me from my certainty about the preciousness of life. I'm not keen on those who are seemingly so anxious to win merit in their personal idea of heaven that they condemn others to their personal idea of hell.

But, I am moved by the souls who tried to come to Earth and were waylaid by whatever means. I am moved by those who are their parents, who miss so much what might have been. My way of seeing mothers and fathers of any child who could not come, or who came and could not stay, derives from having held the sorrowing in my arms, those who have wished for children and were unable to conceive; those who tried to bring a child, but were not able because of miscarriage or childbearing death, death of their infant or older child. I remember the heavy arms and shoulders of those who sagged so under the weight of having said no to a child trying to come through their bodies.

I find throughout my years of practice and listening deeply to people speak of the journey of the soul, that the psyche appears ever filled with imminent love. This word "imminent" means we are "spring-loaded" to love, that our springing into action with love is "about to happen" at any moment. We are, most of us, built to leap to love especially the vulnerable, the beautiful, the in need, the strong, the challenging, the anything and everything. Some say we are different than the animals because of our ability to reason, or to laugh. I'd agree. But far more so, we may be the only creature besides dogs who have an innate and energetic ability to love suddenly and truly, loyally and deeply, and fully alive in any moment. Seated in true self, we love so easily.

That most of humanity is built for "love ready to leap out and encircle so much," is a good deal of what causes pain, when a new life to be loved is not able to be taken up. The soul and spirit are significant aspects of psyche, and cannot easily nullify pain because the ego thinks, "Now is not the time, the place, the right person, or the best moment." I've seen hundreds of night dreams over the decades of clinical work that reinforce: To the soul of the psyche, every moment is the right moment for new life. To the animating spirit that lives within us all, new life is the world born over and over again daily. And, thus, to the greater mind, every time is "the right time," regardless of how the ego or rational mind sees matters.

Think of it in terms of sudden imminent arrival of souls on Earth. Few of us who are here on Earth seem to have been strictly planned. Most all of us seem to have been a big surprise to someone not completely "prepared." It seems most all of us, before we suddenly came to Earth, saw a tiny opening, an aperture in the sunrise of a world beyond, and we leapt through. We took a chance that perhaps a body could be made for us, a body that could survive and be born on Earth. No doubt, in spirit we were impetuous, determined and enthusiastic little souls.

Human beings can often sense this lively life of the little soul trying to come through. Some can sense the one hovering near who is not yet fully manifested, as in a conception. For many a bond seems made before one ever sees the actual child, a mysterious and palpable bond woven in red blood and some kind of sudden sharp memory or glimpse of eternity through the mother's heartbeat.

These and other mysterious factors of childbearing, child-raising, are seldom mentioned by cultures, as though pregnancy is only a matter of biology. It isn't. It is far more the entering into a great mystery in which new consciousness tries to break through at many levels, and for all concerned.

Thus, to tell a woman or man that they will forget child-loss, no matter how that child is lost, is to tell an untruth. If told that child-loss by accident or by being pressured, or by one's own say-so, is of no consequence, that it wasn't meant to be, that the situation was impossible, that it's no big thing—this might be true in one world. Truly and pragmatically true. But, there's a larger relational reality of Souls and Spirits that lies beyond the mundane alone—and that phenomenal sense of holy magnitude and wonder that belongs to new life that suddenly arrived with such promise, is lost also along with the loss of the child.

For that reason: when a living being is taken from its nourishing source, meaning the huge heart of love carried by those who are mother and father, there is no such thing as "no sadness" for most souls. The reality is soul's sadness. Sadness for loss of the "spirit child" that was trying to help mother build a body and come to earth, and then finding it could not be.

This sadness occurs, in part, because the soul/psyche records all events, all choices a person makes. The soul/psyche remembers all things that befall a person, and the higher mind weighs them all; it judges all matters by soul standards of wise support and calmness, even as the ego alone has its own nattering mind that also weighs all matters—sometimes far too fearfully, trivially, helplessly, or darkly.

A truth is, actions undertaken by ego alone regarding any matter, but without consult with soul and spirit, are often based on a lopsided scale provided by not the wisest and most loving in interior or exterior culture, but by those interested most in expedience, or social engineering, or the attempt to carve others' lives so they conform to narrow cultural expectations based in apprehension. These bypass studying and inquiring about opening or blasting open other doors for present and future ways to support new life. Life decisions based on fear—often the least far-seeing function within the psyche—rather than the most visionary aspect given to every soul on Earth at birth, can cause one's sight and insight to be gravely limited. In actuality, each person deserves fullest, soulful counsel, from within, from the Holy, and from those outside oneself who are tenderly loving and experienced in true wisdom.

Freud wrote about "the Death Wish" (a kind of pull to be against the life force.) In my clinical work, I've seen this occur via a patient's jadedness, disappointment, sloth, disregard, devaluation, or other means of undervaluing themselves and the spark of life, the creative and animating force within themselves. But, there is more so, I would say, in most of us, "a strong Life Wish," that is, a high valuation on life, a pull to be *for* Life in any and every way we can. The drive toward Life is protective, thoughtful, vulnerable, and invested in what I think of as the soul's immaculate love—a human version of Holy Mother's Immaculate Love.

Her Immaculate Love derives from a Force Greater that attempts to break through to our consciousness via all usual and unusual opportunities to love. Sudden openings to love truly, innocently and purely are often opened by life-changing events—pregnancy being one of the most vivid of life-changing events, *if,* ego is not feeling overwhelmed by circumstances, and if the culture and others are not exerting so much pressure that the voices of spirit and soul are temporarily drowned out at critical times.

Regardless of outcomes in any matter, in those who have felt a pull toward protecting many forms of new life with tenderness, this often marks the difference between a wise heart muddy with real-life experiences, even though not always easy decisions in the trenches—and a dry heart tempted to function on rote concepts alone.

Yet, I am not a Pollyannista. I do not underestimate that pregnancy can begin with a crime, and that pregnancy can occur to any woman rich or poor in finances, spirit, health, or wherewithal. I've known first-hand, pregnant mothers who are afflicted with late stage cancer and who struggle about who will live if both cannot live. I'm not sure if I can ever convey completely how sacred a silence I was allowed to enter to witness for a young mother who had chosen to forego chemotherapy entirely for it would end the life of her child in utero who could not survive the harsh chemicals. Her beautiful little girl was born alive and well near term, and the mother passed away very shortly afterward in full horrible-blessing love for this tiny new life. That story of such rough pathway, like that of so many mothers and fathers I've known, deserves an entire cairn of its own, with tattered prayer flags flying forever.

Much witness: other mothers took other choices for the sake of their one or three or five living children. There ought be a monument called "For Those Who Made the Hardest Choices." Too, I've listened to pregnant mothers who are drug-addicted and struggle. Pregnant mothers in prison who will egregiously be separated from their children the minute they are born. Over time, I've heard the hearts of a large group of very young and also older mothers and fathers who experienced unexpected pregnancy, and were so frightened of being discovered, so feared disappointing their parents, or being shunned by a certain community, they felt the pregnancy could not be allowed for these and other reasons.

I have listened too, to those who said they didn't care if an unexpected pregnancy was ended. But also, in speaking quietly with them it did often matter to them, but also there were other deep injuries already competing for space in their psyches. I also know fathers who were not told until long after the fact, as well as those who voiced their opinion one way or the other and were agreed to in accord, or contravened regardless.

This is why I see, in all these variations of very tough pathways, that all are worthy of mercy and understanding, of hearing the ways and means and plights each person has walked, each person's desires back then, their longings for peace and congruity between mind, heart, soul, spirit, body again now. This desire for peace in those who have walked the rough road, is the call of the soul yearning for healing and health, remembering that healthcare is not just of the body, but also a necessity for the mind, soul, heart and spirit, the environs, the society within our reach, as well.

I've beheld most everywhere I have traveled, many children who once brought here, were neglected and their lives made horrific by abuse and crimes against children. Holy Mother took me to the orphanages of

Bucharest and Warsaw, and this stays not with, but in me, as does more face-to-face knowledge of harmed children than I ever wanted to personally or otherwise know about. But I do know, and I know to still faithfully try to reach toward true self, for the compassionate One is there, Holy Mother by name for many of us. No matter what we call her, she is here with us, even more so in the most hopeless dark unspeakable corners of the world.

In the real world, the lines are not clear cut as some often shrilly claim about who ought do or think or follow what and how and why, most anything. Sometimes there are no perfect answers. Sometimes the answers are completely lousy. Sometimes we don't know which pathway we are being pointed toward. Sometimes there seems to be no path. And still I find Blessed Mother stands for life and for justice. Ever and now and always. For this she is called Mother of Good Counsel.

Some say, well what has she done for me, nothing. My problems are as terrible as before. My life is still a mess; I have no choices. And she whispers a holy insanity to us, one I believe we can trust in spirit and in soul: *I am with you. I am ever with you. By seeing as I see, hearing as I hear, acting as I act, you will find your way through.*

My first words to those who ask—a mother and father with an "unplanned by ego's measure—but planned by a force greater" pregnancy—and/or to parents or grandparents of young adults or grown up offspring who are suddenly "with child," is this: Do not panic. Breathe. Keep a calm bright heart. Let us think, not only feel. Let us listen to all voices.

I offer that we can, within their belief system, concentrate on the calming influence of higher power. For many this is or can be the Compassionate Mother. Thus, we can encourage each person concerned to take spiritual, not just pragmatic time to think through matters, time enough to reach to others for counsel, protection and resources, reaching beyond one's family if need be. There is time enough to remember that most pregnancies are seldom "the perfect pregnancy" with the perfect mate, the perfect finances, the perfect communal supports—and that one can build outer world structures to support one's future, just as the child is building its little bodily structures within its mother.

It is true a little child coming to Earth will change the trajectory of one's life. A new life will likely, if one attends to and allows it, deeply enrich one's life too, even when there are few difficult tasks ahead; even when there are challenges of many kinds.

And also, as author and poet, I sometimes speak to hundreds, sometimes thousands of people at a time. From the stage in certain venues, at the end of the evening, I sometimes open the conversation about abortion and childbearing loss, and say those who have interest in these matters are welcome to remain with me after the keynote, and we will talk and pray together.

Many stay with me afterward to often weep their way through their stories of dearest love, assault, loss, no choices, harshness from others, abandonment, betrayal, being shamed, and lacks of so-desperately needed support and love. Most still carry direct wounds that may have occurred only last week, or decades ago.

I can, with Blessed Mother's help in that small time-space, help the burdened heart a little way down the road to more reflection, meaningful ritual, more understanding and healing. Sometimes, though our time together is short, I can place a healing medicine into spiritual and psychic wounds. I can reassert for Life, the life of the one standing before me, as well as the spirit and soul of the one who tried to come through the body of the one standing before me.

I am also aware that what I offer is strongly contravened elsewhere in culture by some who have many prominent venues. Some say from their stages they have had abortions and no regrets. I have to believe a person's view of themselves. Some say they are proud to have had an abortion or abortions, and ask women in their audiences to stand and admit publicly they've had an abortion and to be proud of it. Too, I think I understand the radical of that for some. Several women have written that were abortion something men could have, then abortion would be a sacrament. I can sense the underlayment of that too, I think.

But my understanding, and my focus, is different. I don't mean to, but sometimes I draw the ire of a certain kind of person who has a large stake in not looking at the underlying realities of abortion, and the wounding that can come for others from such—or in glossing over how difficult a circumstance a pregnancy can be for a soul. There are also many who hold only women accountable for pregnancies, which is, I think, like saying the Redwood Forest grew from fairy dust without ever being seeded.[3] Most of all, despite various polemics, I think *all* the realities, especially those I see in the walking-wounded who have endured child loss via abortion, have to be given respectful and generous thought and resource.

213

A TINY HEALING REFUGE WITH COMPASSIONATE MOTHER

You can create a simple spiritual healing refuge for the injured also. I began four decades ago, to try to help mend those who suffer so from losses like these. And, the following is only my two cents' worth of anecdotal evidence. If near the end of my reading or lecture, I mention (in a secure environ) post-abortion trauma, the number of women and men who attend afterward (that is, those who are interested and/or hurting for whatever reason) far, far outnumber those who have mentioned to me they feel no post-abortion effects. Regardless of anecdotal ratio of one to the other, overall, those who gather constitute the wounded and untended-to souls.

I have a sense that were we holding others' sorrow with respect to become a new norm, there would also be less severing of new life, and much more familial and social architecture built to serve new life in ways that do not presently exist or barely exist now (or else are hounded out of existence, or starved of funding). But it takes more telling of the true stories of what happens when one prevents viable life from coming to earth.

Thus, when I gather in a quiet space, truly like a workroom of the soul, with either a few or many souls who have suffered and lost, I see through non-societal lenses entirely. I walk into a tiny corner of the post-abortion, childbearing-loss world that is deep and sacred. There, blood has been spilled, and there is such heartbreak. There are no facile answers, but/and there is often genuine desire to reconcile, and in these deep and honest first moments, I first call on Our Lady's presence to be with us. And often just this calling of her to us, breaks open the armored heart of many present, and the waters of the wound rush out.

Over time, I have my own membership in what I call "the scar clan" in many ways: significantly also from having been catcalled, ridiculed, hate speeched, shouted down, and screeched over when, in certain settings, I try to explain holding life as sacred—but, and, yet—my view of those suffering at the side of the road took shape in many ways long ago. I continue onward these many decades, seeking sustenance, and kindly support to keep my troth, to try to just keep going as a mostly quiet protectress of life.

Here, is a little window for you to look through to see one way my views were shaped by a woman of great compassion, someone most assuredly under the mantle of *Nuestra Señora* . . . a woman who had had many abortions.

Many years ago I sat next to a small, elderly woman on an airplane ride into O'Hare Airport in Chicago. She had great big lenses in her eyeglasses that not only covered her eyes, but also her cheeks on her tiny face. Her name was Gwendolyn Brooks and I knew her work well, though I'd never met her in person before. She was the Poet Laureate of Illinois, but even more so, a poet of the people. She wrote about people like us, people of the dirt and broken glass and proud dreams.

I had, long before, read and reread one of Miss Brooks' poems that was entitled "The Mother." The poem electrified me, meant so much to me, as I had fought like a wildcat at age eighteen to keep from being forced and shamed into an abortion. I'd succeeded in carrying my child to full-term, and yet as an unmarried mother, I had also lost my beautiful firstborn living child to a forced surrender.

That very poem meant a great deal to other unmarried mothers I'd read it to, for they too, had been harshly pressured into surrendering their own children—they who had also been poor, often barely educated, and who were unsupported in their pregnancies, all resources withdrawn from them, often betrayed and abandoned even by family, and forced/frightened into relinquishing their firstborn children.

There was one sentence in the poem that was so poignant to us, for it was a cry, a lamentation, like our cries. Our lamentations were like those of Rachel on the hills of Ramah, who after a slaughter of the innocents, "would not be comforted."

Here is the poet's line: *"You remember the children you got that you did not get . . . "*

That was us. We deeply remembered our children, even though older people, including many religious people in the hierarchy of that time, had insisted we would "forget."

This was a bold-faced lie. We did not forget. Not even a little. We remembered with fullest sacred heart of love. We would never forget the children "we got," we carried, we loved, we sang to, we spoke to, we petted through our bellies, we named, we cherished, we ate for, we protected, we understood as new and real Life, we fearfully but gladly suffered to bring into the world alive, most often unpartnered in any way, giving birth on a "charity ward." We young first-time mothers gave birth most often lonely and alone. But we did not get to keep our own children, our precious, precious children. We did not get to keep the Loves of our lives.

Instead, because of "the time of the times," we were led into a narrow gauntlet that carried each young and very often impoverished mother to the same place: lifelong loss, lifelong laceration of the heart.

Forget our own children? Never! *"You remember the children you got that you did not get . . . "*

In Miss Brooks' poem, there are resonances to be found between being forced to surrender one's child, and also other women's experiences of tragic loss of a child—and the poem itself, which is actually a poem about her abortions.

Miss Brooks and I spoke with our heads nearly touching for the duration of that two-hour plane ride, and we agreed that it was clear to any educated heart, that loss of life is loss of life. That loss of life can occur in so many ways, including factor X, meaning no one can say afterward in the case of sudden death and miscarriage, for instance, why life did not "take" or was not able to stay with us on Earth.

Miss Brooks was so gracious and kind. Though I was young in my early twenties at the time, and she was the age I am now, in her seventh decade, and even though her situation was different from mine, she understood that life was Life, for real and for certain, and that loss of life, loss of cheek-to-cheek touch with precious child by whatever means, caused deep sorrow.

Long before there was an anti-abortion movement, long before certain churches began to put in their public two cents' worth by encouraging their members to stand and screech at women going into health clinics (whether they were going there for abortions or not), long before people carried placards showing an image of an aborted child, Miss Brooks the poetess, understood the aftermath of mothers who have aborted, or been forced into surrender, or who have suffered childbearing loss of a much hoped for child.

She wrote about what we understood in our bones: that this child who was severed from its source is and was Life itself, was blessed and creative and filled with love, and that so much of everything dear was shattered when that Life was turned away, or forced away, or mysteriously wrenched from its loving source, by whatever means. This we understood and have carried for life in our holiest mother-hearts.

I've had permission from Miss Brooks these many years to utilize her poem in any way to help others see and/or heal from child loss. It is the strongest, most truthful, most raw writing I know about choices made that were guaranteed to cause lifelong suffering—for often no one was there to help. No one. Not enough. Or not believed in. Often, not ever.

In her poem, written in 1945, you see all the yet unresolved issues for Miss Brooks all those many years after abortion, all her questions asked still, for at the time there was no one to help her, no one to answer her spiritual inquiries. And after, no one was there to help her mend, no one to minister to her soul to carry the bowl of her tears to Creator in such genuine sorrow.

There's a reason poets and readers of poetry often say, "Poetry saved my life," for often the blank page is the only one listening to the soul's suffering, the only small, white paper bowl offered to receive one's tears, the only one registering the story without walking away, the only one receiving all the details softly and without condemnation.

THE MOTHER[4]

BY GWENDOLYN BROOKS

Abortions will not let you forget.
You remember the children you got that you did not get,
The damp small pulps with a little or with no hair,
The singers and workers that never handled the air.
You will never neglect or beat
Them, or silence or buy with a sweet.
You will never wind up the sucking-thumb
Or scuttle off ghosts that come.
You will never leave them, controlling your luscious sigh,
Return for a snack of them, with gobbling mother-eye.

I have heard in the voices of the wind the voices
    of my dim killed children.
I have contracted. I have eased
My dim dears at the breasts they could never suck.
I have said, Sweets, if I sinned, if I seized
Your luck
And your lives from your unfinished reach,
If I stole your births and your names,
Your straight baby tears and your games,
Your stilted or lovely loves, your tumults, your marriages,
    aches, and your deaths,

217

If I poisoned the beginnings of your breaths,
Believe that even in my deliberateness I was not deliberate.
Though why should I whine,
Whine that the crime was other than mine?—
Since anyhow you are dead.
Or rather, or instead,
You were never made.
But that too, I am afraid,
Is faulty: oh, what shall I say, how is the truth to be said?
You were born, you had body, you died.
It is just that you never giggled or planned or cried.

Believe me, I loved you all.
Believe me, I knew you, though faintly, and I loved, I loved you
All.

So here, in this little corner of the world, far from the gabble and gyre of people hashing out who is right and wrong, far from any institutional conferences, corporate or bishopric, religious or otherwise, at which, regrettably, no *La que sabe,* no woman "who knows," is allowed or invited to speak, and thus teach those who can never know the intimacies of childbearing in all its measurements, both mundane and sacred: Far from secular culture where only the same old drones are given the microphone and their predictable words show aggression but no progression of thought in service of the soul . . . far from screechers and verbal assaulters from public sidewalks, and far from people who draw energy by shouting at those they consider sinful, far from those who confuse standing on spiritual principle with slapping the souls of others around . . .

As I write this chapter, I keep thinking I wish there were a way to convey all that is good medicine, all that can be repaired with such precision, and I am afraid I am only able at this time to offer raw material that I know to be *ovarios y cojones* true.

Though I have never had an abortion, in fact stood up to, escaped, and outran those who tried to force me to them in each of my two pregnancies, I most definitely see well-defined parallels in the shattering that takes place in heart and spirit when a person is driven to believe or chooses for their own reasons, that she/he cannot bring this child forward. Those who have suffered any of these need our tending.

I would just say for now that the more often we can tell the stories of all lives with insight, accuracy, inquiry and not be afraid, the more compassionate hearts amongst us will step out onto the road and speak aloud.

There's much more dialogue to come on the subject of post-abortion wounding and childbearing loss from those of us who have witnessed such in others, and yet have either not yet been invited to speak or have been shouted down when we have tried to speak about a humane and heartful path toward all mothers who have ever been pregnant through whatever circumstances.

Even if we are afraid or nervous about saying and telling what we have seen, or telling our own stories, as I can sometimes feel—for so shamed we were long ago, as well as sworn to secrecy, or else—we can instead leap into the unknown anyway. We can do this, mainly because we sense in doing so, that at least one more soul might be freed from a prison of torment, one more soul might be restored and thereby able to walk whole and wise in this world.

OUR COMPASSIONATE MOTHER

Remember? There is a line in the *Memorare* prayer to Virgo Maria that reads, *Never was it known, that anyone who fled to thy protection, implored thy help, or sought thy intercession, was left unaided.*

Those are some of the most beautiful words ever written, for Compassionate Mother is called such because she will not call names, and she will not condemn, and she will not turn away. She will not turn you away. To any who are wounded and by the side of the road untended, I urge you to seek those human beings and angels on earth who carry her attributes, for there will be your help and there will be your healing. There will be the acceptance of you, and the wholeness of soul and spirit again for you. With Compassionate Mother, there is ever profound love of Life—theirs, ours, yours.

...Fierce prayer I sent out with my cry, Mother of God!!
and I threw my rosary with all my might across the waves...
for moments the Lasso of La Virgen hung in the air...

Oh My Lady, please let the stranger
be held above water
until help can come.

CHAPTER FIFTEEN

The Lasso of Our Lady . . . For Saving a Life

The Drowning Man

THE DROWNING MAN

In childhood there are events of both horrifying and mystical proportions. These two sometimes occur at the same moment. Memory
of this kind of momentous eclipse remains with the soul, long past
childhood. These awe-filled moments are evidences that the mystical world
can somehow break through into the mundane world, as well as the other
way around, often by helping to soften or reverse a desperate situation.

Some fear that if they claim the mystical realities, others may think they
have "gone around the corner." Let those who think such things think them.
As my grandmother taught about healing spirit: those who experience
mysteries need no further proofs. And, unending proofs will not convince
anyone who has never spoken with an angel, nor had La Morena as their
Trustee, nor had a fast, true taste of heaven. Let the goodness come as it
will, make what sense of it as one can, and know that sudden blessings are
deeply usual rather than only granted to a perfected few.

◀ Ex-voto: "The Lasso of Our Lady: For Saving a Life"

THE DROWNING MAN AT ROCKY GAP

We dove there . . .
thousands of times,
we were little girls
practicing glamour-girl shots
with plastic Brownie camera,
there at the end
of the splintery jetty.

We sat out there on a ray
of sunset, thighs chilled,
bathing suits cold
as wet clay.
We watched
how sandbars drifted,
how drop-offs shifted,
how everything and everyone
drifted downshore in the water.

But one day, a man—
a stranger to the big water—
ran barefoot to the jetty's end.
I saw him wave to a tiny someone
high on the bluffs above,
a someone who did not see him
nor wave back.
Then the man dove headfirst
into the changing, changeling lake waters.

Suddenly, fierce prayer I sent out
Mother of God!! I cried,
and I threw my rosary with all my might
across the waves . . .
and for moments, the Lasso of La Virgen,
hung in the air.

Finally, the lone lifeguard,
as broad as a slab of broiled sirloin,
finally looked up,
shielded his eyes.
He leapt off his tall wooden tower,
ran splashing into the water,
not swimming, but thrashing at the water
trying to run in the water
to get to the stranger, who
floated with his head
turned upward wrongly.

Our grown-ups tried to hurry
us away so we would not see
anything—
after I had seen absolutely
everything.

Dragged onto the beach,
now on his back,
the stranger vomited.
The ambulance driver kicked
sand over it.
Broken neck,
paralyzed, people said.
I was the last soul on earth
to see this man run
on both legs
for the rest of his life.

Does the stranger still think
of that day fifty-five years ago?
I have not forgotten his beauty,
nor the prayer, *Oh my Lady,*
please let the stranger
be held above water
until help can come!

Someone had to make
the lifeguard look up

and out across the waters,
Someone had to make him
stop looking down,
from his tower,
laughing and laughing
so loud with the older
bathing beauties below.

Does the stranger remember
a dark-haired child
who cried help for him
and would not stop?
Does he remember seeing
the Great Woman's
shining lasso
flying across the waters,
and does he remember
the invisible hands
holding him
above the waterline
until help could come. . .?

CHAPTER SIXTEEN

Holding Fast To The Soul

God Has No Hands: Comforting María, The Ritual of *Pésame*

Why do we have hands? There is a saying from Teresa de Ávila that God has no hands. Thus, the old people say too, we were given hands to bring, protect, comfort, heal, and encourage all Creation. In the ancient rituals to the Holy Mother, there is also a time of literal laying on of our hands upon her body, in order to comfort, protect, encourage, heal, and help to bring sorrowful Mother back to life again.

The ritual is not just for Our Lady. It is to teach us also to lay hands on each other, because we may someday be brought down and imprisoned in a long grief, too. Isn't it true for most everyone that there comes a time in life when it seems anti-creation is taking place?

The door to hell swings open, a huge wind blows us backward like the backdraft from a huge explosion, a tall iron jail door clangs shut behind us. We are locked into a sudden brutal descent.

The ladder leading downward does not hold our weight. The rungs fly apart. We cry out. No one of this world hears. No one comes. And we fall headfirst, catching the most tender of spirit and soul of this world on the most lacerating crags.

This harsh descent challenges every sweetness in us. It can cause us to mutter that only becoming hardened and growing bitter will get us through. We find ourselves not only in a fight to return to true life, but a battle to keep our souls rooted in our greatest gifts, in the nearness to the Source without source, the creative force, and innocence.

─────────────────────

◄ Ex-voto: "God Has No Hands But Ours:
Las manos de la gente quien la ama, Hands of the People Who Love Her"

We struggle to resist surrendering our tender natures. We fight against becoming a half-dead unfeeling, ungiving, unforgiving frozen corpse who turns away love and all its potentials, who leads instead with the heart of fear, or the eye of anger, or the unfeeling hand of control, or all of these.

So, we are not "pulled"; rather, we are dragged through a long, intense, lonely darkness. "Pulled" is too polite a word. We are dragged into spaces too small to rest spread full-out, forced to walk with blistered feet spans too wide to cover in a mere day, and often we are given no clear map for the way out.

We stumble dumbly forward, taking the blows, finally not even trying to defend ourselves. We stagger, fall, lie still and near-dead of heart and mind, so hurt with spirit bleeding.

THAT SOMEONE, ANYONE, OF SOUL BE WITH US

Yet, in this time, somehow, someone of flesh or a force of spirit reaches out and lays a hand on us lightly, to let us know that someone, or Someone, is with us. Perhaps this person, this creature, this angelic force stays with us, not allowing us to be alone in a time of such pain.

But perhaps it is just one momentary touch, and then that person, that force, that creature of Nature, leaves us, and we are alone again. Yet in that single touch of beauty they've granted us we find intense nourishment. We ration that out minutely over and over, remembering the brief touch that so comforted us in our dying times, our helpless moments. And we go forward, despite sensing we are in some way mortally wounded.

And in the days and months ahead, that small but memorable moment, of being touched by love and with love, provisions us to keep going.

Whomsoever comes to us in our *agonistas*, spirit or human creature, is blessed . . . and we are irradiated with their goodness. Just enough to somehow take strength, to continue finding our ways forward and eventually out, upward, and back into an above-ground life again. Scarred, yes, but often even more alive to soul and spirit, to creative genius, than before . . . ever wise in and from our scars.

DARK NIGHT OF THE SOUL

Some call such hard descent "the dark night of the soul," after San Juan de la Cruz, who wrote this phrase in his prison journal. He had been forced to submit to an unjust imprisonment by the very religious order he worked for and with.

Many of his fellow priests were jealous and were ego-glued into their thrones and lavish lifestyles. They wanted to silence San Juan's humble and fiercely holy ideas, which urged a return to the life of the soul, rather than the empty repetition of the word "soul" over and over whilst heavily pursuing only the appointments and privileges of kings.

And fighting to put soul, not ego appetites, at the center of one's life may be the *anlagen*, the exact living center of the dark night: That one decides for the soul, no matter what. That no matter what torment, what doubt, what "not knowing," we too, in our dark nights, find our ways to hold on to the most radical essentials, often modeled by One Greater. Essentials such as . . .

- Abiding love that even though sometimes faint and failing, rises again and again.
- Inquiry into depth of meaning with real guts instead of by rote.
- Instruction on how to grow the soul, that is, the curiosity and willingness from the often least "institutionally qualified" sources, which are often the most soul-qualified sources.
- Unfurling creative fire in joy, not fear, and in original instead of copyist ways. The soul is ever the original thinker, actor, lover, peacemaker, inquirer.

It's often our time spent wandering in hell, in the aftermath of sudden assault, the having walked the *via neglectus,* the way of neglect of the soul by others or self; or the *via squaleo,* the way of being covered over by dirt through neglecting to watch and cleanse and renew; and/or the *via incultus,* the way of the empty but fertile field longing to be sown with seeds of new life—it's time spent on these rough roads that often brings us in a zigzag, wandering back to home again.

REMEMBERING TRUE HOME

Home: understanding the little and often ramshackle shed of spiritual life that holds such immortal treasure of soul and thereby vast energy for being and doing—and this little testudo, little refugio, like a turtle's shell,[1] even though it often looks far less promising, is a beautiful protective carapace for the soul, and far exceeds burying oneself in the secularly appointed castle filled only with "treasure" of ashes with no phoenix.

And too, what comes out of a true dark night, a true wandering in the "way with no way out except for going inward" and learning anew, is a state of *memoriter,* instead of the former state of *excidere.*

Memoriter is Latin for knowing something by heart. More and more, the way of the soul through any dark night is now written on us. The revitalizing moment, a holy hand or sight has been laid upon us. It is inerasable in its goodness. *Excidere* is Latin for an idea that is forgotten, not held, having no emotional, spiritual, or mental fastening to our being.

And this state of being fastened to a Force Greater often revolves around *memorizing by heart* the knowing that cannot be unseated, due to having traversed hell as an eyewitness. One realizes there is something in the instinctual spiritual nature that wants not only to be comforted when in pain, but massively wants to comfort others in need also. Thus scar becomes calling to help others.

And thus one is changed, charged with, deepened to understand, to make or remake what is found in ancient ritual—the beginning of healing in the next phase of the life/death/life cycle, the night between two days. When this occurs after dearest beliefs and dreams have been massacred, there will follow thence, in some new way, a rising of bright soul once again.

THE RITUAL OF PÉSAME:
LAS MANITAS, THE COMPASSIONATE HANDS

Amongst many Latinos and those of other ethnic groups who still keep ancient ritual alive, this gathering together to comfort those who suffer is know as Pésame; to give condolences to one who is taken apart by pain and love and grief, all combined. The people gather in vigil so as to not leave such a soul alone in travail.

This ritual of comfort is still meaningfully engaged in many out-of-the-way places, as the ritual of Good Friday, the day of the torture, crucifixion, and murder of Jesús, God of mercy and love for all. In the ritual I know from rural backwoods, the big statue of La Nuestra Señora, the Blessed Mother, is carried down from her *nicho,* her alcove or altar, and placed in *la tierra de la gente,* the "land of the human souls," the "ground of the people," which lies outside the altar rail in the nave of the temple.

There she stands or sits then. Soon, many someones will have draped a soft *rebozo* or shawl around her shoulders to keep her warm, and a *mantilla* or ten will be placed over her head and down along the planes of her face to give her privacy to grieve. She's present in her *agonistas* because her son has literally nearly been beaten to death before being nailed to two heavy wooden beams in the shape of a cross.

Her only Child, whom she suffered to give birth to alone on a cold desert night, and with whom she fled in the middle of a raw night to avoid a slaughter of innocents, this is the radiant Child who is dying now. She watches as the divine dream that was dreamed so well and so hard is slaughtered.

She sees the end of her Child's life as she knew it, an end she would never, as a mother heart, ever, ever desire for her Beloved in any way. She watches helpless, as her gentle, loving Son of God child, the miracle-bringer, the healer with touch, the uncanny, knowing Child, is dragged through hell on earth.

WE ARE ALL WELCOME TO COME STAY WITH HER

In ritual pésame, people come to the iglesiacita, the little church to be with her in her time of torment. Nuestra María, Mary, Mir-yam, Mar-yam understands this and she receives with gracious sorrow all that we have to give to her . . . our literal condolences in words and remedios . . . and not only our comforts, but also our own personal sorrows, which in so many ways mirror hers.

Thus, as we come to stand guard over her wounds, to shelter her lacerated heart, we can also sense our own wound rising too. In this way, we are brought body, soul, mind, spirit, and emotive being to the underlying meaning of loss—which is reduction of us to soul only—and then, eventual rebirth.

In *pésame*, we do not witness the Passion with intellect or even only eyes, ears, and heart. We share in it all the way down to our grief sinew, and all the way down into our courage bones.

So, one by one in *pésame*, mothers come forward, their chests crisscrossed with the straps of giant diaper bags; fathers leading two little children with each of his hands, like a brace of beautiful little ponies trotting to keep up with their father; teenagers carefully stylized into the latest clothing that speaks street talk or else poverty; young adults in first grown-up suits; *los viejos*, the old ones, all shuffle into church with rosaries enough to outfit an army.

And the welders come in their suede work jackets with tiny holes burnt through from flying embers, and the *mecánicos* come smelling like gasoline, and the shy ones come, the waitresses still in aprons, and the liquored-up ones, and the veterans in green government-issued clothes, and the just everyday everybodies . . . they all come to squeeze into the old wooden pews. Everyone wants for a change to sit up front where La Señora sits in such sorrow, the closer to her the better. And they will not leave her.

Some from the south bring *floripondio* flowers and tape them behind her head to bring rest. Some bring fresh-scraped bark to lay over her hands and feet, as though she is wounded there too, like her Son.

Some bring her water in a tin cup with Jerusalem thorn added to clarify the blood. Some bring sweet well-water in an old washed-out tomato jar. Some bring the food cooked by the grandmothers since time immemorial: *con chocolate y cilantro y los anchos,* hot peppers.

But Our Lady will not eat or drink, for she has lost all appetite; we all know this. Yet it is the offering, the tender preparation of that green chili, that *posole,* that *té,* that matters as the source of caring shown in ways that can be truly seen.

THE VIGIL KEEPERS

So too, the hands of the vigil keepers: their hands are considered to act as the hands of God . . . for the God Who Has No Hands.

After a time of praying, rosaries swinging over the rails of the pews like Spanish moss in a light wind, gradually then, each person will walk, slouch, hold on to balustrades and pew backs to get there slowly, lurch, genuflect, crawl on hands and knees, so as to come to María, to the gigantic, living, loving force of Holy Mother who stands behind any beautiful painting, mural, sculpture which acts as aperture to her.

The vigil keepers with and for Our Lady may perhaps wipe her feet with their tears. They will for certain touch her, tell her in their own words how they understand her grieving, for they too have their own grief for her, and about the killing of the Radiant Child come, amongst many other reasons, to lift the world away from those who scorn the many souls via exclusion and power madness that prefers coldness of heart over Heart as Limitless Love. This compassion flows from having suffered so, and it is as much offered for our own suffering souls as for the unknown souls who suffer in the wider world. For our belief is, we are all one. As we pass one another, if you are happy, I am happy. If you are sad, I am sad.

But most of all, each person will put their hands on La Señora's body. There will be hands, many hands, all at the same time. On her brow, on her cheeks, on the crown of her head, cradling her face like a baby's, on her shoulder, on her back, on her hips, over her heart, on her knees, on her belly, on her legs, and on her feet. Hands pouring healing *rayos* of the animating force into her, but also into all the people, known and unknown, gathered there in vigil and the world over.

People will ask her please to await patiently the resurrection of her Beloved Child, and thereby the world's sunrise into new awareness, freshly born again—and they will ask so humbly to please also receive a resurrection of health or heart or mind or soul or spirit for themselves and for any of their ill or troubled or lost loved ones, too.

Many a time a man or a woman will whisper to the Great Woman, and we will not quite hear what is said. Often a teenager or a child, an old woman or old man, will break down sobbing while speaking to La Señora in a broken voice, or a barren wasteland kind of howl.

And the rest of us, well, you can feel it course through you like one giant collective sob pushing back the walls of the church—as all of us are so deeply touched to be in "the hell place, that is, the place of desolation, the Golgotha with others' sorrows," to somehow let no one of us be alone. Rather we remain with one another—in mysterious ways there.

Not one hundred hearts, but rather one heart. Not one hundred minds, rather one mind. Not two hundred eyes, but rather one strong lens seeing the inner and outer worlds merged. Not one hundred souls in vigil for each other, but a seamless garment woven of souls in vigil for all.

The way it is supposed to be: the way it is in the terrain of all that is holy in the manner of Limitless Love.

OUR LADY, LITERALLY DEFACED

Some time ago at Georgetown University, a person under cover of night came to the white marble statue of Our Lady of Fatima that stands on the lawn at Copley Square. According to police reports, this stealthy person painted Our Lady's face and a bow-like ribbon running down the front of her white gown ... dark charcoal black.

There was a terrible outcry about whomsoever did this defacement of the statue of Our Lady. Press releases flew. Bishops spoke out. Police converged. Websites billowed.

But far more notably, there was an immediate reaction in the minds of many of the young: more than wanting any tracking down of presumed predators, more than chasing the legal aspects, they wanted to go be with Our Lady, to hold a twenty-four-hour vigil with her.

Some said they wanted to protect the statue from further vandalism, but we old believers would say the drive to "be with" Our Lady was for another reason altogether—that is, "to be with Maria," to not leave her alone, to not let her suffer by herself, instead to remain near. It is an ancient instinct to not let a loved one suffer alone.

And so a vigil was touchingly undertaken by many students and faculty. And in the next few days, someone would try to wash away the dark paint on the statue's face, and in that first effort, this only made her face look smudged light grey.

And yet ... when I looked closely at the photos of her face painted black, I saw how that whomever had painted her, had done so carefully. It was not a flash spray-can job, as is often done by desecrators, for the sake of sacrilege. Instead, the person stayed within the curves of her mantle, almost as though perhaps someone wanted a Maria who either looked like them, or a Maria who was not portrayed as so frozen, but one who had more than one visage.

I am shocked by vandalism to images that are sacred to anyone. But I wondered. And then, when I saw the "before" pictures, I noticed that this statue of Our Lady already looked worn and injured on one side of her face in the cheek and mouth area. I wondered if that hadn't come from years of being set out in winter ice, sideways sleet, and hot sun? She seemed already, in many ways, becoming less statue, and more earthy.

I kept thinking, this is like us, too. The statue of Our Lady in the midst of restoration looks like us. This is how we are. We begin as a pure something, and then go through a dark night, and afterward we are not restored to our original look or ways. We appear instead, to show right on our faces, that we have been through a great something, through a no-small thing. We are smudged; we are scarred. Our faces are deepened.

And like the rough-faced girl in the old folktale about a girl who was burnt and yet had the most radiant soul, I think the old believers would say that, though for whatever reason, this statue of Our Lady was altered, nothing, absolutely nothing, could alter her courage, her endurance, her continuance, even were this an attack—that she was, is, and will ever remain radiant . . . that the outside looks hardly ever match one's inside incandescence.

THE *IMITATIO MARIA:* AS WE LEARN TO BE LIKE HER

About all these matters of vigil keeping with the wounded María, about Pésame, I suppose some passers-by might say, "These silly people are playing pretend with a statue."

But it is not the statue, it is the *memoriter:* the remembering one knows by heart, that those devout souls who touch her cheek, place compassionate hands on her body, pray to and for her, feel the ancient and timeless Mary, Maria, Mir-yam, from far away in time but coming directly up beside them now; her flesh warm, her tears wet, her love deep. It is this. It is not the statue, that is only the tuning fork for recognition of and reverent resonance with the living saint.

Any who hold Mary to their hearts will tell you she comforts them as they comfort her. And some of us will say that in return, she prays her ancient blessings and mendings over the parts of our lives that are torn, too.

May all of us then, with infinite tenderness, comfort each other in this special lacuna of time of Pésame, and escape for a while or forever the hubris of either withholding comfort from others or else suffering in silence, refusing to be comforted.

This learning through Pésame, through tending to the Great Woman, by my sights into the worlds "here and not there," is what I would call an *Imitatio Maria,* a following of Our Lady's ways, insofar as we who are only human can become a Mary on this earth.

By attempting to be a little satellite-Maria, these are some of her traits that we can manifest each in his or her own way: we can give birth to the Holy Child of Love and healing of soul and world every day, protecting, guiding, helping, learning, even if and when we suffer unspeakable loss of the precious light for a time. If and when we are grieving, bewildered, wandering, following her pathway, we know we will finally find the Holy One again, one way or another. Again, we learn to see the fully human-fully God child, only this time in an entirely new way—not in a corporeal way, but through direct touch, soul to Soul, heart to Heart.

Thus, by staying with Our Lady, in imitation of Maria, through her joyous, sorrowful and glorious way of seeing and being, we walk the zig-zag path striving for holy responses at center. Holding hands with her, we travel through dark toward Light, that is consciously lived life with Soul at radiant center—even if we forget, even if we are bowed, we strive to return to the incandescent Heart. As we stay in reciprocal compassionate and loyal relationship with the Holy Woman, we become to the earth, to creatures, to her, to one another, the most insightful and humane hands possible for the God Who Has No Hands, but for ours. Our protective, creative, blessing hands.

REMEMBERING OUR BILLIONS

You are not "removed"
because you
cannot reach *all*

suffering humanity
all the time.

Hold all souls as whole
in your heart,
not just their horrors
and losses.
This is the stronger prayer:
Wholeness despite
holes through and through.

Hold all the injured as whole,
and on the torn red
beribboned slingshot
of your heart . . .
aim, draw back hard, harder,
and release all your holiest
and most healing thoughts
to fly across all divides,
to fly across all big waters,
to vault across all insanities . . .
Bid the holy to fly—
and to land at this moment
in exactly the places
most needed.

Souls sense
being fiercely
prayed for,
on, over,
with, daily.
Add to that torrent.

Knowing that someone
who knows you not,
is nonetheless praying lariats,
risers, invisibility, perception,
being heard, along with
pouring will and strength
into you, for you,

into and for those you pray for:
This is inestimable medicine
for the soul.

Continue then,
like the farmer farms
his little land
outside his door . . .
washing the seeds,
turning the soil,
planting right depth,
watching over,
weeding out,
counting the tiny
progressions.

So too,
tend to the poor in spirit,
the poor in soul,
the poor in health,
the poor in want,
right before you:
the ailing kin,
the street man
the road mother,
the broken friend,
the innocent child,
the torn,
the wondering,
the wandering.

I tell you,
those who would care
across the oceans only,
and not care for those
they can wash
who are standing
right before them,
are not fully caring yet.
I know you understand this:

That we desperately
want all humanity to not hurt . . .
and that this is one of the worthiest
prayers we know.

Thus, we bend to tend,
in whatever ways we are called,
to those within our reach—
wherever that reach reaches . . .
for there are times
when Creator has no hands,
only ours . . .

Thus, in this tending,
we keep the greatest
blood compact with Creator,
with Our Holy Mother,
our souls
have ever signed . . .

So may it be for thee
So may it be for me
And so may it be for us all

Aymen
Aymen
Aymen

And with oceanic love . . .

Our Lady of Fatima statue at Georgetown University
before her face was painted black

Blessed Mother Africa

CHAPTER SEVENTEEN

The Great Mother Inspires the Little Mothers

The Marys of Mother Africa

THE MARYS OF MOTHER AFRICA

Like the Great Mother, Mother Africa for hundreds of years has groaned under many humans who have harmed her by looting her treasures, setting enmity between peoples, and by forcing stones atop the people's greatest minds and hearts so the people could not grow into their full magnitude.

But, also I sense from knowing many souls who were born into the earth there, that in Mother Africa, there is rooted a mysterious Heart of the World, a Heart of Humanity that ever beats strong no matter what, and that is oddly ever vulnerable . . . yet ever invincible . . . ever wounded . . . yet ever covered with flowers of acacia, the honey of which flows like deep amber sweetwater.

Though the crown that Mother Africa has been forced to wear is made of piercing thorn branches, because of her immaculate generosity of heart those barbed branches are ever bursting with fragrant blossoms.

And always present anywhere there is so much death and so much resurrection, there are the Marys.

◄ Ex-voto: "Holy Mother Africa"

THE MARYS

"The Marys" are what we old believers call souls, both men and women, who have been sorely wounded, yet carry such depth of sight and generosity rather than bitterness of heart, that they make you want to weep just to be near them again—or for the very first time.

As in other parts of the world, in Africa there are millions of Marys hidden in refuges and out-of-the-way places. Contrary to the brutal African dictators, Robert Mugabe, Idi Amin, and others who have purposely driven their nations into poverty and slaughter, the Marys are the rememberers and restorers of "what the soul is truly fashioned from." Africa is filled with the Great Mother of Humanity, even when wounded, even though not yet completely healed.

Like many of the icons of Holy Mother throughout Africa, what we sometimes call the "Black Madonnas," these living Marias of many skin colors are often some combination of the finest delicate pink-ivory, and the blackest most enduring ebony—the strengths of the soul fashioned into living beauty in the African people. This endures even when that beauty of red heart and deep soul draws predatory interests from those who once again want to enslave and exploit Mother Africa.

The Marys everywhere in the world are the ones who endured despite, and in a way because of, all attacks, all indecencies, against them. The Marys are the ones who were made to carry the World Heart in a basket woven strong from one's own courage bones, from spiritual brawn, from scar tissue, from the coiled hairs of one's own head. Beautiful.

Creator knew the pulse of the world would be safe with those who had suffered and yet persevered. Creator knew they would pass forward "that which cannot be allowed to perish from the face of the earth," hand to hand, heart to heart, generation to generation—hiding the Great Heart next to their own hearts during night treks from village to village, no matter what crosswinds.

And most especially, the Marys would pass the Heart of the World soul to soul through stories that tell not just what is treasure, but that tell exactly how to hold to the strong center of the Mother no matter what.

TINY MAGICAL TREASURE BOXES FOR AFRICAN VILLAGES: A NEW MAGICAL STORYTELLER APPEARS

It has been a long while since I met with a particular group of Africans. I was enthused to help with their work. "Wait! Listen to this sister," they'd say to me. They were trying to start their own radio broadcasting stations in their home villages in various African nations. They were creating a winged miracle of sorts, for they wanted to make words fly through the air.

I'd published a dozen audio books, many of them broadcast over National Public Radio and community radio stations in the United States and Canada. I was recording radio commentaries on a weekly basis and it was that last, deep involvement in community radio broadcasting that brought me into direct touch with the Marys of Ghana, Angola, South Africa, and other African nations, where I met some of the most kind, most gentle people I've ever touched lives with. And all these Marys wanted to be radio mavens and mages.

I gave them encouragement and was able to help them raise a little money to birth their endeavor. I kept saying to myself: just think of it, as in the days of eld: stories flying through the air invisibly but now landing in full timbre and tone far away in little villages. How amazingly low-tech, and yet blazingly modern.

Just think of such a miraculous way to teach, tell, remember others back into themselves again—for unknown and anonymous Marys to be teaching village people who couldn't read but who could speak. And oh what beauty of warm poetry they spoke just in everyday talk—to be able to broadcast by themselves, wholly independent, without the censorship and silencing of their voices by whichever regime.

Thus my African friends went back home and set up Rube Goldberg-esque studios in their cooking rooms, and begin broadcasting through the air to villages far off—villages that had nothing but hot sun, dry dust storms, a few clay pots, and the true riches of the land, human beings with deep souls.

It was arranged that a number of villages would be given a precious little treasure chest that was to be kept safe by the headwoman of each village, for this little box was the most rare of magical objects and one that would be magical to us, too. It was a little plastic radio with a crank, in reality, a tiny radio receiver that was powered by . . . the sun!

Solar cells. Leave the little radio in full sunlight for several hours. Let it "harvest the sun." Then, when a pre-arranged afternoon arrived, twenty, forty, one hundred villagers stood and squatted in a circle to listen to one more magical storyteller coming into their midst through the little radio.

Solar cells at that time would allow a radio to receive broadcast for perhaps up to twenty minutes at a time. Thus the radio gave out stories and spoke to the people in their own down-to-the-bones manner.

As it was in the beginning, it was now again—except for one thing: the old stories were still told by the old ones in the village sans radio. But now there were new stories too, magical new stories from the radio-teller that seriously and concretely educated the villagers about how to chase away the Demons of Death. Seriously.

CHASING AWAY THE DEMONS OF DEATH

The never-before-heard stories on village radio were little skits with heroes and monsters. We'd written storylines around overcoming monsters that soiled the water, and a hero/heroine who then cleansed the water, showing how to keep it clear by keeping refuse and bodily functions away from the water, never letting these meet where fresh water flowed.

The stories' underlying motifs were about teaching the way to prevent typhoid, which killed those who drank tainted water, and ways to prevent the monster Dysentery, who killed so many babies and elderly through dehydration. In the dysentery saga, the hero taught how to keep the village from being touched by the monster to begin with: a kind of folkloric science based on reality.

The stories' heroes and heroines taught how to properly wash a leg wounded by a machete while chopping brush, and thereby how to chase away the monster called Infection and Tetanus.

The Africans are story people who have not forgotten their ancient tales. They have also not written them all down so they are fixed like dead butterflies in a box. Rather, they hold stories as the blood flows to and from the Heart of the World, to and from the Mother Drum, the heartbeat of the World. Stories are an essential, rather than a mere entertainment.

Whereas we might hear the solar-radio stories about monsters and heroes and health, and learn their values, thereby thinking we'd not need to hear them again because now we knew the precautions, many village people in Africa had a different idea about it all.

The people of the villages began to tell the radio stories themselves—to each other and to visitors and distant relatives who lived outside the villages. The mask maker made masks portraying Dysentery, for example, a mask that was made of withered, gray leaves.

Thus, the new stories made their ways into the tribal mind, into the hearts of mothers, fathers, babies, dancers, artists, musicians, and became part of the village life of story hand-me-downs. Thus it was just as important to tell the tale of how Typhoid was vanquished in the village, as how the first dawn of creation took place and First Man and First Woman were born.

One set of stories from time out of mind were thereby melded with stories that were of this time. And their commonalities were that simple words, whether broadcast or spoken in person, were telling the how-tos: how such and such is made, how something else is avoided, how this is turned this way in error, how this is corrected, how to protect, and most especially, how to save the lives of the soul and the body.

The stories taught the how-tos, step-by-step, so everyone had a chance at a full and far more educated and conscious life, but without breaking any of the tribes' spirit bones.

THE POPE ON AFRICA'S WOMEN, AND THE NECESSITY OF STEP-BY-STEP WISE INSTRUCTION RATHER THAN JUST EXHORTATION

On his trip to parts of Africa, Pope Benedict XVI did say that Africa ought treat its women more decently. And that was good. Unprecedented, really. To recognize all the Marys of Africa as precious, worthy of protection and care.

But there is a rub: we had hoped the how-tos would be addressed. Perhaps the next trip, the Pope will assess, more clearly and say: Be respectful of women. And also say how and in what exact ways? How would this look were one to do this? Where have we already gone wrong, specifically? What are the exact steps to helping, healing, mending, correcting the unaware heart?

My Ghanaian friends knew what the issues were for many women throughout much of Africa—how hard a woman's life is—but the prevalent and unquestioned mind for abusing women, especially by some men, was also enjoined by some older women and others, who had their own son's "best interests" in mind by blindly demeaning and often physically beating the son's wife themselves.

During the Pope's visit to Africa, many of us were hoping he would become a Mary himself, broadcasting to the huge crowds about how to reverse all this turning away from the humane soul—how to, step by step, reverse a backward de-evolution that was implanted long ago in the psyche of Africa—not only by crass colonization, but also by ancient and modern African warlords who had no good in their minds with regard to souls in general for men, and for women and children in particular.

In the psyche there can be, under pressure to survive, a strong tendency toward identification with the oppressor. This is often seen in those who have been colonized, their nation over-run, occupied, and/or conquered.

If what one learned while surviving an oppression is not carefully examined afterward and measured against a strong spiritual norm of what it means to be humane—as held for instance by The Mother of All Life—the once severely harmed sometimes mimic their own oppressors, enacting harms on those persons within reach who are not in any way oppressors themselves—or are sincerely no longer oppressors themselves.

Eventually, as deleterious and inhumane attitudes are handed down generation after generation in a culture, those taking demeaning attitudes toward others—often have learned to also easily disrespect women and others, with such self-appointed impunity that they no longer even register their own cruelties and exclusions. Thus, worthy souls continue to be exiled and harmed because they have, for generations now, normalized brutality toward themselves—seeing oppressors as a certain class of "others" who are somehow annointed to threaten and harm others. And often it takes long for the oppressed to even think/remember they have an inalienable right as souls to be treated decently.

When I'd asked my African rookie broadcasters which was the biggest issue faced by their people, one of the Marys, a soulful gentle man, said it was adults who acted like "children with great power who had not overcome their greediness for all the butter in the world."

We worried over this matter of "ravenous child within a man's or a woman's body"—ravenous for power, for influence, to be seen as important, to take all the people within reach by force, to make them walk in a crouch of fear, instead of unfurl and develop into full flower as human beings, as was their birthright.

As we tried to understand the non-understandable, at least with heart intact, as we turned over the attendant matters of abject inhumanity, we agreed I'd weave a story from all the hours of heartfelt testimony I'd heard from my African friends in order "to tell the story of it all." As long as it took to tell it, but also "as short as need be," in order to be heard in full on solar radio with its tiny span of "receiving time." This is that story.

THE STORY OF GREEDY BOY

A little boy was sent to bring butter from a neighboring farm. "Bring it quickly so it does not melt," said the mother. So the little boy walked to the farm, was given fresh butter in a crockery pot, and the child set off for home.

But somewhere along the path, the boy thought the crockery pot sort of looked like a crown, and so he turned it upside down and put it atop his head.

Thus he strode through the brush emulating what he'd seen and heard of kings, tromping around, ordering the weeds to bow down to him, and trampling on small creatures. He felt so powerful.

But also, the heat from his head under the "crown" made the butter begin to melt and drip down his forehead, then nose, then right into his mouth!

And the more the boy dallied, marching about pretending to be king, the more the butter melted, and the more the butter ran into the boy's mouth—and he lapped it all up very enthusiastically—until finally, all the delicious sweet butter was gone.

And that is how a child pretending to be king became a tyrant, nearly overnight.

For the taste of something sweet that came from the hard work of others (but that he kept all to himself without offering any of it to other souls) had twisted his heart.

Even though his first intention was good, to bring the butter to his mother who in turn would share it all around, he wound up depriving all others of the sweetest tastes of life, taking it all in for himself, only—while caught in the net of wanting to rule over all.

"Before we can ever be free," said my friend, *"the moral decay of such butter-carriers has to be faced."*

I'd agree with my Ghanaian brother: confronting the endlessly greedy child if it ever suddenly tries to spring up in ourselves after a tiny taste of power over others, no matter how benign or malignant, must be questioned, measured, transformed. For to keep such an impulse "to eat up everything" only leads to a head full of snakes.

We agreed all practices must be put in place to protect the vulnerable, but also, there needed to be a return of the old ways of being impeccable in character and judgment, premises that were intact in many ways in most African tribes before they were over-run by others, and their ethics and ways of seeing and being with the Mother in all integrity were forbidden. It was far past time for some of the ancient ideals of Holy Mother's dignity toward others to be brought back, to be taught openly to the young as they had not been for eons out of fear of torture, retaliation, and exile. Now it was time to practice and remark upon in good light, all the virtues of Holy Mother: constancy, protection, patience, compassion, vast insight, healing heart, right conduct, beautiful soul, verve for life, endurance, respect, standing up for, to, and with however needed for the sake of the souls of the Just on earth.

Vaguely spoken words are rarely effective to teach how to help to mend a deep wound. The churches across Africa too, must continue to decide whether to help free Africa and lift her people away from Greedy Boy, or buy right back into some boys pretending to be kings, self-centeredly consuming all the sweet butter, thereby suppressing all the gifts of the Holy Spirit meant to be shared with and by all others.

Espíritu Santo, Holy Ghost, insists on respect toward women, instead of shouting and scowling at women as a matter of course in order to try to intimidate them.

Espíritu Santo insists that a man request clear permission to court or be intimate with a woman, rather than telling falsehoods and/or forcing himself into a woman or a child sexually.

Espíritu Santo requires that neither woman nor child, neither man nor elder before, during, or after day's end, be beaten or shunned for not acquiescing to unreasoned demands that harm body, mind, heart, spirit, or soul.

Espíritu Santo insists that a man bend to do his just share of what is for the common good at every level, rather than imposing servant-slavehood on vulnerable others under the guise of "do this for Jesus" . . . or because any male or female is bent on pretending to be a king tromping around in the bush, exploiting others to undergird the fantasy that he or she is the one and only crowned butter-eater of all time.

All these issues and more are to be brought into the open and spoken about, not once, but rather many times, as many times as needed to lift all souls back into place. Moving from being unconscious of harms that one does to others and moving instead into conscious ways of acting that do not harm others, is indeed heavy lifting that one can hire no slave to do for oneself.

Each soul has to pry their unconsciousness out of the primal ooze and develop consciousness—to allow The Mother of the Heart of the World to take their hands, heart, and head in order to lead them to enact these new life attitudes and practices for themselves out of mercy for others.

That would indeed be a move from being a monster-in-the-making, to being a hero on the mend.

WISH LIST FOR THE POPE, ANY SPIRITUAL LEADER

Pope Benedict, despite the fact that there are more thorough instructions to be given about safeguarding the souls and lives of women and children and the vulnerable in Africa, still and yet, he seemed to display a consciousness in himself and about others that might be understood to be his assertion that Africa still has too many greedy boys who want a pretend kingship.

I wished he'd said something about how abusive actions derive from disrespectful underlying and unspoken attitudes—that these have to be questioned, and the deleterious ones changed to ones that would make Creation and Holy Mother smile. I wished he'd told how women could better protect themselves theologically from some men who wear the gown and the pomp, but act disgracefully toward men, women, and children.

I wish the Pope had listed the common offenses: Forcing sex on others. Beating women up repeatedly, pushing them, slapping them in the face, whaling on them with their fists and with sticks, breaking their bones and cutting them. Calling them whores. Enslaving them, disallowing education for them, pressing them into menial service in order that some men live like kings. Forcing the women and children to service the men's addictions. Throwing bellowing temper tantrums that insist the man is supreme when he hasn't earned the status he falsely claims. Treating the women and children as property to be used, sold, traded, and degraded, just as they were in times past, without cease.

Kindly words help, but Our Mother wears a Heart of Seven Swords. In respect, Pope, sometimes it is time to draw a sword from one's heart, slicing open ill matters for all to see. Let us insist: *Do unto others only as Holy Mother would do unto you. Courage of a lion, touch of a lamb.*

Yet I can see also, that what the Pope left out of his speeches is and will continue to be the huge and holy work of the Marys of Africa: what was left unsaid, and what even more so, the Pope did not perhaps know how to define point by point and clearly: the how-tos, the step-by-step, the vanquishing of the monster by the heroic soul. I can see, and I think you as old believers can see too, that the step-by-step will be carried by the Marys, the Marys of the Heart of the World.

BLESSING-PRAYER FOR THE MARYS OF THE WORLD . . .

In one of the most powerful Hadiths (prophetic sayings), Muhammad was to have said, "Paradise is at the feet of the Mother." Thus, that you find your ways through, as you see best, led by Holy Mother, universally understood as oceanic, as river water, as water welling up from a spring, as clean, clear ground water, as sudden rain. From Bible: "the mere scent of water" can bring the withered plant alive. Thus, this I wrote to bless your way . . .

RAINMAKER: YOU COULD BE THE WATER . . .

By the scent of water alone,
the withered vine comes back to life,
and thus . . . wherever the land is dry and hard,
you could be the water;
or you could be the iron blade
disking the earth open;
or you could be the *acequia,*
the mother ditch, carrying the water
from the river to the fields
to grow the flowers for the farmers;
or you could be the honest engineer
mapping the dams that must be taken down,
and those dams which could remain to serve
the venerable all, instead of only the very few.
You could be the battered vessel
for carrying the water by hand;
or you could be the one
who stores the water.
You could be the one who
protects the water,
or the one who blesses it,
or the one who pours it.
Or you could be the tired ground
that receives it;
or you could be the scorched seed
that drinks it;
or you could be the vine,
green-growing overland,
in all your wild audacity . . .

El Cristo de La Llave, Mary's Miracle Child

CHAPTER EIGHTEEN

Refusing the Holy: No Room for You Here

The "Oh Yes, There Is Too Room for You Here" Ritual of *La Posada*

LA LLAVE, THE KEY[1]

With the Key of Love
Whatever is locked, will be opened;
Whatever ought be held closed, will be locked safely inward.
The Key Itself knows what is needed . . . when . . . and why.

EL CRISTO: EXILE OF THE HOLY

Who has not been locked out, sent away, or heard someone in charge say, "There's no room for you here"? We creep or crawl or walk away hopefully in dignity, keep going, trying again and again, taking the next chance, and the next, until we discover a way that meets the need—often a surprising way comes to us, and it is a blessed one.

◀ Ex-voto: "El Cristo de La Llave: Mary's Miracle Child"

Some would try to quash this determination of the soul who keeps going, keeps going, no matter who said what, no matter who did what, no matter what twist of fate befell us, no matter what doors are closed to us.

Thus, it is not unusual in our modern cultures to see miles of crass overwriting atop the beautiful natural impulses of the soul. Then, all holy impulse is pushed, down into last place—ridiculed, turned away, ignored, scorned, covered over, made into petrified wood rather than living cambium.

But all these derogations, including rote holy-izing that is not sincere, all such efforts to caricature or expunge the holy, are like vain efforts to try to banish the blue out of the sky.

This is how *La Posada* acts as a candle in the dark. *La Posada* is a ritual that asserts, despite all blather and disheartening from self or others, "I will find a way through; there will be a place, a person, a shelter. I will keep going."

We believe that no matter who tries to exile the genuinely holy, it will never work for long, for it is seeded innately in the psyche, in the spirit, soul, and body. The holy is not something placed into us. It is a radiant light that blossoms from us.

THE GREAT SOUL HIDES

The Great Soul hides as a stranger
yet in every crowd . . .
and often it's the littlest Child who
recognizes the Stranger immediately . . .
The Child suddenly smiles and smiles,
waving arms in sleeves too long,
wiggling pink-tipped naked toes,
reaching, reaching, reaching out,
tiny hands opening and closing,
opening and closing . . .
wanting to touch,
wanting to bring closer,
wanting to taste the Holy One.
What is that longing
the Child carries

that can detect the Presence,
the direction, the closeness
of Pure Love?[2]

THE STORY BEHIND *LA POSADA*

Rituals exist to try to blast away the cultural cement laid down incrementally or inexorably over our heartfelt longings for the holy. Rites are meant to create protective barriers against society's harms which are often meant to half-hearten or dishearten the people toward the holy. *La Posada* is a ritual for transforming the overculture's cold shoulder toward the sacred . . . back into warm, open-armed welcome again—like a child's enthusiastic waving and open-armed embrace.

Sacred *Posada* ritual is based on an ancient story about the night the Holy Family tried to find shelter at a wayside inn during a mass migration of tribal groups. The dusty-haired travelers swirling across the desert lands were trying to meet the demands of the Emperor Augustus. He had ordered that all persons return to their birth villages to be registered in a census so they could be taxed.

The rapacious Emperor's decree imposed hardship on the poor shepherds, farmers, and family people living far from their birthplaces. They had to carry their newly born babies, and the pallets of their sick and dying with them, had to dig up enough food, had to find enough linen to keep everyone from freezing in the cold desert nights.

All travelers dearly hoped—no matter how slowly they had to walk to keep together all their children, livestock, their lame, their elderly—that when exhausted, they could find shelter of even the most rude sort to rest in.

The *natividad* story of La María, the Great Woman, goes like this: She who was pregnant with the brilliant little Light of the World, desperately needed a resting place. She was in her ninth month of pregnancy, and she had bumped for miles over rough terrain. As any woman knows who has carried a child, walking can bring on labor even more ferociously, necessitating even more need for shelter—at the least a tree, a steadying post of some kind, in order to give birth.

But, there was no room at any hostel where hugely-laden María and her spouse, Santo José, begged for shelter.

Then as now, now as then: Some speculate there were no rooms because of the huge migration of tribal peoples at the same time. Some say the innkeeps turned the poor away because they were holding out for

255

rich travelers who would pay inflated prices. Some say the innkeepers turned away those belonging to racial and economic classes, tribes, and gender they destested.

Regardless, the doors were locked against Maria, her carpenter spouse, and the radiant Child in her belly.

Yet, as ancient and modern Posada ritual demonstrates again and again, it doesn't take money, it doesn't take education, it doesn't take being from "the right tribe," it doesn't take prescience nor foretelling for an inkeep to open the door to the Holy Traveler.

All it takes is to have mercy on those laden with Perfect Love, and to remember one's own longing to be united with Love: thence the key turns in the lock automatically. The door of the heart flies open. The Holy Travelers enter.

IMITATIO MARIA: THE PRACTICE OF GIVING BIRTH TO THE CHILD OF LIGHT EVERY DAY

La Posada literally means making one's own heart into the inn or "place of shelter" for The Light of the World, for the God of Love, to be born.

There are practices for each soul to become a shelter for the Divine Child and his Mother and mortal father, for ways of seeing with the soul rather than the ego, that will better cleanse our own fed-up minds and half-poisoned bodies, our fatigued souls and disheartened spirits, bringing them into vibrant, receptive, welcoming, sheltering refugios, again.

There'll be no following tired routines. Rather, we'll make again special places in our real lives for Love to literally be born into the world—through La María, La Lumina, The Carrier of the Light, Blessed Mother—with us, for us, through us, time and again.

Not just once a year. Rather, a daily practice of remembering to grant first place to Love without barriers.

If there is a prayer that commemorates the true love of true Love, I'd offer this: "Creator, impregnate me every day present, and every day future-tense; impregnate me with the Child of Love."

In a man or woman who prays such or similar, I think there begins a gentle fissioning of the spirit cells—a dividing, adding to, rocking, developing, just as in a human pregnancy. A flutter occurs that feels like a butterfly's beating wings clinging to the vermilion of a truly stalwart heart—this growing a kind body and gentle mind of Love that will become, and then must be born daily. With us, for us, through us.

During Posada, fear that loving the Holy is somehow dangerous or deluded is wiped away as society's foolish lies. Fear that loving must be hoarded like string; or that love might make one sick if one be found too lovable or too loving: All this plaque is chipped away from the chambers of the heart.

In becoming a Posada, a little inn at the wayside, a refuge in the wilderness of our own cultures, Love is only dangerous the way warmth is dangerous to things that have grown too frozen in scowls, or in you-can't-hurt-me smiles.

So we specifically try to wrestle our love-fears out to the dustbin, and instead increase our actions in the world that are of a *hospitable* nature, meaning we make welcoming gestures for and to Love. We strive to find and live in ways that are favorable to Love. We respond—even to difficult situations and people—with first thought, or at least last thought, of being Love—which is the opposite of being parsimonious.

Posada: To reject the overculture that harps about how it is unrealistic to teach unfettered Love, when in fact to reach for Love is the weapon against, and remedy for, so much that is so tedious, too hard, too soft, too short, too long, too vague, nearly too anything because it's been gutted of simple dignity.

Rejecting the overculture's demand that we all be cross and impatient, often means to stop, just stop, and examine where in life we bristle and defend, acting as though we are going to be left duped or impoverished if we dare to give away what we carry in endless abundance innately: Fully lit Love.

The idea underlying Posada is to re-enter the rapture of and with Love again—to unlock our ways of love based on examples set by the miracle Child, the Mother and the mortal, loyal father. That is, we act as close as possible like this little family who are affectionately called "First Family," they who see through the eyes and heart of Love alone; the Ones who have few armed fortifications; the Ones who understand sacrifice and determination; those who protect others; who know the healing touch and those who teach the ignorant with patience; who know how to breathe as perfect rest. Those who keep going.

And more: we develop the *Imitatio Maria*, an Imitation of Mother Mary, acting as she acted—not nibbling at life, but living fully unfurled: as one who carries the God of Love through dark of night, through tempests, through travail, through taunting, through all the tremors and cultural attacks—during which the God of Love is ever cared for and protected by Holy Mother . . . and by us.

Acting that way exactly gives birth to the Child of Love, every day.

FURTHER PREPARATIONS TO BECOME A REFUGE FOR LOVE

Ancient understandings about the life of the soul are wrapped into Posada. Primarily? I'd put it this way: The Soul knows the way to live. The ego might . . . but not for long. First and foremost, re-learn to depend on the soul's point of view.

It's the soul that urges us to name aloud what needs refurbishing in ourselves, in our homes, in our families, our friendships, our politics, our spirituality, livelihoods, creative lives, concerns with hearts and souls across the world. It's the soul that urges us into then doing, in each of these arenas within reach, what it takes and whatever can be done now to help "to clean it up." To cleanse each area of life focuses on the idea of making room for the Divine to find shelter with us, with others, in every workroom, every meeting, on every riverbank, at every table. Here are the many time-tested ways to make generous room and refuge for the Holy Ones:

- Cleansing the inner rooms of the everyday mind: one's own viewpoints, inventory of one's attitudes toward one's spirit, soul, and body. Thus, each person applies, in their own ways, or in time-honored ritual ways prescribed by dreams, inspirations, or local customs.

- My grandmother used to call this ritual cleansing, "unrottening the ripe," meaning to retreat back a few steps to flowering and fruiting in one's life—instead of allowing continuous deadfall of withered fruits into our lives—that long over-ripe but unpicked ideas, material goods, outgrown savebacks thumping to the ground. Instead, one can trim, prune, gather up, and create with these right now.

- One cleans out not just the mind and heart, but also the home, the workplace, "the squirrel's nests" of cupboards and cubbies, goods held back for no good reason. These goods now can be released and passed on to others who will put them to often grateful use. Thus we unlock ourselves and our environs—laying the truckload of material ghosts that bring no value to our lives, and on the other hand, making far more room to receive the Holy Guests.

- This means, too, unlocking and clearing out all the locked, up impatience, tenseness, expectations, projections, grudges, chaotic schedules that we've closed ourselves in with by forgetting "to clear out" as a regular practice, thereby choosing to live with "not one jot of space left over" for the Holy People.

- In refuge-making, some souls include ritual bathing to literally strike the body and therefore the spirit back into original shape again. This may include prayerful but sudden immersion in cold winter streams. Some cleanse by fasting—meaning not starving and torturing the body, but rather staying away from what hurts or poisons the body's ability to feel the soul fully in all its sensations, perceptions, and riches.

- Some take on slowness in tasks—on purpose—in order to rest in the kind cloud of timeless time. Some truly telescope down into just whatever is before them, to re-sharpen one's holy gift of focused seeing and attending to.

- Some write a little *bookicito*, a little journal of "self-examination," going over all one's own faults—real but sometimes, in the over-zealous, imagined flaws. However, I'd advise about the latter: a person's *imagined* sins can only be *imaginarily* overcome. I think, if inspired by Creator truly, better to wait until the imagined sins are *real*, and then *really* overcome them.

- In making Posada, souls prepare the refuge for Holy Presence by welcoming their trusted spiritual advisors to sit knee to knee with them, perhaps over honey tea, and then talk about how one might improve life, mind, heart, and soul, specifically. They sit with one another and just talk candidly, in full love for the Life-giving life of the soul.

- In essence, all are building a Posada by measuring and remodeling, by naming and confronting foibles, by repairing weak fence lines, diluting overly prideful strengths, correcting lacks of loving responses, through expressing long-winded bitternesses if need be, and pinpointing one's brevities of real care and regard for self and for others.

- The sweeping and dusting and taking down and laying in, is fine-tuned with special attention given to our inattentions—to people and matters our egos have mistakenly deemed unimportant.

- Also, out go our impulses to spend too much time looking at insignificant imperfections of whatever, and not enough seeking the whole Holy Being. Gleaned too, are failures to gently mend breaches insofar as we can, to reveal the depths of our true hearts no matter what we do or do not receive in return, to put one's toughness on the inside where it belongs, the softness on the outside where it belongs in the sacred algorithm of the holy—not the other way around.

• To literally acknowledge and honor one's teachers, to revere the memory of the blessed departed who, often enough, still lean through the door frames between the worlds from time to time, trying to point out something useful to us, and with love.

• To move forgiveness forward at least a few spaces.

• This *temenos,* that is a place designated as a holy refuge, is swept clean inside and outside by our examining and cataloging other conditions: treasures laid up but not cared for, riches hoarded for "someday," a day we know will not likely come; stuck doors needing shaving; doors perhaps lolling open too wide, so all goodness rolls out before it can be contained in a finer form and put to creative use.

• In our communities also, as well as those we do not live in, we ask the question: "How can I become more shelter for the power of the Holy?"

• All this self-questioning is not meant to be punitive nor self-deprecating, but rather in the spirit of the birth of the Light of the World, that is, in the spirit of loving and en*light*ening our tired, burdened, and stale ways of thinking/acting in the past.

In us during the time of La Posada, all these prepare the rooms so that Love will find its place to be born to the World—*with us, for us, through us.*

THE ETERNAL RHIZOME

The *kind* of Love that is needed
for everything needing to be saved, to be saved . . .
everything needing to die, to die . . .
everything needing to be sheltered, to indeed be sheltered . . .
is goodness capable of growing goodness.

THE RITUAL NIGHT PROCESSION TO
FIND SHELTER FOR LOVE

In Posadas I've been part of, the intent is to travel with José y María y El Bebe, to not be separate from their travails and desperation in searching for safe haven for the birth of the Gift of Love.

This is not an imagined travail, for today, as in times past, we can feel we are exiled from the mainstream culture, and societal rules which the soul often finds bewildering.

The sense of being *los exilios y los destierros,* the exiled, the banished, is not play-acted in Posada. Each Posada pilgrim, in some way, truly is an *exilio* seeking to find shelter from the world for the Child of Love they carry in their hearts. The underlying elements of the ancient story—being reviled, looked down upon, being told, "There is no place for you here"—are still too often very real for many souls in our time.

Yet La Posada ritual seeks to re-enact the spiritual and psychological process of not being welcomed despite being or bearing a great Gift. The procession of souls proceeds through the dark winter night, not in the hope for, but rather in the fierce belief that somehow, somewhere, an abiding shelter for The Gift will be found. It must be found. It most assuredly must.

As with all other rituals, Posadas are practiced somewhat differently depending on locale, the familes or the parish, the country of origin, the venerable and cranky old women's say-so.

There can be nine nights to La Posada ritual and so, beforehand, it is arranged at nine pre-chosen homes that when the pilgrims dressed up as the Holy Family come to their doors, they will be sent away. No room for you here. Myriad people will refuse to give shelter to María and her family.

The ritual commences then, at night, with a procession often beginning at the parish church, often accompanied by singing the "Litany of La Virgen." Then, with the lassos of rosaries swinging, and handheld candles lit, the procession of souls walks into the night toward the first of the homes that will turn away those bearing the Christ Child.

THE PEOPLE HOLDING LOVE CLOSE
AGAINST THEIR BODIES

In some Posadas, different people are chosen to portray María and José each successive night. Sometimes a different child is chosen each night to portray the coming Child, or else a beautiful little *muñeca,* a doll or doll-like marionette of the Christ Child, the exact size of a newborn baby, is swaddled and held close by people of various ages.

I still smile in my heart to remember during one Posada, when I lived in Albuquerque in the 1960s, a sweet staggering toddler carried the Cristocito with his *mami* and *papi* and *abuelita* waddling behind, crouching over the child to make sure the little Christ Child would not be dropped accidentally.

I still remember the old people in their soft, dark slouch hats, old ragged *mantillas,* woolen headscarves, and woven sash-bandannas, who walked with side-to-side swaying because of this bad hip or that bone-crooked foot, that cartilage-thin knee.

And I remember one old one's hands, which were like end-sawn lumber from his years of labor. Those old hands had touched and learned so much about life and death—and they now held the little Christ Child muñeca, doll, so tightly against his barrel chest, as though he alone had sole responsibility for protecting all that could ever matter—that if he didn't carry and hold on tight to the radiant little Child, the entire world would somehow disappear into the dark forever.

Thus, the traveling procession proceeds from house to house.

When I lived in Taos, La Posada is in dead of winter, so some people dressed in burlap "biblical clothes" they'd made, and then wore their combat or flak jackets over that, or their long black overcoats with the big celluloid buttons over house-dresses that were patterned like cabbage-rose wallpaper. Women sometimes wore their husbands' old Navy pea jackets or wool-on-cotton-warp *rebozos,* shawls, over their heads with fringes trailing down over their hips.

Can you imagine a cloud of dark overcoats singing? So covered over were people in their scarves and mufflers. So much singing and crowding together on the side of the road, here and there stopping for old knees bending into a Pueblo semblance of shuffle dance. A drum. A flute. Voices. Cristocito. The eyes of so many of our tired, worn-down people filled with hope and happiness in the candlelight.

At each of the nine houses: loud—*knock, knock, knock. Silencio* till the door creaked open. A gaggle of dimly lit people behind the door—uncles and aunts, *abuelos y abuelitas,* other elders, the neighbors, kidlettes. Whoever answered the door would take one look at us, and in some form of "high dungeon" theater, or snarl, or bellow, "No, no, go away."

Some pretended harshness: "No, no room here for the likes of you!"

Some answering sadly, "We're full already. No vacancy. I have no room for you."

Some acted brittle and bitter: "No! Go away! Don't let me catch you here again!"

And we would all hang our heads, but go away singing and waving our rosaries and holding up our candles, for we knew. We knew we ourselves were carrying the ultimate room at the inn inside ourselves. That no matter what anyone said, we knew there would be room for the Child of Love, for we were the inn itself, the exact chamber needed.

LOVE EVER UNLOCKS THE HEART'S LOCKED DOOR

So Posada goes. We are supposed to be turned away from homes eight times. But often Love intervenes early, and the ritual tilts, goes haywire (only according to the rigid minds, though), and the planned order veers all awry instead . . . or as most of us think, goes completely right after all.

On one occasion, one of the grandfathers of the house where we were to be rejected, had a bit too much to drink early in the evening, and instead of being able to hold the harsh stance of "Get out of here, we have no room for you," he was in his love heart. He forgot his role was supposed to be to refuse the weary travelers a room at the inn.

Instead, he disrupted Posada by bellowing from the kitchen table through the front door open to us in the snow: "Ah mio Dio, yes! Come in!"

A woman's voice was heard from the kitchen, "No you old fool, we're supposed to say 'No! Go away!'"

The grandfather bellowed again: "Come on, come one and all. We got plenty of room, what the hell you talking about? Come. Come."

A child's voice was heard in the kitchen, "No, *Abuelo*, we're supposed to say 'No.'"

"Oh, hell with no. Say yes! Say, '*Sí, se puede.*' Say, 'Yes, it can be done.' Come in, we got a cot, we got the Stratolounger, we got a floor! What's keeping you!?"

We, out in the cold then, felt what María y José y Cristocito might have felt too—at the inn, the innkeeper and the wife arguing "Yes/no, yes/no, let them in, no don't, yes do, no no no."

Another time, another year at Posada, the bearded man who answered the door, tentatively said, 'Noooo, I ummm don't think so. I don't, no, no room . . . well . . ." He had Down syndrome, and he and his mother had rehearsed his Posada speech for days. Now, he spoke his part as planned, and his dear *mami* patted him and pulled him away from the door frame. We, the troop of once-again rejected Posada celebrants turned to fade back into the night. But the young man suddenly ran out onto the porch stoop in the snow, crying out from his heart of love, "No no! Come back, come back! You can have my bed!"

The unlocked heart will ever let love in. Ever, ever. Some might say this young man was "broken," because he blurted out "the wrong thing." But, in fact, this young soul was radiant-whole: Love ever finds shelter in the heart of one who is so permanently unlocked.

POSADA GOES ON

Even though some of us had called to the young man, "Yes, oh thank you and your big heart, we will be back, thank you so much," we had to continue being rejected. And so our little ragged Posada group of dark crows, face-lit by the candles we carried, all flew in formation away from that house, continuing to have to decline any other of *abuelos'* so dear and tipsy invitations. No, to the children trying to talk sense to their parents about letting us in, and even no to a grown man-child filled with such a permanent heart of love.

So, we trudged back into the dark, searching for the place for María and her family, searching while remembering our own exiles, merging them in some measure with those of the Holy People. To remember what was most important to shelter, that unity of us all with ancient María y José y Jesús in a real way in the real cold and ice, the real snow and wet, rather than to somehow divorce ourselves from the root instead, loving in ways I suppose might look to a modern audience as though we were stumbling through an ancient stage play.

But, regardless of how others might see us, time and again the people who vowed to protect the Light, the Child of Love, knocked at doors, and sang the songs asking for shelter. And were turned away.

It is amazing what emotions, memories, thoughts, and feelings come up for souls when their egos think they are, in one sense, only participating in a pageant. I see it occur at *Pésame* also: the time when after Christ's crucifixion and death the statue of María is brought down from her altar or alcove to the nave beyond the altar rail, and prayerful people come to her on their knees to give her comfort and condolences.

Then too, you see men weep, and women tear up, and little children cry because they are in some mysterious way moved and torn by the loss of the Light of the World. The night between two days. The darkness without knowing for sure if the Light will be allowed to be born again, if the Light will make it through alive. We never know if it's the story or the longing for the story that causes us to remember where we came from, and how dearly beloved is the Light that makes so many weep.

And this element is in La Posada as well. A child answering the knock and saying in a sweet little voice, "No, no room for you here," can strike at any parent's heart who is trying to let go of a beloved child because it's time, any parent who is estranged from his or her child, any parent or grandparent who has lost a child, any squadron member who has lost a buddy, any person suffering from feeling shunned. And you can hear the tears in the dark then; the tears come through the singing voices that suddenly go wavering, in the loss of timing, in the dropping out of half the singing voices down into the whisper range.

And if the door is answered by a bent-over elder, one so frail who cheeps out in a little voice like a tin flute, "No, no one can stay here," you can be sure that those of us who have lost our mothers and fathers, those of us who have no elders left, those of us who long so badly for a mother or father who is real and loving to us, those of us who know the evanescence of life and always want to say to the very old, "Don't die, don't die, don't die." Well, then the pilgrim song asking to please give us shelter deteriorates into some serious howling and sobbing.

And it's alright. We're together. It's all alright. We hold onto each other, we comfort each other, we hand Kleenex all around, hold candles for others while they dry their faces. Arms over shoulders now, arms around waists. A tribe of heart-wounded sailors, we act as crutches and bandages for each other as we row on to the next house, the next.

FINALLY

Until finally, the search is ended. Finally, we come to the last house, where at the very end of the long search, those cast to be "the compassionate people" welcome the weary travelers in out of the cold.

Sometimes different old women stand as midwives in the last house, and hurry to take María by the arms and help her to lie down about as well as any nine-months-pregnant-and-in-labor woman can lie down on a straight-back chair when she can no longer fold in the middle. María instead sprawls with legs straight out, ankles clad in wool socks the same size as her calves.

This brings on much laughing and shy reminiscences then about "The time I was ten months pregnant and big as a house," and how "Her water broke, and I was so scared, I tried to put the house key into the car ignition to get her to the hospital," and other stories of the birth of someone's precious light in someone's precious world.

In this last house there will be *las servietas*, special snowy linens folded just for this moment, and cakes and sweets and often a *piñata*, and there will be much rejoicing that at last there is a place for the soul to rest who is pregnant with New Life. And for José, the often-bewildered protector, he will be congratulated and given some fiery tequila to numb his anxiety about his wife and the little Child. His arms will be pumped in congratulations, mustaches will bob up and down with, "I was waiting for my first *hijo*, son, to be born and I thought I would grow wings." They will give Joseph the big strong recliner, and faces will soon be red from laughing and drinking hot tea with chiles in it. And in all this last house on the road is a place of honor—no matter how humble. A place has been prepared for the Child of Light to be born.

Again.

Right there in each person's weeping, happy, exhausted, frozen, but warming-up-now heart.

And we are changed. We have gone through the dark desert, and we've been whipped around by memory—ancestral and common, personal and momentous. We are not separate from María, we are not separate from José, we are not separate from the Cristocito.

We are together in all this. No one will be left stranded, for we are the new innkeepers.

LA POSADA: THE WELCOMING INN AT THE SIDE OF THE ROAD

Since time out of mind,
forces rise up from the dark
spewing black sand everywhere
trying to douse The Light of the World . . .
trying to destroy the sons
and the daughters of the Light.

Sometimes, begging from door to door
is the only way
to find shelter for the Holy.

Even when doors slam shut,
one will open eventually,
And the firelight inside

Will jump through the dark,
So that light meets Light,
Like steel sharpens Steel.

Yet, even if no one comes,
Even if no one opens the door,
no one human, that is . . .
Hold tight, for
angels will come then . . .
and using the key of Love,
all doors will fall open
or else be locked securely
protecting all within . . .

all this *for* you,
rather than against you,
for you who persisted,
you yourself now, and every day
being born as the *i*
at the beginning of the word
miracle . . .

In this way, you yourself,
in your own human and soulful ways,
are forever Mary's miracle child.

CHAPTER NINETEEN

Letter to Young Mystics Following Holy Mother

Our Lady of Guadalupe: The Path of the Broken Heart

Dear Brave Souls:

Listen, my young ones, you have written me saying you feel called as mystics. Some of you have had several visions of the Blessed Mother or just one little one (which can be enough to last a lifetimwe), or you have rightfully swooned in some other way for La Nuestra Señora, Our Lady, in one of her many forms.

And now you've written to me because you have heard we endeavor as a group of social justice activists to walk as contemplatives in, but not of, the world.

You wish to know what to call the experiences you have been having. The old-fashioned words are *appearances* and *apparitions*. But I offer to you and advise you to call them by simpler words. They are *visits,* as from a great and beloved sister-mother, who comes because of long-standing love and familiarity with you. She comes through the door without knocking in order to deliver some sweet or strong *dulces o carnes,* sweet bread or meaty nourishments, to you.

I have heard you state seriously that you have no access to rocky caves where you can take up immediate residence in order to pursue your love

◄ "Letter M Is for La Mystica"

of her in a solitary way. *M'hijas y m'hijos*, daughters and sons, understand that wherever is your bed, that is the right cave for you. Your own cellar, your own table, your own street corner, your own bicycle, your own alley—these are all the right rocky caves. It is true that some people teach that mystics live in out-of-the-way places, but many, many across the world live exactly as you do—in the most hidden way of all—as very extraordinary souls living inside very ordinary circumstances.

This is right and proper, for although it is lovely to think of retiring from the universe—perhaps to a faraway place of great beauty and serenity where the outer world hardly ever intrudes, Our Lady grows her strongest roses in the earthy ground where she is most needed—amongst horns honking, ambulances careening, children crying out alternatively in joy and in pain, all the people groaning and dancing and making love, the complete *trochimochi*, every which way, of humanity whose singings, sounds, works, and actions are part of the exact basis for the harmonious cacophony—the music of the cosmos.

Some say that sudden knowledge of mystical matters is accomplished only in complete quietude, or that Creator, in one of God's many forms, appears only in orderly ways that are beauteous and picturesque, or that the mystical appears only in completely silent ways. All are true. Except for the "only" part.

For instance, the great mystic Jakob Boehme saw a sunbeam glint on the edge of a pewter plate, and some say he was transported into a lifelong religious ecstasy. Madre Castillo entered a convent to guard her visions and ecstatic poetry. Others developed under what many might call "privileged conditions." But the best visionaries, *m'hijos y m'hijas*, grow where they are seeded. Exactly. No matter in humble or elevated ground.

You ask, since your visits from her were not calm or decorous like those at Fatima or Lourdes, or even episodic like those of our dear relative now often known in history only by his colonized name, Don Diego, are your experiences somehow wrong?

No. No, my hearts, they are not wrong. They are completely righteous. I assure you most definitively that the Beloved One comes in complete calmness to some. But, in my experience, more often, she appears in times that are not calm, and in clouds of dust that are not particularly picturesque. She comes skidding to a sudden stop in dark cars on even darker gravel roads. She stands in the midst of broken glass at curbs. She walks in every street, stands at every street corner, even those where it seems that, as my grandmother Querida used to say, "Maybe even God Herself ought be cautious."

To be a contemplative and follower of Holy Mother, I believe, for you she will appear in myriad ways. She will appear to you as much in the midst of noise, upheaval, and times when we feel the sky is falling as when there is peace all around, at least in one's own little universe—for she is often most present whenever there is most need for order, strength, endurance, a new idea, fierceness, hope, and vitality.

Now, you write that all around you seems often in complete mayhem, and this causes you great sadness. I would agree completely. Our own sorrows seem heavy enough, even when lifted by certain long-term joys. But watching others hurt is the breaker of most any heart. Yet, She is clearly with you, for the kinds of lives we have led would lead many to become thick with cynicism and biting—and yet, we are still here with our hearts still unruined.

This is a very good sign.

Too, I would like to say to you that there is great power in the broken heart. Unlike many aspects of psyche that might close or hide when hurt, the heart broken open stays open.

Though painful for certain, the heart broken open can be a blessing beyond compare. It not only allows you to see others, it allows you to constantly see her.

Just recently, one more time, my heart broke again. How many times must a heart break in a single lifetime? When I ask this question, I always receive this answer: "A thousand times a thousand, for anything worth having, or safekeeping."

Allow me to tell you this story from my little life, and perhaps this can demonstrate to you two useful things: First, that ministering in her name is very, very simple. Second, for many, the essence of Creator does not occur in silent and golden appearances, but more often in the midst of mud and dirt, in the storms and thunder of daily life.

I had spent an entire morning preparing to go on pilgrimage. This kind of pilgrimaging I have done many times over thirty years' time. The pilgrimage I was going on had not an ending of which I know. I go to the shrine where most people never go, to a dark, dark hovel filled with the most imploring souls imaginable, the most brave, the most innocent of almost any—a place filled with people who exist, as poet W. B. Yeats puts it, " . . . where all ladders start / in the foul rag and bone shop of the heart."

Although I have for part of my adult life looked longingly at the colorful brochures of pilgrimage sites that are popular in each era, those advertising group tours and exotic voyages to faraway sites—the Aegean Islands, the Temple Sites tour, the Stonehenge Gathering, the others—I have grown into the midst of my seventh decade and I have not yet been to any of those wondrous places. Perhaps someday. If I hear her call me there.

For now, I prepared to go to that place where no one asks for much other than only to endure, and to one day be freed from all that oppresses. It is a place where no soap, no rag can wipe away the history of anguish there. It is a condensed world made from the distillation and packing together of many souls, all ready to either unfurl or run or pounce. It is a shrine to the profound humility of the wanderer, and instead of being filled with hope, this place is filled with misled hearts, with cruel twists of fate, with broken promises from coyotes, and worse.

I am a pilgrim to the immigration jail. As I write this letter to you, all the people to be deported are being held there, and cannot go back home to their Haitian, Mexican, Irish, or Puerto Rican families, for the Republicans in the 104th Congress have threatened and made good on a shutdown of the entire federal government, meaning all paychecks, funding stops, and federal workers are taken off their jobs.

Thus, many souls will be held in jail for many months forward, some longer. Their parents, loved ones, their *novias* and *novios,* betrotheds, will not know their whereabouts for a long and chilling time. There are many frightened mothers and sisters, fathers and brothers praying at the *iglesias,* churches, in Mexico, Haiti, Ireland, and Puerto Rico for the safe return of their loved ones. Praying scared, for most are stonewalled about where exactly their loved ones are being held.

Extra charges placed on prison phone calls, calling collect to Mexico alone, with hookup fee and all the rest, can cost more than five dollars a minute. Most here do not even have fifty cents. It is a joke amongst us all about who ought to be put in jail, our *hermanos y hermanas,* our brothers and sisters, or *los políticos,* the politicians.

I pack my *bolsita,* little bindle bag with various small treasures, holy cards, various tiny *remedios,* herbs and teas that the guards will let me bring in, rosaries for those in greatest need. Lastly comes the tiny container with the much-used cotton ball saturated with chrism. Before Father Melton, a giant black priest teaching a Midwestern parish of astonished Euro-Americans his deeply ethnic form of Catholicism, graciously gave me his own personal container of healing oil, mine was made of a bullet shell casing that my great-aunt swore came from Emiliano Zapata's own rifle during the *revolución.*

There is something else I take with me on pilgrimage also, the most important something that has no object attached to its memory. I take a mandate from *mi* Guadalupe, one given to me long ago as a child. Every time I go on pilgrimage to prison, or to the street, or to my writing table, I think of events from long ago that were influenced by Holy Mother. And this is what I will now relate to you here. For why else should I leave my warm bed to travel to a cold jail in the midst of winter, to see many whom I will never see again? You, already having your own visits from her, already know how she moves. Let us see.

When I was seven years old, the grown-ups from my home and school life told me that I had at last reached "the age of reason." Apparently, in spite of my many childhood jailbreaks (running away from the house to be in the massive cathedrals of the forest, or baptizing flowers and children smaller than me in the talking-water of the creek, or staying late in the forest at night to see the eerie swampfire), in spite of these semi-terrible transgressions, I, the little ecstatic child-wanderer, was now qualified to be "reason-able."

In our immigrant and refugee family, several of our old ones did their own blessings and ablutions after the more formal ones done at the parish, whether this be baptism, first confession, or Holy Communion. Back in those times, members of the family carried three times more sacraments than the parish had, including the old ablutions for childbearing and childbearing loss, for recovery from failed love, repair of the body's inner sight and hearing, repair from wars of many kinds, and pledges of loyalty and foreverness for the betrothed, and other kinds of blessings on many, many other matters of life and death and rebirth.

So it was not unusual that after this talk about having reached the age of reason, one of my aunties, Kati, whom I loved the smell and sight and sound of, leaned near and joked that this whole passage should really not be called "the age of reason," but rather be called "the ache of reason." She was my cohort in little mischiefs, such as staying too long gazing at the sunset over the fields, letting me take my grisly shoes off, which were heavy "corrective" ones that went in directions my feet and ankles did not. Those kindly sorts of things.

But now she gazed at me seriously and instructed that as in certain novenas, now too for two weeks after my consecration to Our Lady, I might be able to know my future. That the curtain between the worlds would part for two weeks only. That I might be able to see across the void to the other world. That I should pay deep attention to what I would see, for whatever events, matters, comings and goings in particular would capture my heart. And that these special noticings could be understood as pointing the way toward my future life and work.

This whispering and rustling of my aunt's spirit bones, and that of the wings around her, did not disturb me, for what is a Católica born to strive toward but the charisms, the gifts of the Holy Spirit? We try to take our spiritual understandings both seriously and with good humor. We know we sometimes appear to others as followers of odd rituals and requirements. But we nevertheless strive toward what we hold to be true—our insights, intuitions, visions, prayers, dreams, and prophecies that surround the intercessions of and by the Great Holy Woman.

Now that I was old enough, sentient enough, I received my lifetime consecration to La Mujer Grande, the Great Woman. Ah, it was a ritual that I think Thoreau would have approved of, even though he cautioned against occasions requiring new clothes. I had a new little shawl my aunt had crocheted for me. There was no pomp, but there were avid and earnest askings and blessings. The old women and nuns all seemed to wear the same kind of black shoes with Cuban heels. There were fog banks of incense, the chanting of the most vivid adorations to Santo Niño, the Child God of Love, and much swinging of black rosaries, some with beads made from the walnut tree, some made of seeds. All of this I loved from the very center of my being outward and back again.

With my arms outstretched to their fullest extent, and my eyes lifted to the Great Holy Mother, I knelt for what seemed like hours on the coldest brick floor imaginable, until that terrible ache from cold, like a pneumonia in the knees, began. I was asked to repeat after the adults many things—words and supplications and praises—and I remember also repeating words that pledged my virginity to Blessed Mother for all time. I said the holy words earnestly as I had been taught—"with thinking, but without blinking."

I knew what a virgin was: Firstly, it was, in some quarters, Guadalupe's first name. Like my own first two names, or like one of my friends, María Cecilia. Virgin Guadalupe. Secondly, to be "a virgin" meant to try to be as she was—brilliantly colored, fierce, watchful, with the loyalty of a good dog.

My aunt had told me that in the next thirteen days I would see thirteen things that would affect me for life, things "that will call for your help, your hands, your heart—for the rest of your life." I now tried to keep my eyes truly open. She had said, "You are a little child, and you can still see what most who are older no longer care to see: you can see what needs your help."

In that week I saw many things. Most were not out of the ordinary for our lives and times; they were either arrestingly beautiful or arrestingly violent (as a child I lived in the Midwestern rural backwoods, and these polarities were unrelentingly normative). There, many feasted on the beauty, and many, many had fallen into or become injured by violence in its many forms.

In efforts to repair themselves from having been victims of violence, some became hardened, some fell lower still, some bowed their heads and went on in resignation, some escaped, and others endured. Anyone who has lived through such terror knows exactly how it is. I know many of you understand this.

So, many things did I see during those thirteen holy days that my aunt had prepared me for. But one of the most startling came as I wandered down a dirt road through the far woods. A little ways down the road, a big sheriff's car, in an even bigger cloud of dust, skidded to a stop at the side of the road. Right there, a little deeper into the woods, was a stick-pole encampment of some of the hobo people who regularly jumped from the freight train uproad, and stayed for periods of time in our neck of the woods.

I think there are times when you can smell mal-intention coming. I quickly jumped into the field at the roadside and lay down to hide amongst the dry stalks there. The deputies jerked aside the canvas flap of the stick-pole tent and charged right in. Less than a minute later, amidst all hell breaking loose and with the terrible sound of cooking pots clanging and falling, scuffling sounds and much crying out and epithets, one deputy dragged a half-naked man in manacles from out of the canvas hovel.

The poor man was dressed like many who lived hidden in that part of the woods, many who had come up from the hills of Appalachia with their rustic Elizabethan English, some with whom I had made best friends. His torn strappy T-shirt was gray with oil; his trousers were stained with paint and dirt. He was unwashed, unshaven, uncombed, and, like a bull roped to the ground, his eyes were rolling, his mouth slobbering, as he cried out what sounded to me like, "Milady! Milady!" The deputy shoved the disheveled man into the patrol car, and slammed the door and ran back to the tent.

As I watched frightened and horror-stricken, I thought I heard in my head a calm and gentle voice asking, "Do you love me?"

"Love you? Love you??" I wondered. My anguish over what I was seeing was so great I could hardly comprehend the words being spoken into the ear of my heart.

"If you love me, comfort them."

"What!?" I implored, trying to understand. Before I could react, the deputies dragged a screaming woman from the tent. She struggled against their manhandling of her. She had a short, lit cigarette between two fingers, and she wore only one shoe, a broken-down black flat, which made me think of crickets and shiny beetles.

The men had hold of her so-thin arms, arms like a skeleton's, almost, and right before my eyes they bent her arms backward to angles not truly possible. She was flaming words and flailing limbs. She screamed and screamed and for one breathtaking moment I felt she looked directly at me, appealing directly to me, though surely she could not have seen me in the overgrown field across the road. "Help me, help me," she cried in the most pitiful voice.

One officer had pulled her head back by her long hair. Another was trying to pull her sweater up out of the back of her trousers to pull it up over her head like a hanging hood. "Help me, help me," she screamed again and again.

I heard a calm voice in my panicked heart ask once more:

"Do you love me? If you do, then help Me."

I felt deeply confused, yet I shot up like a quail. I had sudden turbines in my legs, and with my arms reaching ten feet ahead of me, my lungs filling with a gigantic thundercloud, my head back, I ran like a crazy child down and across the road. The deputies were pushing the woman into the car. They were slamming the door on the couple. The officers piled into the front seat and slammed their own doors. I could still hear the woman screaming.

"Help me, help me."

Completely panicked but somehow able, I thought, "Yes, I will help you." Agonized still, but in a new way, I thought, "But how? How?"

I came up alongside the back end of the big sedan just as the car began pulling away. I yelled out loudly—I hope I called out in a voice that could be heard from earth to the heavens, but I am afraid that I was so filled with fear that maybe I only croaked. Yet, I felt I pulled in the breath of windstorms and that I thundered out as strongly as I could, just as I had witnessed the old women do in the healing rituals. I cried out:

"In her name and all that is holy, do these people no harm!"

The deputies startled and braked the car hard. I had just enough time to throw myself across the trunk where the faces of the two haggard and manacled souls gazed up at me with what seemed like excellent wonder. I had just enough time, one split second, to use three of my fingers at once to make the Sign of the Cross on the dusty back window and cry out, "These souls are under my protection."

Now the car window was rolling down on the driver's side. I skidded off the car and fell to the road, seeing my own reflection in the mud-specked hubcap. Now the door was opening on the driver's side. I scrabbled to my feet, and ran as though a demon were chasing me. I ran and ran like a crazy thing far into the wild field of broken *gordo lobo* wands.

The patrol car slowly pulled away, gravel crackling, and it kept going. Over my shoulder I could see the crosses on the dusty back window of the car. I had made them big, all three of them, all intersecting, big and bold. Like her. *Igualmente,* equally. Like the hearts and souls of the man and the woman they took away. *Igualmente.* Like the true hearts and souls of the unawakened men who took them away. *Igualmente.*

I did not know exactly what I had enacted then or later. I am not even certain yet these many years later. I only know I followed rather than led. After the sheriff's car was gone, I crashed deeper and deeper into the forest until I found a way to the creek. There I sat down, fell down really, and could not get up again, for my legs shook so. My stomach was sick just like the time I once, in a childish experiment, mixed together milk and grapefruit juice and drank it. Now, I finally rolled over onto my side and threw up.

Then I crawled over into one of the hanging scrub-oak warrens, lay face-down for a long time, breathing in the rich, healing fragrance of the iron-filled earth of my home. I cried many tears about matters that I could hardly explain. Later, I walked into the river with my big awkward shoes on. I lay in the loving water, not as Ophelia, but as baptism, reburied into the life of the living once more.

I do not know what the man and woman did wrong. Likely nothing. Vagrant. Talking too loud, making love too loud, or just by their presence disturbing the gentry who had come to build big houses out in the woods, and who we knew were made uncomfortable by us, the truly rustic. I only know that the sound of fists thudding on bone is a truly sickening sound and sight, and the sound and feel of these were not unfamiliar to me before or after. And, life went on. But for me, not as before.

Though I could pick self up for a thousandth time, millionth time, and go on because there was nothing else to do, because it was a cruel blank time in the culture of that time, wherein there was no direct help, no aid, no looking to see what was wrong about the injustices I had witnessed that day and more before and after. Still, I could never forget.

I had a strange moment in time then, what I someday would come to understand as the "transformative moment," as when lightning strikes, and all vision and knowing is charged and changed in an instant. One's electricity of body, mind, heart, soul, and spirit, is altered in an instant. Made more prescient, more capable of carrying current. On the road with people in the woods, I thought I had seen the holy people being manhandled. Through the back of the car window, in those poor imprisoned innocents, I thought I saw for a split second, saw in both of them, *mi* Guadalupe suffering. I thought I saw her being assaulted. This was the end of my life as I had known it to that time.

"Do you love me? Then help me." This was one of my thirteen postconsecration callings to the "age of reason."

When I told my aunt what had happened, she cried and took my hands. "You do not have to ask who says, 'They are under my protection,'" she said. "You already know."

I felt I did know.

Twelve years later, when I was nineteen, I heard this from her:

"Do you love me, my sister?"

I answered, "Yes, my Dear One, I love you."

"How much do you love me?"

"With all my heart, my Beloved."

"Will you then visit me in prison?"

"In prison??"

I was afraid to go to the prison at age nineteen. But I went on my very first visit to prison in Michigan City, as I would go on pilgrimage in the ensuing years to many other prisons, those made by government, and to those many, many soul prisons, human-made, and to my own imprisonments, as well, some by choice, some by hard twists of fate.

I promised then as a late teenager that if I kept hearing her call, I would try to keep going where sent. As you can see, I am a fool for her completely. I am still going. This time it was the immigration jail, other years it has been pilgrimages several times a year to other places—the locked institution for boys aged eighteen to twenty-one, the locked institutions for girls and boys aged twelve to eighteen, the men's penitentiary, the women's federal prison, the city and county jails, the state prisons, and sometimes ministering to patients at city hospitals brought in chains for a needed surgery.

It goes on, as it always has.

Do you love me?

Yes, I love you.

Will you then come visit me in the home for unwed mothers?

I would—and there the next sword was run through my heart.

Do you love me?

Yes, I love you.

Will you help run a shelter for battered women? Will you lick the wounds of the wounded?

Yes, another sword.

Do you love me?

Yes, I love you dearly.

Will you walk with me through Skid Row with alcohol swabs, and wipe hands and feet teeming with bacteria, the cuts and hurts of the men and women who can hardly be told apart? Will you do that for me?

Yes. A big sword.

Do you love me?

With all that I am.

Will you stand in the cold of a Chicago night in the dead of winter dressing a stranger's wound as the old man tells you his life's tale with the worst breath you could ever imagine?

Yes, this I can do.

Do you love me? Do you love me?

Yes, yes, a thousand times yes.

So, *m'hijas y m'hijos,* now I am at the close of this letter to you. You have asked me the way to continue and to deepen your devotion to her. I have this great feeling in my bones that you already know the way and just need a tiny little reminder. She comes in untidy ways mostly, often in very big and very bold form rather than demure.

> You will recognize her on sight,
> for She is a woman
> who looks just like you
> and all that you love.
> Remember?

CODA: MI GUADALUPE IS A
GIRL GANG LEADER IN HEAVEN

Mi Guadalupe is a girl gang leader in Heaven.
She is unlike the pale blue serene woman.
She is serene, yes, like a great ocean is serene.
She is obedient, yes, like the sunrise
is obedient to the horizon line.
She is sweet, yes,
Like a huge forest of sweet maple trees.
She has a great heart, vast holiness,
and like any girl gang leader ought,
substantial hips.

Her lap is big enough
to hold every last one of us.
Her embrace
can hold us,
All . . .
And with Such Immaculate Love.

"Aymen

(as my grandmother would say),
and a little woman."

and with love,
Dr. E.

CHAPTER TWENTY

Los Inmigrantes, *We Are All Immigrants:*
The Undousable Creative Fire
They Tried To Stop Her
At The Border

PART I
THEY TRIED TO STOP HER AT THE BORDER

She ran on the *Camino Real* in Mexico, but
they tried to stop her at the border.
No visa for her kind, you know . . .
undocumented, some were certain.
Border guards, *la migra,* didn't like the looks of her.
No one cared that her many, many relatives
were waiting for her back home in Santa Fe
and in surrounding little villages with names
like La Cienega, over near Chupadero, and Española.

Her so many relatives, holding babies in their arms,
were praying daily, nightly, for her safe travel
and especially for her clear passage at the border.

Her *familia* already had all their kisses ready on their lips,
just to give to her.
They had prepared the special water to ritually cleanse her
for having made this perilous journey successfully.

◀ "Letter M is for El Milagro de La María, Miracle of Our Lady"

But fate would not have it, their prayers were not answered.

Stopped at the border; the frontier guards swarmed the truck,
their reasons now seeming so clear,
for her girth alone, was so great . . .
a peasant woman, not a svelte city woman,
she was just a *campesina* girl grown up . . .
and now pregnant, seeming so bigger than usual.

And just trying to make her way over the border . . .
carrying, as *las parteras,* the midwives, say, "way out front."
She could hardly be expected, being with child and all,
to fold herself into a woman the size of a gnat.

So, no, she stood out, that belly in certain lights, you know,
looking quite suspicious and all.
Clearly she was from one of the oldest villages.
One could tell by her odd clothes and bare feet.
Why would such as she be wanting to come into our country?

So Immigration and Customs nabbed her.
And the truck driver who was bringing her,
Became scared and faded away.
And Customs interrogated, wanting to see papers:
Papers and papers and more papers yet.
And money too.
But she was not carrying *la retícula,* a small purse,
and did not even have coinage.
She could only answer
with the treasures of her beautiful eyes.

They took her then, to where all suspicious people are taken,
to a warehouse made of holding cells;
and there alone on the cold floor she laid her head.
And they put their hands inside her maternity clothes,
certain she was carrying contraband.
"What about that belly, real or fake?
Maybe filled with cocaine probably . . .
Ah these people will try any trick to bring in drugs."
And so they forced her to be X-rayed, just to make sure.
And after, she just looked at them through the fence

of the cage they'd put her in.

Would someone, anyone, come and free her?

No one came.

The next day.

No one came.

The next day.

She was lost.

But not forgotten.

PART II
DESPAIR BACK IN THE VILLAGES IN THE USA

How lonesome they all were for their jailed relative, for since forever in what was once Mexico, now the United States, *la familia* had grown to thousands—blood, not blood—thousands of aunts, uncles, *comadres, compadres,* cousins—especially cousins—*mamis, papis, abuelos, abuelitas,* neighbors, everyone who ever traded tomato plants with each other, friends, everyone who cultivated gardens amidst the chamisa and scrub piñon across the Santa Fe hills. All had become family by virtue of food and Faith.

Now this huge group of "families within a Family" prayed and prayed, hoping to hear word of their lost relative's whereabouts, praying to see maybe even an old Mexican truck with the little religious flags and red chenille berries waving across the truck's headliner. They imagined how such a truck would come chugging across the border, tilting sideways with the effort, carrying her home at last to her people up north . . . .

Everyone there waited.

Many wept for her being lost.

PART III
AND THE PREGNANT MOTHER WAITED IN JAIL

And waited . . .
having committed the crime of trying to come
across a line
that someone claimed was holy . . .
a line drawn in the sand

along the banks of the Rio Grande
by fewer than ten men, long ago.

The pregnant mother waited in her jail.
And waited.

PART IV
MEANWHILE, AT THE BORDER,
MEN AND WOMEN THRONGED,
WAVING PAPERS

Phone calls flew through the magic wires, demanding she be found. A holy man was called in to do the things holy men do, to negotiate the young mother's release from the holding tank. To bring her home to her people.

And finally it was done. Somehow the grim blood and the prayer sent out over the Sangre de Cristos and the Sandia mountains, the sudden appearance of these gentle yet fierce souls at the border, led to her release.

And now, allowed to go free, she was brought the rest of the way in a big red truck from the United States, fittingly called by its manufacturer's name "El Ariete," the Ram.

And you have rarely seen such rejoicing, teenagers holding camera phones high, elders weeping, those scarred by life weeping and laughing, children bedecking everyone with flowers.

PART V
AS SHE CAME FROM THE TRUCK,
SHE WAS GENTLED AND SOOTHED

. . . kissed and touched as though souls
had at last met Soulmate.
Singing broke out, the old hymns . . .
as *la familia* extraordinaire, were reunited once again . . .
From dream to reality, she had made it across the border . . .
on the same trail that all ancestors journeyed upon long ago . . .
La Nuestra Señora Guadalupe, with the Cristocito in her belly.
She made it to her people, to all souls who hold a place for her.

And her little Son, "the radiant contraband Baby," who is invisible only to those who have not yet the eyes to see, the ears to hear. Invisible even to X-ray machines . . .

At last she and her little One were here, safe in the arms and eyes and hearts who love her, those who have always loved La Conquista, Mother of the Conquered, Mother of the Americas, who ever comes bearing her Precious Cargo.

PART VI
AND TO MORE THAN ONE OLD PILGRIM IN SANTA FE WHO COULD HEAR LA SEÑORA GUADALUPE'S WORDS WITHOUT HER SAYING THEM ALOUD

Guadalupe whispered that she was touched by the people's fears and by their great love—but that she was never really lost. Just had a little work to do . . . at the border . . . in a warehouse

. . . maybe with one of the poor old men who swept the floors there
. . . maybe with one of the young who came to graffiti a wall there
. . . maybe with an official who saw her and remembered the generous heart again
. . . maybe with a young mother who didn't know if she could make it, but seeing Our Lady through the fence, lying on the floor but in all dignity, felt suddenly filled with bold grace and knew she could make it after all.

A momentary pause. Not a lifetime peril after all.
Our Lady, on the way home, stopped for just a bit,
for she had important business at the border.

THEY COULD NOT DETAIN HER AT THE BORDER

Several years ago, the padrecito *of Our Lady of Guadalupe Parish, now Shrine, in Santa Fe, New Mexico, Father Tien-Tri Nguyen,* along with deacons, parishioners, and many people on both sides of the border, began seeking an artist to fulfill a vision to create a living statue of Our Lady of Guadalupe.

The *comadres* and *compadres* were literally overjoyed to find just the right sculptress, La Señora Georgina Farias in Mexico, a tiny woman about five feet tall and in her sixties. She agreed to create the heroic-sized statue of Our Lady in bronze. When completed, the beautiful statue would be twelve feet tall and weigh two tons.

The *Camino Real* is an ancient roadway that stretches from Mexico to the United States, up through Texas, New Mexico, Arizona, and Nevada, all the way to California. It was the road most of the ancestral Latinos, Native Americans, Mestizaje (born of both Spanish and Native American blood), and Nuevos Españoles (Spaniards from Spain, now domiciled in Mexico) traveled on to the north, beginning in about 1400 AD.

The little Vietnamese priest of Our Lady of Guadalupe Parish in Santa Fe, knowing all about destruction of families, conquests in war, and love of heritage, planned that Our Lady would be brought home over the same road trod by the ancestral people of his parishioners.

The huge statue of Our Lady of Guadalupe was indeed confiscated at the border on its way from Mexico to the United States, but it was not allowed the usual Customs detainment of a day or two. Rather, because she seemed suspicious somehow, at least to the authorities, well, they ordered that she be pulled off the truck, all twelve feet tall and four thousand pounds of her, and lugged to a warehouse. She was indeed X-rayed to make sure she was not carrying contraband.

But afterward, Customs officials claimed they had no record of where she had been taken. Thus, for many days, her whereabouts were completely unknown—or whomsoever knew where she was, would not say, likely working up to demand *la mordida,* the "bite," that is, a big bribe.

For several days, the hundreds of people of faith waiting for her in the United States—having already rented buses to drive to the border to greet her, to stay with her, and to bring her home in triumphant procession—were so frightened that they had "lost" her for good.

Like many other families on both sides of the heavily guarded US–Mexico border who do not know where their loved ones are, they too kept a heart-rending vigil.

Customs authorities continued to claim they did not know where they had put Our Lady. The "right hand at US Customs" said one thing, and the "left hand at US Customs" said something different—as though she had become a missing person, or as one addled officer opined, thinking she was a real human being, "Maybe she ran away."

But of course she did not run away. Our Lady never runs away.

Yet, anyone knowing the border-crossing terrain and tactics as we do, knows it sometimes seems the Tower of Babel must have been built right on the banks of the Rio Grande, and that Babel can come startlingly alive again with "very official" disinformation, misinterpretation, and downright suppression of facts—facts that would normally be kept in a notebook by any rational being who is supposed to keep track of what's what, and who's who, at the border.

So, in order to find Our Lady of Guadalupe and free her, along with his posse of devotees to Our Lady, Father Tri, as he is called by his parishioners, journeyed from Santa Fe to the border.

There he and the determined posse (in Latin, *posse* means "to be able") found officials in Customs who helped. Then they found a warehouse guard who was a door-opener rather than a foot-dragger, and no doubt by the *padrecito's* purity of purpose poured into him by all the longing and gentleness and fierceness of the parishioners, deacons, candidate-deacons, old people, young hearts, middle-aged soulful people, and others who loved Our Lady—they were able to secure her release.

Thus, she was lifted onto a giant flatbed trailer, secured safely, and with the red Ram truck, El Ariete, pulling with its strong engine, she came finally to roll forward on the rest of the old road that led from deep in Mexico all the way up to and through Santa Fe—that road called El Camino Real.

Thus, she entered into Santa Fe—literally with police motorcycle escort, sirens and horns blaring from the long lines of fine cars and battered cars, newer trucks and broken-windshield trucks in the processional that had formed to bring her home to Agua Fria Street, at last.

And too, just as I said, the people literally wept in joy and gratitude, and most of all, in love, in immaculate love for her, as they touched her, kissed her, sang to her and for her, danced for her and with one another.

And the blessed workmen raised her up to the perfect outdoor sky room they'd prepared for her—an outdoor room where, were you to sit at her feet for one entire day and night, you would see the strongest living symbols associated with Our Lady: drifting clouds, the sun, the moon, and the stars. All these celestial lights traversing the planet and peeking through the many windows made by her wide-open *los rayos,* the rays of flaming light all around her body.

> She is, after all, not a fence to keep souls out,
> Rather, she is an open gate, to let souls in.

COMING HOME PRAYER

> Let this be the prayer, then, in every heart,
> that every month belong to La Nuestra Madre, Our Mother.

If you can, let there be a little procession to crown Our Mother,
as in times of eld,
let that *procesioncito* be on the *Camino Real* of our hearts
the ancient red road where we remember all mothers,
who walked before us,
no matter how they appeared,
no matter in what condition . . .
Let us honor all who carry in their own hearts that which,
no matter whatever else, remains striving
toward Immaculate Love for all.

Let her, let us, let all of us be found,
be freed to be brought home
to a place of Love for one another,
on all sides of every kind of border, at last.

Let all of us know how and when to stay
to teach others at the borders,
Let us learn how to take down fences.
and how to become ourselves, wide-open gates . . .
just like her.

We are all, in some way,
los inmigrantes, immigrants
crossing borders to true home,
with proper papers issued
only by the Soul.

La gente, *the people who love*

Our Lady, 12 feet tall, 4,000 pounds. Perfect.

CHAPTER TWENTY-ONE

Mi Madre, Tu Madre, La Madre de Ella,
La Madre de Él, Nuestra Madre:
My Mother, Your Mother, Her Mother,
His Mother, Our Mother

The Truth about How Very Hard It Is to Get into Heaven

There's a story told by the old women in our family, the ones whose hands smell like bread dough and rose water: according to them, these two fragrances are the "scents of Heaven."

How hard is it to get to Heaven if you don't fit the culture's home-made ideas about who goes up and who goes down?

Though they meant no disrespect, in the Old Country, some prelates who were condescending with their interpretations of "the Godness of God," as I call it, were often cause for much hilarity amongst the villagers—after a certain priest had ridden away from the village, of course. The people themselves held to a far simpler sort of Godliness that is, seeing Creator as better than the kindest person they had ever known on earth. And they depended on that to be true . . . in ways and means that might surprise some. This is how we tell the story with levity in our ethnic family.

Listen . . .

◀ Ex-voto: "A Door To Heaven"

THE UPSIDE-DOWN, RIGHT-SIDE-UP HEAVEN

God the Father was strolling through Heaven one day when he came across two old Roma, Gypsy men down on their knees, throwing bones burnt with dots and betting piles of coins against each other.

God the Father was shocked. Shocked.

Shaking his old white curls, he continued onward, and suddenly came across an old Indian woman sitting under a big shade tree, enjoying a big fat black cigar.

"Harumph," said God the Father, "this isn't right. These people don't belong here!"

Next he saw an entire gaggle of little children jumping in mud puddles, and the dirtier they became the more they were filled with laughter and joy.

Then, to top it all off, he saw lovers so deeply in love, kissing each other and swearing their allegiance to each other's souls—on a holy book that was not the Bible.

The next thing, though, put him over the edge. A group of painters were painting frescos on the inside of a small chapel, and believe it or not, each one was painting God the Father a different color and race and even gender from each of the others.

"Abomination! This makes me sick!" said God the Father. "This simply cannot continue. I cannot understand how all these people can possibly have taken up residence in *my* Heaven."

And God the Father made up his mind to find Saint Peter, who obviously was not doing his job properly.

"Saint Peter, I demand an explanation. On my way here, I saw soldiers shaking from withdrawing from drugs. I saw child-prostitutes who were singing and washing their new little wings. I saw men and women who had destroyed their children being comforted, people who are still wearing pain and shame in their eyes from having drunken binges, from severing life from life.

"And of all the nerve, I saw a group of some prelates who were carrying on about who was right and who was wrong in church matters on earth. And . . .

"I came across a woman praying a prayer I've never heard in my life. She was chanting 'Oh my dearest God, my Mother, holy is thy name.' I came across priests who were catching their children in the air, dancers and revelers who begged me to join them, and one fellow who was brewing beer that smelled so good I almost almost caught myself saying, 'Mmmm-mm.'

"Saint Peter, has Heaven gone to Hell? All over Heaven there are men and women who have their low-rider cars pulled up onto the front lawn of Heaven, tinkering with their engines. There are girls in short skirts, and kids who you can tell by their eyes they have seen more years of life than their years lived.

"Saint Peter!!" God the Father boomed. "*Why* are you letting these people into Heaven!? They're not the right sort. They should have gone to Purgatory first to be cleansed, some of them need a hell of a lot of cleansing. It's not right that they're here in Heaven."

"My dear God the Father," said Saint Peter, "you don't know how hard it is to keep them out. Why, they come to Heaven's Gate and I look in the Book and I tell them what their judgment is—and they look at me and say, 'No, no sir, Saint Peter, you must be wrong. I am supposed to come to Heaven. I have been told I would be welcome here.'"

God the Father, who was aghast: "And so, Peter, how do they get into Heaven despite what I've decreed and despite you telling them they're not welcome?"

"Well, God, you see, it is not easy to explain this to you. It is very complicated."

"Come now, you can tell me, Saint Peter. You know, I am God, and God is a very forgiving force in this world. You can tell me."

"Okayyyy God," said Saint Peter, "but you're not going to like it."

"What do you mean I won't like it?" snapped God the Father. "Just tell me already."

"All right then, you asked for it, God. These people come to the gates, and I send them away, and I send them away, and I send them away . . . But then they go around to the back of Heaven—where your Dearest Son and His Blessed Mother let them in."

The Blessing of Guadalupe

Have you forgotten?
I am your mother.
You are not alone.
You are under my protection.
Anything you need,
ask me.
Do not worry about anything,
Am I not here-
I who am your mother?
Have you forgotten?
I love you, and
you are under my protection.

CHAPTER TWENTY-TWO

That You Be Watched Over and Kept Safe
Until We See Each Other Again

Closing Blessing: Have You Forgotten? I Am Your Mother

Here are the back and front of the first holy card I created and printed two decades ago. This special little *tarjeta* was made to raise funds for our own little charitable foundation, La Sociedad de Guadalupe, which is devoted to La Señora's works in the world—that is, to broadcast strengthening stories through many means, and to promote the importance of adult literacy amongst impoverished people in our world (including literacy for mothers especially.)

I placed this card here so you can see La Virgen's most beautiful words. Though some persons seem to have, over time, assigned some horrific words to her mouth, or claim she incessantly rains down invective and disaster warnings, I do not know the woman those others claim to know. With an attentive heart and clear mind altogether, most will never know such a spectre.

Rather, they will know the La Conquista of deep substance, the Mother of unending Compassion and Love. In this small token of a holy card, to me, to many, these words from Our Lady of Guadalupe are the most beautiful words, the most perfect, the most *inspiriting* our Mother has ever spoken to us.

◄ Holy Card: "Blessing of Guadalupe Through Cuauhtlatoatzin, Santo Juan Diego"

Have you forgotten?
I am your mother.
You are not alone.
You are under my protection.

Anything you need,
Ask me.
Do not worry about anything.
Am I not here—
I who am your mother?

Have you forgotten?
I love you,
And you are under my protection . . .

On the front of the card is pictured La Señora de Guadalupe in her dark green mantle, signifying the earth in perpetual springtime, the time of new life arriving. Her mantle is covered with the golden stars of the cosmos. This signifies she is not just here or there, but everywhere. One can never live outside her domicile.

She is wearing her red gown, its color portraying the Immaculate heart coursing with life. When standing very close to her, you can see her gown is inscribed with living roses outlined in gold. Her roses are said, since time out of mind, by scent alone, to be able to lift the human spirit, to help the embittered or one-sided mind to remember higher ideals of Love and Love and more Love—and to help heal the afflictions of whomsoever takes in deeply the scent of the rose.

La Virgen de Guadalupe wears a woven dark belt around her waist. It is the color of black fertile earth, and is tied in a bow to show that she is a mother who ever incubates Life and brings it forth. The little *angelita* below, holds up the hem of Our Lady's gown in one of the oldest courtly gestures, showing respect to *La Dama*.

We see the horned crescent moon, the beginning of the new cycle of Light to the world, behind her. La Nuestra Señora stands in a bower of violet flowers that are emblematic of the mysterious spiritual light that is said by mystics to emanate from the wounds we endure—lighting a new pathway, carrying us into an often unexpected flowering that can be so surprising in terms of bringing forth in us a new kind of mercy and creative life.

Her *los rayos,* the fire emanating in a piscus, an almond shape all around her body, is the fire of El Espíritu Santo, the Holy Ghost, who is the inspirator of souls. In the old Aztec / Nahua times, the one who flames and inspires was called Firemaker. Now, Our Lady's *los rayos* ignite *Espera, Caritas, Humanitas, Veritas, Unitas* in souls who have gone dim for lack of Love for and from. Hope, Tending, Humanity, Truth, Unity.

Los Rayos represent the presence around La Señora by the One who delivers the fire of ideas and actions of goodness into the soul. Los rayos via Espíritu Santo, also represent the flames of rendering, that is, the burning away of any egotistic dross not needed.

Yet also, her rayos of Espíritu Santo, in our ethnic knowing, represent Our Lady's fireside, which will warm whatever of the soul is pushed away by self or others—whatever of soul has been wrongly exiled or treated harshly and without love by others; whatever of soul has been banished or left to die in the cold. La Señora will not abandon her sons and daughters. Her fiery rayos are her signal fire to summon the weary to rise up out of the wreck, and stumble toward her to be held and healed.

The words on the back of the holy card are the gentle and fierce words spoken by Our Lady when she first appeared to the frightened little Aztec Indian on the Hill of Tepyac in Mexico in 1531. That dark-skinned, brown-eyed, shiny black-haired Indian is now called "Saint Juan Diego" (only recently recognized as a saint, nearly 500 years after La Señora's visitations to him). Juan Diego's original Native American name is Cuauhtlatoatzin, translated by some as, "one who sees and speaks like the eagle."

I like very much a reference he is said to have made about himself when first confronted with the grand mercy of La Señora's sudden appearance to him. I thought you might like to hear it too. He said to Our Lady, *"I am a nobody, I am a small rope, a tiny ladder, the tail end, a leaf . . . "*

FOR HER:
WE TOO ARE THE NO-BODY, THE SMALL ROPE,
THE TINY LADDER, THE TAIL END, THE LEAF . . .

May the Being in each of us who is the "no body,"
that is, *La alma pura,* the pure Soul,

ever remind us that no matter what else,
we have a loving Mother, gentle and fierce,
who expects us to learn, to commit to
being gently fierce, fiercely gentle . . . like her.

And we who pull and hoist each day,
let us go slack for a moment,
and remember with hearts turned homeward,
that it is our Mother,
the most beautiful Bell ever forged,
whom we small ropes
toil to ring . . .
so that memory of her singing voice
chimes throughout our bodies, our minds,
our spirits, our souls, our works and our lands daily.

We are the tiny ladders used to climb up and peek over,
used to breach every wall set against Our Lady.
We stand on the humble wooden rungs
so as to never lose sight of her—
no matter how sequestered by the jealous,
no matter how appropriated and made small,
no matter how forbidden by Caesars,
or hidden away by any means, for any reason.
We will climb down or up or sideways
To behold her wherever she lives.

We too, are little leaves,
and just for this moment,
let us float down the rapids of her Love,
poured and dunked, drenched and half-drowned
in Holy Mer, Holy Mary, Holy Mar,
and let us be glad for this wild and wise ride
up the strong, watery shoulders of our Beloved Mother.

May we ever serve her memory,
And ever be the little tail to her starry kite,
become the last little bite of her sweet cake,
accept a small but powerful role
in her best and most blessed stories.

May we remember her words daily
and never feel alone.

For with her, under her, within her blessings,
I say to you dear soul . . .
May you from this day forward,
ever be watched over by Our Mother,
ever be guided by her,
and ever be kept safe by her . . .
until we see each other again.

In her name, La Nuestra Madre Grande,
and in the name of her precious little Child,
The Love Light of the World.
May you remember you are swirled
in her mantle of stars,
surrounded by the scent of her living roses,
that you are spiritually protected,
and most especially,
that you are truly loved.

So may it be for thee,
And so may it be for me,
And so may it be for all of us.

Aymen
Aymen
Aymen

(And a little woman.)[1]

CHAPTER TWENTY-THREE

Beautiful Words About The Mother

Some of the Ways Other Creative Souls
Understand Relationship with Mother

Lyric writers often understand the sanctity, the great gift of being a mother on Earth to others, whether the children are born through one's body or through one's mind and heart. To me, the definition of "Mother" is mothering a world, a child, anyone or anything precious that cannot be allowed to perish from the face of this earth. In these ways, we daily cleave near to Our Mother greater, also. There are writers who I think write and often act as the Marys of this world. Here are some of them with their ways of seeing, being, evoking the Mother. So many of these writers, I think, are literally embedding poetry of Her into their prose.

A mother's concern for her child pervades all . . .

Karen Armstrong in *Twelve Steps to a Compassionate Life*

May all mothers and sons be reconciled, May all mothers and daughters be reconciled . . .

Jack Kornfield in *The Art of Forgiveness, Lovingkindness, and Peace*

[Speaking of Mnemosyne, Memory] . . . As mother, she taught . . . about all aspects of culture and creativity that left legacies of beauty and well being.

Angeles Arrien in *The Nine Muses: A Mythological Path to Creativity*

The Church ignored her too until about a thousand years ago. Then the mother of Jesus was consecrated as the mother of humanity and . . . in the eleventh century . . . in France [alone] eighty churches and cathedrals sprang up in homage to Mary.

Eduardo Galeano from *Mirrors: Stories of Almost Everyone*

My thanks to women not born to me but who allow me to mother them.

Maya Angelou, in this line, which reads like a holy prayer of gratitude, speaks of the honor of mothering, blood, or spirit genealogy, either one. From her book *Letter to My Daughter*.

Coleman Barks, foremost interpretor of the Persian poet Rumi's works, and author of *A Year with Rumi: Daily Readings*, one of his many books, offers that Rumi says, when the soul is empty, one's heart suddenly "becomes Mary, miraculously pregnant."

Though I may stumble and fall, I know that this universe mothers me, that I am held on the lap of infinite compassion, infinite patience, infinite unconditional love.

Michael Bernard Beckwith in *Spiritual Liberations: Fulfilling Your Soul's Potential*

Robert Bly, in his book *A Book for the Hours of Prayer*, translates Juan Ramón Jimenez who speaks about his mother's face. In psychology we sometimes call "the primal gaze," wherein mother and child gaze into each others' eyes so deeply during nursing, that they bond to one another as one being only, rather than as two separate beings. Bly, who's held a "great mother" conference yearly, shows how Jimenez is so imprinted with "mother," that as an adult, he speaks of his own mother's face sailing him to safety through all storms.

[In Latin America, amongst the poor] . . . They cultivate a form of prayer that the modern mind is likely to regard as primitive, if not downright superstitious. But . . . it would be a serious mistake to stop at a superficial analysis . . . Deeply rooted as it is in this popular devotion, while also drawing nourishment from the wellspring of protest against repression . . . the prayer life . . . in the process of liberation, possesses great creativity and depth.

Father Gustavo Gutiérrez, who holds the John Cardinal O'Hara Professorship of Theology at the University of Notre Dame is known as father of liberation theology. In his eighties now, he resists romanticizing the poor: "Poverty is not a condition, but an injustice." He notes in his book *A Theology of Liberation: History, Politics, and Salvation,* that some have an aversion to the very idea of devotion, including to Holy Mother, and he calls them to see more deeply into the mysterium, rather than into the superficial. We see it too, some too quick to pounce and call devotees "muddled." This cynicism, (the word cynic deriving from Latin, meaning *doglike/churlish*) is misplaced, for Holy Mother models the reaction most warranted for growth: trust in the sacred . . . not the paltry-sweet, but the fiercely intelligent, wholly miraculous reality. Father Gutiérrez, says we can walk in this world not just as contemplatives only, but steep ourselves in the ancient practice amongst old believers, that is: *es in actione contemplativus,* "as a contemplative *in action.*"

[A] healthy mother . . . toward her child . . . her selfless desire to encourage his or her best potential. Such a mother naturally sets limits and speaks her mind, but always with the greatest respect and love.

Joan Borysenko offers this as "a seed thought" in *A Pocketful of Miracles: Prayers, Meditations, and Affirmations to Nurture Your Spirit Every Day of the Year.*

Seeking greater simplicity and purity, they fled into the deserts of Syria and Egypt, first in trickles, then in droves. And they took the [poetry of the] psalms along with them . . . These spiritual pioneers became known collectively as the Desert Fathers and Mothers.

305

Cynthia Bourgeault writes about devout people striving for a holy life but up against monarchical structures, fleeing to protect the intense poetry of holy words to keep them alive. Rooted in the regenerative, as is The Holy Mother, these protectors could have been called many things, but are called by the most venerable of earned titles: Father, Mother.

Our Dark Madonna of the Americas is not a docile meek mother. She is a warrior with her roots growing deep in the Nahuatl Tonantzin of the sacred hill at Tepeyac, and deeper still her roots connect us to Coatlicue, Serpent Skirt, the darker fierce mother goddess of the Aztecs. "In her name—Whose Love is Endless, Who has never abandoned us. On the contrary, we have left Her too long . . ."

Ana Castillo writes of the warrior woman that she herself is and the One she loves in *La Diosa de las Américas*. Her book *Massacre of the Dreamers: Essays on Xicanisma* was where I first heard of the legend by that name.

In a world struggling against senseless violence and growing economic disparity, Mary offers a feminine antidote to the poisons of poverty and war . . . Where society demands competition, Mary teaches cooperation.

Mirabai Starr in her book *Mother of God: Similar to Fire*, tells how Holy Mother's relationship to the soul, is not based in the tenets of consumerist ideologies, rather in the truest heart of mother who first and foremost thinks of the thriving of her child. The author says Mary skirts consumerism "for compassionate service" instead.

Some women would describe their best friend as a cross between Mary Poppins and a Godmother . . . the ones who witness your life and remember everything that happened, "my only non-judgmental confidants" . . . "replacement mothers who you can trust with your secrets . . ."

Dr. Phyllis Chesler, in her book *Women's Inhumanity to Women*, writes about how women lean into friendships where the mother imago is so central to heart, mind and living spirit . . . She writes that "many more women, of all ages . . . do value the importance of female relationships." When she asked women about their definition of "best friend," they defined most of the tone underlying, as mother.

Real friendship then, requires two things: the transparent disclosure of the self and another's single-minded appetite to hear it and abiding commitment to treasure it.

Sister Joan Chittister in *The Friendship of Women: The Hidden Tradition of the Bible,* writes about how relationship in friendship with human beings and with the Holy can be so nurturing. She is, in a sense, describing the relationship between what we call, in Spanish, *comadres,* which means we are mother to each other . . . transparent, treasuring.

You have three minutes to answer. Make sure you are specific. Nothing vague. You might want to begin each answer with "I remember." Give me a memory of your mother, aunt or grandmother . . . Be detailed.

Natalie Goldberg in her book on memoir, *Old Friend from Far Away: The Practice of Writing Memoir,* has the above beautiful "I remember" exercise that is filled with life for, to, and about any mother, but also the most neglected Mother of all, the Holy Mother, the presence of Shekhinah in one's life.

Canyon walls crack and break from the mother rock, slide into the river, now red with the desert. [Seeing] a spiral and what appears to be a figure dancing, her arms raised, her back arched, her head held high . . . There she is, the One Who Gives Birth . . . I place one hand on her belly, and the other on mine. Desert Mothers, all of us, pregnant with possibilities, in the service of life, domestic and wild . . .

Terry Tempest Williams writes soulfully about giving birth to herself in the desert, in her book *Red: Passion and Patience in the Desert.* She also speaks of a certain rock ravaged along its petroglyphs, suffering from rifle fire and yet sees the spirit woman in the rock with the belly filled with life.

In brief, may I offer benefit and joy . . . to all my mothers, both directly and indirectly . . . may I quietly take upon myself, all hurts and pains of my Mothers.

Nawang Khechog, the strong and tenderhearted Tibetan flute player and musician spent many years as a monk, and he writes this so caring elegy to the essence of mother, in such a beautiful generosity in his book *Awakening Kindness: Finding Joy Through Compassion.*

. . . mourning the recent death of a mother, my sister-in-law, created a spirited line dance that assured me that, though we have all encountered our share of grief and troubles, we can still hold the line of beauty, form and beat—no small accomplishment in a world as challenging as this one . . . Hard times require furious dancing. Each of us is the proof.

Dr. Alice Walker (Alicia) writes in her poetry book *Hard Times Require Furious Dancing: New Poems* (A Palm of Her Hand Project), speaking of the ancient urge to ritualize, to regard, and to lovingly create around the comings and going of the mother spirit.

At birth, we fall in love again with our mother through our visual and physical senses . . . ground that recognizes mother. Our survival depends on it.

David Whyte, poet, speaks of how the newborn and by inference the reborn through the mother, is made new again, in his book *The Three Marriages: Reimagining Work, Self and Relationship.* He goes on to say that this primal relationship also means, in the human sphere, that the child will grow and eventually leave the nourishing breast, the guiding hand . . . but the experience of the mother's love will be fastened within the person now, even though they were once only a pip, even thought they are now grown-up.

We may not yet have maps . . . but . . . progress seems to have similar stages: first, rising up from invisibility by declaring the existence of a group with shared experiences; then taking the power to name and define the group; then a long process of "coming out" by individuals who identify with it; then inventing new words to describe previously unnamed experiences . . . then bringing this new view from the margins into the center . . ."

Gloria Steinem speaks about banishing invisibility in her work *Doing Sixty and Seventy,* she herself making so much of the invisible visible in the overculture. Her grid can most certainly be applied with forward hope regarding the visibility of the force of Mother in the world being seen in new ways.

We all think there is a formula, [but] as long as we love our children, that's really the only solid thing I know that works across the board . . .

Jada Pinkett Smith displays the center of the mother imago in that quote. Miss Pinkett Smith is an actor and a nurturer of talent in others. She is speaking about a quintessential "mother-heart." Her inference is that when facing any matter in the flurry of life, this center place she is fastened to—loving the children— is the very thing to weigh and decide all else. From that center, the instinctual mother watches over, springs immediately to give aid, sorrows with, and celebrates with. Both the mother, and Holy Mother, are known for reacting entirely to give succor to "the spirit of the child," whether in an adult or in the young.

We tease my oldest daughter Thandi. Although her nuclear family is small, she always cooks as though preparing to feed the biblical five thousand . . . This reminds me of my mother, who even when we were at our poorest, always made enough to feed several unexpected guests. This habit of generosity was not one that was overtly taught, but it is one that I hope has been well learned.

Archbishop Desmond Tutu and his daughter **Reverend Mpho Tutu** write about the essence of love in their book *Made for Goodness: And Why This Makes All the Difference.* Meeting Archbishop Tutu, I saw he was an *hombre con pechos,* a man who is also a fine wild mother. His speaking about mothers and food, reminds me too of Dr. Angelou, and Dr. Walker, and other "women of the food," who fix enough fried chicken, boiled peanuts, and greens to feed all souls who might suddenly appear out of the mist at their doors. Archbishop Tutu, in the same book, refers to being a midwife, the role of mother, since time out of mind. This kind of language tells that he and his daughter are two of the many Marys of the world. "As pastors, Mpho [Archbishop Tutu's daughter is an Episcopal priest in Washington, DC] and I find one of our roles to be midwives of meaning. We guide those in our care to discern a purpose in their challenges."

There are three kinds of friends: those we cultivate for the sake of the good times they give us, those we seek out for what they can do for us, and those we love for their own sakes.

Aristotle wrote in a vein that sometimes sounds brother-to-Shakespeare across time, in terms of his poetical insight into the psyche. And, regarding the Mother, we can be in relationship to her in all three ways listed above, the last being first.

Holy Mother seen with what were long ago called with respect, "island eyes," is protectoress of health, breath of life. In the islands, she is sometimes called by the same word as "palm frond portico" where tribal healers of the people, Hawai'ian and Samoan, touch-sing over the ill and the distressed. In the Maori tongue, one word for "mother" sounds to my ear like, "Maurii." There are other words in the most beautiful mouths of island people to call her: ocean in which the child is rocked until born; the greater ocean in which all life lives. Holy Mother is fresh, clean-smelling ocean water. Akua tells me the people find plastic anything a "bad food," that makes people sick. Clean blue lagoons and clear air heal. Thus, the Mother is understood by the precious old women here, like other old women all the way across the ocean, understand and entitle her also: Maria Madre, Health of the Sick.

C. P. Estés, notes from speaking with elderly Samoan and Hawai'ian women as we awaited a bus near San Francisco, circa 1975.

[As] our Chinese sisters and brothers prepared to face the tanks . . . the poet-demonstrator completed the message to his mother: "At present, we are all fainting, we may fall any moment. But soon trees of enlightenment will grow up where we fall. Cry not for me, mother. Shed no tears. But do not fail to water the trees with your loving care. Surely god will bless the growth of enlightenment in China that soon will shelter All its people."

Dr. Vincent Harding is professor at Iliff School of Theology. He is a civil rights friend and colleague with Dr. Martin Luther King. Dr. Harding wrote a book called *Hope and History: Why We Must Share the Story of the Movement,* which is about Dr. King, President Obama, and other heroic black Americans. But with typically Hardingesque compassion, he bridges to other cultures too, offering his thesis that we are all one. Thus he shows us the letter of a hunger striker at Tiananmen Square, who calls down, not the army, not the wrath of the gods, but calls on his mother to rise, the spark of venerable Mother residing in his mother, to water the trees of enlightenment should he, the young poet, be murdered—so that all Chinese might one day be free.

Rahulabhadrea's "Hymn to Perfect Wisdom" is one of the masterpieces of Mayayana Buddhism: Homage to Thee, Perfect Wisdom. Boundless, transcending thought, all thy limbs are without blemish faultless those who thee discern. Spotless, unobstructed, silent, like the vast expanse of space; . . . then art Thou, O Blessed Lady, Grandmother thus of beings all. All the immaculate perfections at all times encircle thee, as the stars surround the crescent, O Thou blameless holy one.

Andrew Harvey studied under Hindu, Tibetan Buddhist, and Christian spiritual teachers and has written several translations—interpretations of the Sufi mystical poet Rumi. In his book *The Return of the Mother*, he gives poems and prayers from Hindu, Sufi, Buddhist, and Christian teachers. The above are some of the beautiful—and familiar—praise lines which are given as attributes of Holy Mother, since time out of mind: that she is without blemish, that she is immaculate, that she is spotless, and here, that she is the oldest mother, the Grand one.

Choose a sacred word . . . asking the Holy Spirit to inspire us with one that is especially suitable for us . . . Example: God, Jesus, Abba, Father, Mother, Mary, Amen . . . other possibilities: Love, Listen, Peace, Mercy, Let Go, Silence, Stillness, Faith, Trust.

Father Thomas Keating O.C.S.O., in his book *Open Mind, Open Heart*, gently suggests each person choose a sweet sacred attribute to focus on in "centering prayer," the list of attributes he suggests so closely flowing straight out of the mother lode of compassionate virtues, most of which are touted for centuries as the traits of Holy Mother.

Sally Kempton, in her book *Meditation for the Love of It*, speaks of "the seed of blue light" as carrying the ability to transform all in an instant . . . like the Mother. She explicates the difference between what one might call plastic impressions of shakti/mother as a mere thing, rather than what the shaktis/the mothers really are, a massive impulse that one follows, one that leads into the powers of knowledge, divine will, bliss, witness, and more.

Inadequate love from her mother in early childhood . . . but how to find healing? . . . Her healer may begin by simply placing her hand on her patient's chest . . . extending her awareness into her hand, and then further beyond herself, . . . she can feel, very clearly, the tightness, the congestion, . . . She just rests in this experience. In the course of twenty or thirty minutes, her patient may report that she feels a kind of relief, as if something cool and soothing is developing in her chest.

Reginald Ray, student and friend with the late Tibetan Buddhist master Chögyam Trungpa Rinpoche, in Ray's book *Touching Enlightenment: Finding Realization in the Body*, speaks of how contemporary research validates that a free-flowing relationship between body and mind is how we receive healing and awareness. I was taken with his parallel to ancient hands-on-healing, where the lack of mother in the body, is remedied by the laying on of patient, loving hands. In curanderismo, one would say a healing of a wound made by an earthly mother, is not accomplished by the compassionate healer alone, for she or he is "the hollow bone,"—only the tunnel. Rather it is what stands behind the healer, that is, the force of the Greater Mother who then flows through the blessed passageway of the human mother instinct and intuition.

[My mother] and I have sometimes not known quite what to do with each other . . . she makes me these big pots of soup, and when she leaves sometimes I cry. . . . in Franny and Zooey . . . Franny is lying around having a breakdown, starving herself . . . trying to find something holy in the world . . . and Zooey finally explodes in complete exasperation, crying out . . . that she should simply drink her mother's soup, that her mother's love for them consecrates it, makes it holy soup.

Anne Lamott, in her book *Operating Instructions: A Journal of My Son's First Year*, makes, in her own unique writing style of levity-gravity, the connection between the compassionate generosity of her mother wanting to make nourishing soup for her, and something else, that stands behind that reliable gesture—that the mother can act in ways that are beyond this Earth alone, holy and consecrated in this most simple act.

Father and Mother of Orphans, Planted Law, Truth Speaker, God's Secret Plan, Space between Everything, Through Seer, Attentive Heart, Sacred Wounding, Softener of Our Spirit, The One Sadness, Our Shared Joy . . .

Father Richard Rohr, in his book, *The Naked Now: Learning to See as the Mystics See*, created this "Litany of the Holy Spirit," which contains many of the attributes assigned to holy Sophia, Ruach, Shekhinah, and Maria. Father Rohr says poignantly, in engaging with the Holy, to be curious, not rejecting: ". . . to learn to appreciate and respect these matters in and for themselves, not because they either profit you or threaten you."

I always feel supported by my mother who died four years ago.

Thomas Moore, in his book *A Life at Work: The Joy of Discovering What You Were Born to Do*, wrote the above line in his Acknowledgments. Some are born with the talent, and some learn the skill nonetheless, of being near that which is invisible but palpably felt. In this simple sentence, Moore tells that this organic bridge between the powerful spirit of mother, holds firm for the mother's son. It is not different with Holy Mother. There is a bridge. At its center point, one meets the Other.

Vincent undertook to nurse a victim of a fire in the mine. The man was so badly burned and mutilated that the doctor had no hope for his recovery . . . Van Gogh tended him forty days with loving care and saved the miner's life. Vincent [said Gauguin] "believed in miracles," in maternal care.

Ken Wilber tells this story in *The Eye of Spirit: An Integral Vision for a World Gone Slightly Mad*. This portion of the story brings "the mother in the man" to the fore; the nutritive nurse as healing and unifying principle in a man taken by creative fire of another kind.

Vincent Van Gogh, consummate artist, used his vermilions and violets, his scarlets and gris and cobalts so that up close, his paint marks make no sense whatsoever. They only looked like random slashes of buttery color upon the canvases. But, moving back from those deliciously knifed and brushed marks on Van Gogh's canvases, one can see how each fragment merges with the next and is related to the whole, making a greater reality apparent to us, in depth. I offer that Holy Mother and all matters of time, nature, sense and space—and all the carbon dots who represent us here on earth—are related in a similar kind of atomic-spiritual pattern, the same way Van Gogh's paintings read. Up close, without the farther focus, we seem in chaos. But

through the lens of the farther gaze, that is, a larger sight, we can "read the paint" of our many worlds of consciousness, and our place in them, as an enormous harmonious portrait.

C. P. Estés, in my manuscript *The Creative Fire*, I write about how within the creative work, moving one's focus to either telescopic and magnifying, can reveal "the many ways of creative seeing". . . the meaningful and fragmentary and temporary, but also the meaningfully connected, external and eternal, all at once. It is not by accident that Holy Mother is called a human being in microcosm, and also a magnitude in macrocosm.

In India . . . a great physician and sage named Charaka prescribed some sunlight for all diseases, along with a walk in the early morning, and his advice will never grow stale. If I find a green meadow splashed with daisies and sit down beside a clear-running brook, I have found medicine. It soothes my hurts as well as when I sat in my mother's lap in infancy, because the earth really is my mother, and the green meadow is her lap. You and I are strangers, but the internal rhythms of our bodies listen to the same ocean tides that cradle us in a time beyond memory.

Dr. Deepak Chopra, in *Quantum Healing: Exploring the Frontiers of Mind/Body Medicine,* calls on the spirit of ancient and primal mother to remind of return to health through the ministrations, as he says later in the same piece, of exposing oneself to both mother sun and also mother moon, which also happen to be appellations of Holy Mother: She who shines like the sun, She who is clothed with the sun, and She who stands on the Horns of the Moon. Too, Dr. Chopra relates the greatest peace to "the inherent rhythm" of the first ocean all little zygotes first experience, the oceanic and beautiful warm and perfect-temperatured mother.

Most Reverend John Shelby Spong is a theologian and author of twenty-plus books. He writes in his book *Eternal Life: A New Vision Beyond Religion,* that "Mother Church" and the rise of the cult of the Blessed Virgin were the medieval "breakthroughs" of the feminine, and that today, she is embodied in the peace and environmental movements worldwide. One of his other books entitled *Born of a Woman,* is about Holy Mary and how he sees that the past records of her and her Child, ought be interpreted with the knowledge of our most current times. He is retired Bishop of the Episcopal Church Diocese of Newark, New Jersey.

We deny that which is Eternal when we deny our own depths . . . be passionate, be holy, be wild, be irreverent, to laugh and cry until you awaken the sleeping spirits, until the ground of your being cleaves and the Universe comes flooding in.

Geneen Roth, in *Appetites: On the Search for True Nourishment,* is saying that leading a false life that denies additional realities other than corporeal ones, leads to one ignoring one's own corporeal life and the life of Spirit. This is true with regard to living presence of the Holy, as well, to deny one's being built body and mind for being influenced to the good by forces beyond the concrete, is to deny that the eternal lives everywhere and anywhere, and has your exact address.

. . . those who advance on the spiritual path . . . beyond that level of understanding [of revering and fearing a divine lawmaker and judge, now] . . . are to come to see God as Father, as Mother, Source of all being, in other words, as One who transcends all such images. Thus Ptolemy invites those who previously saw themselves as . . . servants . . . slaves . . . to come to understand themselves as God's children.

Dr. Elaine Pagels, in her book *Beyond Belief: The Secret Gospel of Thomas,* details one of the many ancient appellations of Creator as Mother . . . and as important, the movement of consciousness from a slave relationship in relationship to Creator, which in reality is a brutally unloving relationship of fear, to understanding one's soul and life as a cherished one, one held with the tenderness of a Mother who is far more than mundane.

Here in South Africa, we are plagued by street vendors at every turn . . . I turned to this woman politely refusing her . . . she suddenly beamed the most sweeping, beautiful and heartwarming smile I have ever seen. . . . I knew it came from her very soul. That . . . lifted my heart and touched my very being . . .

Caroline Myss, in *Invisible Acts of Power: Channeling Grace In Your Everyday Life,* telling about a woman who had met more than just another human being in the streets. In the many legends, stories, and witness accounts of Holy Mother, too there are stories of her momentary or sometimes lifelong embodiments in actual human beings, and most always, the first effect is startling and penetrating in a meaningful way.

God's instruction is clear, but with us, it has to first pass through mud.

Thomas Aquinas. This quote attributed to him is one of my favorite maps, for it is true; the clearer the mind and heart, the more swiftly can flow through the ideas, presence, and gravity of the Mother. This reference to mud and clarity might be from writings during his time in Italy when he was speaking about mud being filterable as mud from water, but once fired, became hard and opaque. In any sense, it is a beautiful non-formulaic reminder to be fluid in seeing and being and not half-baked opaque.

One of them painted the toenails of the Blessed Mother that sat on the altar . . .

Dr. Christiane Northrup, physician and author of *Mother–Daughter Wisdom: Understanding The Crucial Link Between Mothers, Daughters, and Health,* has an eye for the quixotic as an element of health. She tells of a girl at a Catholic institution where her mother went to school who seemed to have given a nail-polish pedicure to the statue of Blessed Mother. The decorating of Holy Mother in ways others think honorary and beautiful, is a long tradition across all continents, including hats, shoes, dresses, facial tattoos, markings of many kinds, pierced ears, belts, necklaces, rings, and bracelets. Often the infant-sized Cristocitos from Peru are made with each tiny little toenail painted a cheerful bright red. Some say Holy Mother likes only simple garments. Some say otherwise. It would seem more so, Holy Mother shows up in whatever way people can see her best, understand her most . . . including painted toenails, if this is compatible with the sincere heart and soul.

The feast of Our Lady of Guadalupe with the predawn celebrations are the great affirmation of the new life that she continues to bring about. In the early morning chill of December we experienced the warmth of being together as a united people, almost as if we were one body, one soul, and one heart.

Father Virgil Elizondo, in his book *Charity,* calls the cultural fiestas surrounding La Señora, Nuestra Madre, Our Mother, and other holy events, "the force of our Survival and the source of our Joy." Think of The Mother's teaching: survival in joy, joy in survival, a kind of sunyata of its own: an emptiness which is full, a fullness which is empty. Father Elizondo is a progenitor of the theology of the *mestizaje*, which means a mixing of two or more groups of people, biologically, culturally, and religiously, as many of the peoples of the Americas are today as a result of invaders and conquerings and takeovers. When I met Father Elizondo in San Antonio long ago when I was studying at the Mexican American Cultural Center, we spoke of mestizos (mixed blood people that many of us come from, who are both native and European), and I was clear that here was a man who knew Our Mother and followed her in full heart, not like a lamb, but like a lion.

I am telling you all this now because I want you to know from the outset that I am a normal, rational, well-educated, well adjusted woman not given to delusions, hallucinations, or hysterical flights of fancy. I do not drink or do drugs. The only voice I hear in my head is my own. I want you to know from the outset that I am not a psychologist, an eccentric, a fanatic, or a mystic. I want you to know that I am not a lunatic . . . It all depends, I suppose, on how comfortable you are with uncertainty, how fond you are of mystery, how willing you are to make the quantum leap that faith requires . . . This is definitely a novel, and Mary has never paid me a visit. But, if she ever decides to, I am more than ready and I know exactly what I'll make for lunch.

Diane Schoemperlen, from her novel, *Our Lady of the Lost and Found*, and the last quote is from an interview with the author, as quoted in the *Readers' Guide* to the same work. Her protagonist puts forth, with humor, almost exactly the same kind of "self-examination litany" that many young and older persons go through when first they find that the Holy leaks between the worlds.

[The Hebrew word] Chesed/Love . . . instinctively reaches out to help, heal, teach, feed, and soothe . . . Chesed is likened to the surge that a nursing mother feels when her milk lets down. As any lactating mother knows, milk lets down when the baby's hunger hits, regardless of how far away Mama is, how many bottles Grandma has on hand, or how beautiful the chiffon evening dress she is wearing when the call comes.

Rabbi Tirzah Firestone in her book, *The Receiving: Reclaiming of Women's Wisdom,* describes what she called "the nurturing quality of *Chesed* [built] into our very molecules . . ." This mothering element is what I'd call profound bio-spiritual imperative of mother for her child. Rabbi's words poignantly point to one reason why the intense hiding, over the centuries, of one of the most maternal elements of Holy Mother in art and sculpture—that is, the Holy Lactation—impoverishes us, rather than saves us from anything. Rabbi speaks of the Love that is without boundaries in the Holy, and that we as women and our lover-mates too, witness this spark of the divine way of loving the innocent and hungry. Rabbi points out further that being in full rooted relationship with the underlying Tree of Life, makes it so the divine spark does not become depleted.

[I painted] Traditional Madonna and child side by side . . . [It is the] image of a Latina mother cradling her fallen gang member son.

George Yepes, mural artist painting down in rough and tough East Los Angeles, specializes in yards and yards of linear feet of murals outdoors and inside buildings. This is his commentary on his mural called "El Tepeyac de Los Angeles," which covers the front of Saint Lucy's Catholic Church, in City Terrace, California. Many of his paintings are—not "portraying,"— that would be too weak a word: Rather this muralist is illumining Holy Mother in the ways she is most get-down real to so many who live in grit and endless backbreaking labor to carve, clean, consecrate daily life in all decency, whether the over-culture agrees or not. *El maestro* Yepes is the painter of *La Nuestra Señora Guadalupe* on the cover of this book.

The Irony of writing about such an experience in the modern era is such that, if I say to people, "This really happened," not unreasonably, they will be inclined to doubt me. They might suspect me of boasting or assume that I have lost my mind. If I say, "I imagined it, I made it up, it's fiction"—only then are they free to believe it . . . I used to feel the dissonance whenever I heard Mary described as both Virgin and Mother; she seemed to set an impossible standard for any woman. But, this was narrow-minded on my part. What Mary does is to show me how I indeed can be both virgin and mother. Virgin to the extent that I remain "one-in-myself," able to come to things with newness of heart; mother to the extent that I forget myself in the nurture and service of others, embracing the ripeness of maturity

that this requires. This Mary is a gender-bender; she could do the same for any man.

Kathleen Norris, wrote these words in *Amazing Grace: A Vocabulary of Faith,* wherein she speaks of how via various means, cultural, and otherwise, people are often robbed of—not "believing"—but *knowing,* and instead are given to superstition about spiritual facts, rather than the simple holiness for the good to be found inside each person. She also does a beautiful mending of polarized duality, saying one need not be stuck in an either/or, having to somehow choose one side or another. Rather as I read her work, she suggests an and/and, meaning one can choose both ends of a spectrum as a woman. Too, she casts her net toward men, with the inference that one can be a father and a virgin also . . . a person/soul to and within himself, as well as a father who leans out the window of soul and ministers to others in meaningful ways.

Rabbi Zushya . . . once said: My mother didn't pray from a prayer book, because she couldn't read. But she knew how to recite all the blessings by heart . . . In the lower worlds, in "creation," God's Presence is the Shekhinah. Here on earth, the Shekhinah, The Divine Spouse, Who is our Divine Mother, is in Exile, just as in the world of Atzulut our Divine Father is in Exile. The Shekhinah is held prisoner in innumerable little sparks, awaiting redemption at our hand. Whenever a minyan is convened where She is: "She radiates so powerfully that an angel, even from the highest of angelic hierarchies, would be annihilated."

Rabbi Dr. Zalman Schachter-Shalomi, writes these words in his book: *Wrapped in a Holy Flame: Teachings and Tales of the Hasidic Masters,* Nataniel M. Miles-Yepez, editor. First he speaks of the accessible earthy mother who is a sweet thrower of sparks in the ancient oral tradition: one who can say the prayers, even though she cannot read: The essence of the Holy can be carried by anyone of sincere heart. Then, Rebbe tell us that the very idea of "the highest of angelic hierarchies, would be annihilated" in the presence of Divine Mother. We've observed she is often reduced by some, to a mere idea but without the numen, and without the living incandescent lumens. Yet Rebbe offers atomic truth enough to make the ego faint from sensing such huge magnitude of Blessed Mother . . . and as ego is down for the count, thus Soul can again be fully born into full consciousness again in those moments . . . a taste of the Greater reality that Soul seeks and knows it when it sees it. After, though the numen can wear away, be corroded or forgotten in the day-to-day of groceries, car repair and work, that witness to the fact of her magnitude . . . that even the highest angels would be made into atomic dust were they to behold her in all her glory . . . that is ground note, touchstone of the reality of Holy Mother. Our Holy Mother. We belong to her. She belongs to us. No small tenet can hold her. No admonition high or low, can keep us from her. As is meant.

Claribel Alegria, great exemplar of the protective Mother, was born in 1924. She is allied as a non-violent protestor against dictators and their armies in wars in El Salvador and Nicaragua. Writer of many books I'd call "witness-poetry," in her poem entitled *Salí a buscarte*, she speaks of going out over mountains and seas, *"asking of the clouds/and the wind"* the whereby and wherefore of the central heart of Being. She says such a sojourn was useless, for *"You were within me."* One of her books is called *Saudade,* translated by Carolyn Forché. This word *saudade* has no direct translation, rather is a cry from the heart. Alegria's *"saudade:"* it is a kind of "pain for home". . . the moment, even during joys, when we can still suddenly remember loved ones who are lost or missing yet. Just as we can have *"saudade"* for Holy Mother—pain for home with her. In all, *La Claribel, mi Alegria,* repeats endlessly in 29,000 forms that Life with the true Center of sheltering Mother, even in the face of death, is worth everything.

The West remains so out of touch with its own mystical tradition . . . Carl Jung warned us that ". . . we westerners cannot be pirates thieving wisdom from foreign shores that it has taken them centuries to develop—as if our own culture was 'an error outlived.'" There is great wisdom in Western spiritual traditions, but this needs a new birth . . . the crises we find ourselves in as a species require that as a species we shake up all our institutions . . . reinvent them.

Reverend Matthew Fox, priest and theologian of Creation Spirituality, in his book *Christian Mystics, 365 Readings and Meditations,* one amongst his thirty books, says "Change is necessary for our survival . . . and we often turn to the mystics at critical times like this. Jung said "only the mystics brings what is creative . . ." Rev. Fox holds that the mystic is not a rare bird, but rather an ordinary person with extraordinary insights and sincere and brave inquiries into the mysteries of our universe . . . and protection of our universe.

Demetria Martinez, poet, activist-heart, also expresses her beliefs in *el santuario movimiento*, to aid those souls, as I'd put it, who attempt "to cross [the border]," without being "nailed to the cross." She often writes with tender-anger about how the holy freshet that flows is cemented over gradually, more and more until "how it was once," regarding fresh-born understanding about Creator and Theotekos, Mother of God, is only dry weedy "filter," no longer sacred materia. In one of her poems, "Untitled," she speaks of how the numinous names of the Mystical ones, including Holy Mother, have been made clinical, and have, over time, been *"smoked down to a stub."* She notes another truth: that when a culture no longer has a word for Light, *"we live in shadows."* Her inference is that the opposite is blessedly true: when we have many words for She Who Shines Like the Sun, the Mother Who Is and Who Brings Light, we no longer live small and in narrowed consciousness.

Every time the incrustations of an overly established Christianity have been broken open, the faith has spread . . . increasing exponentially . . . [in] reach as a result of its time of unease and distress. Thus, for example, the birth of Protestantism not only established a new powerful way of being Christian, but it also forced Roman Catholicism to make changes in its own structures and praxis.

Phyllis Tickle on how more fresh, vivid forms of understanding the sacred and holy, emerge after having become deadened by various means . . . and then spread in fresh ways with new practices, that do not merely "allow," but give birth to true life in spirit and soul. This, from her chapter entitled with her signature serious historian intelligence garnished with humor, "Rummage Sales: When the Church Cleans Out Its Attic," in her book *The Great Emergence: How Christianity is Changing and Why.*

Israel, one of the doormen in my building, was beside himself. Israel is Puerto Rican. It was winter. What had just happened? "I seen J.Lo. On the street!" he whispered. "And I seen her and she just went like this." And he put his finger

to his lips, "Sssh." He was practically blushing. "I said, 'Cool. Cool.' And she just walked on by; I was like, 'I got you covered. Cool,'" he said. His eyes were twinkling. "That woman," he said emphatically, "There needs to be a picture of her in the dictionary beside the words 'Latin woman'!"

Anna Deavere Smith, consummate actor, tells this dear story in her book *Letters to a Young Artist, Straight Up Advice on Making a Life in the Arts— For Actors, Performers, Writers, and Artists of Every Kind*. She was speaking about physical aura, that is, presence, and relayed this story about Israel, who is a so humble man, still touchingly capable of awe in what I'd call "the presence of presence." Miss Deavere Smith goes on to say: "Presence doesn't have to do with likeability. . . . Often people who have presence know that *you* are there before you know *they* are there." This last, a perfect description of charismatic human presence, but even more so, describing the mystical Presence of Holy Mother when she appears . . . she is aware of souls often long before they are aware of her. And it is often the most humble and sweet, like Israel, who "perceive her best" would be the wrong phrase, for she belongs to everyone—but rather who protect her best, seriously move to preserve her beautiful essence.

[We have the custom in our tribe] for the pregnant mother's neighbors to visit her every day and take her little things, no matter how simple. They stay and talk to her . . .

Rigoberta Menchu Tum, of the K'iche' tribal group of Mayans, Nobel Peace Prize awardee, and survivor of the horrendous killing wars of *los indios* in Guatemala. Here she speaks so tenderly about how a mother is recognized as a special being, gently tended to within the tribal groups, remembered daily, not left alone. This is how Our Lady is often seen across the Americas; as ever about to give birth to the Divine Child of Love, and so worthy of being visited every day, brought a little "something" . . . like a flower petal, a special stone, a ribbon, a string . . . being spoken to every day, spent time with, kept company. When Rigoberta and I worked together at Peace Jam, we talked about "The Black Time" in Guatemala, the slaughter of the tribes. I'd been a witness to far too much of this horror in the 1960s and 1970s. But we suddenly began to speak about *las madres y La Madre Grande* . . . how Holy Mother was often the solace for the mothers and fathers of los desaparecidos, the "disappeared," who were torn from their cornfields, or kidnapped on the dusty dirt road on the way to market, and never seen again. Still and now, amongst other saintly watching over, it is understood in true heart that Holy Mother sees all and has cared for and tended to all who have been so egregiously routed and taken. Sees them, still. Holds them, still. Holds their hurt families, still. They speak to her. Daily. Still he speaks back to their hearts. Still.

. . . My daughter . . . fourteen, had an after-school job . . . I spotted her right away, kneeling on the floor in the toothpaste section, stocking a bottom shelf . . . I noticed two middle-aged men walking along the aisle toward her. They looked like everybody's father. They had moussed hair, and they wore knit sport shirts the color of Easter eggs . . . My daughter did not see them coming . . . the men stopped, peering down at her. One man nudged the other. He said, "Now that's how I like to see a woman— on her knees." The other man laughed.

Sue Monk Kidd, in her book, *The Dance of the Dissident Daughter: A Woman's Journey from Christian Tradition to the Sacred Feminine*, speaks of how she confronted the men accosting her daughter. We recently heard similar words, as WOW, the Women in White, mostly elder women, peacefully protested the walling over of the huge folk mural of *La Lupita*, at Our Lady of Guadalupe Parish . . . A man screamed at the praying women: "The only place for Mary is on her knees at the foot of the cross!!" Miss Monk Kidd too, is a stand-up hermanita: regarding the two men saying similar words to her daughter, she said she felt the words forming in her, "unstoppable by any earthly force". . . and she defended her daughter, telling the men, "You may like to see her and other women on their knees but we don't belong there. *We don't belong there.*" Her dear daughter was blessed for life, no matter what else, by her mother then. And, surely the mother was taken up and blessed with words by the Mother in those moments too, for She is the one who is indeed, "unstoppable by any earthly force."

[About those who are too grim and stuffy, let those] . . . who make life difficult for their fellow human beings and themselves . . . be given rather more genuine joy in life. . . . For me especially, that includes joy in nature. I got this from my mother; I can still hear her voice in my ears: "Look how beautiful it is . . ."

Father Hans Küng, in his book *What I Believe*, says that "there are people, even educated people, who get no enjoyment from nature." He says that it was his mother who tuned his ears, who focused his eyes and senses to beauty and the joy of beauty. I don't doubt his mother was a great "church" in and of herself for teaching the most acute form of Holy Mother Love, gratitude and joy in all creation. Father Küng is professor of ecumenical theology at the University of Tübingen, and says that when a fine scientist would reduce nature to biological stats, to chemistry only, then the luminosity, the radiance, the joy of holy Creation is missed completely.

. . . how we are affected by historical fluctuations: We stretch the limits to . . . convey our views of the world and the spiritual status of our consciousness. For the last three years this feeling of Constant vs. Change has been accentuated by current events, war, age, menopause, relationships, and each other. I need the ancient icons of my Mexicanidad *to keep me focused. [This] allows conveying feelings of freedom, incarceration, capture, redemption and wonder . . . The fleeting illusion of "capturing what can never be captured."*

Maruca Salazar, artist, arts educator, Veracruzaña, Executive Director of Museo de las Americas in Denver, Colorado, is speaking here about collaborating in artworks which for her often include "boxed" art with tiny statues of the holy people and saints, including La Señora de Guadalupe. She speaks particularly about what underlies our sense of images throughout the centuries, and how one sees differently, depending on what stage of life one is in, what challenges one faces, what happinesses . . . that all these inform one's way of seeing what cannot be seen with eyes alone, knowing what cannot be known by brain alone. She speaks of falling in with the living, fully alive, "mysterious mysteries." For her, Holy Mother and all that underlies the sacred *Mexicanidad* is vital memory. For her, the ever-changing ways of seeing spirit, mean "home is ever where the art is." I think of her beautiful words, their oppositions of "imprisoned" and "free,"—a long-standing set of metaphors amongst those in love with Holy Mother.

We too, can be captured in good ways in the thrall of the Holy, and also saved from the ego's superstitions and the cultures' derogations, all at once thereby. This phenomenon of being captured and freed at the same time are experiences that many report when living near and with Holy Mother, who it is said in our native heritage in Mexico, "captured" the Child of Love via her pregnancy, the little divine prisoner who is then set free in the world to do

goodness, to teach, to tell of the worlds within worlds. We too: Incarcerated, captured, freed, redeemed, reborn, practicing resurrection all in one wonderment: The Mother-Heart. So may it be for us all.

C. P. Estés

CHAPTER TWENTY-FOUR

Aymen, Aymen, Aymen . . . And a Little Woman

The Highest Prayer

Long ago, I wrote a poem that carries my grandmother's eccentric ending to her prayers that blessed and comforted and gave rest to we who prayed with her: "Aymen, aymen, aymen . . . and a little woman." Aymen/Amen, means "as it will be," or "may it be so," or "so it shall be," or "so be it."

Aymen and Amen could be said in any number of tones and in a number of places, including while walking around the fields saying "Aymen, Aymen, Aymen," meaning, "Grow flowers! Grow corn! Grow wheat! Grow cayenne!" It could also be used to chastise and pin another into new behavior: ". . . and you will stay put and not do that again. Aymen Aymen." And it could be said to love people forward: "May you be watched over always. Aymen Aymen Aymen."

LEARNING TO PRAY THE HIGHEST PRAYER

I learned from the Church, if one
says a perfect rosary,
one will receive a reprieve
from the usual sentence in Purgatory.

I learned from my grandmother—
herself a great and simple church—
if one creates a prayer of poetry,
heaven will send for you by name,
bypassing all theological detours . . .
for God so treasures poets.

It was night.
We were kneeling,
saying our prayers together:
old aunties, uncles,
daddies, mommies, children,
and one old, old one.

It sounded like this:
"Hail Mary full of grace," we intoned.
But grandmother said under her breath,
Hello, my most holy Sister.
(It sounded like this: Elo miy most holeh see-stair.)
You are so filled with the light of God
(Djou air so feeled wit te leet oav Goad)
I can hardly bear to look at you.
Soften your light just a little
so I can see you more clearly Dear One.

And we droned on,
"The Lord is with thee,
blessed art thou amongst women . . ."
and grandmother whispered,
You were pregnant with the Lord,
oh the glory day of it all!
You are filling my womb
with holiness as we speak.

And we bleated onward,
". . . blessed is the fruit of thy womb, Jesus."
Grandmother went on,
Oh my dearest sister,
I am so sorry you had to give birth
with only the poor animals,

your poor distraught husband,
with only the night sky to hold you,
for, What did Joe know?

I know this feeling, and I commiserate.
If I had been there, I would have held
your thighs for you, cut the cord
of our beloved baby Jesus.

We bellowed on into the home stretch,
". . . Holy Mary, Mother of God, pray for us sinners . . ."
Grandmother murmured,
Oh, my sins are many my sister,
but without your love
they would have been so many more;
if not for you, for your advice,
for your great love for women such as me.

Then, we began the final bugle,
crashing now into the finale
like moose in rut:
". . . now and at the hour of our death, Aymen!"
Grandmamma was still whispering:
I have had many hours of death in this lifetime.
Without you my sister, my mother, my child,
I would never have known that pain, joy,
and strength are one.
You gave birth to me over and over again.
You are not the mother of all life; you are life itself.
Thank you for my life my Child, my Sister, my Mother.

Aymen for now, says your old daughter, Katerin.
Aymen . . . and a little woman.

Notes

INTRODUCTION **Opening Blessing:** *Totus Tuus,* **I Belong to You, Blessed Mother**

1. **Blessed Mother Blessing:** This is a prayer I pray every day along with the Angelus. As I lift all the dear brave souls up, so Creator, Jesu Cristo and La Señora can see what is most needed by each to lead them. I ask particularly of Blessed Mother that all souls be given signs, angels to walk with them, directions, for strengths, and grace in ways they can understand and immediately put to good use.

CHAPTER TWO **Untie the Strong Woman**

1. **Imitatio Maria:** In imitation of the Mother, who in ancient tradition accepted without knowing her destiny to become the God-bearer. This means, as well, to live *Totus tuus,* as totally hers: to inquire of her wishes for us, her instructions to us, her problem-solving on our behalf, her surprising insights, her opening of doors, her intercessions with Creator and with her Child.

2. **"One-Eye, Two-Eyes, and Three-Eyes"** is an idiosyncratic folk tale told by the Magyar people of my families. It is about seeing the world without seeing the soul (one eye); seeing what everyone else sees with no amazement attached (two eyes); and seeing in uncommonly brave or insightful ways. In other words, it is about seeing the worlds of soul, spirit, and matter as all interwoven (three eyes).

   In the tale, people are tested by an angel in the disguise of an old woman who asks merely for a drink of cool water from the farmers' "deepest wells."

Those who scorn her plea experience sudden negative changes to their bodily functions and to inanimate objects nearby—thus revealing how those who scorn are, in fact, put together inwardly.

Those who willingly fetch water for the "angel in disguise" are rewarded too, by sudden beautiful changes to voice, senses, and surroundings—these revealing outwardly how those who serve are also in fact put together inwardly at heart.

The transformative aspect of the tale is found in the characters who failed to recognize the angel/old woman the first time, but who plead to be given another chance to care for her more generously, more consciously, the next time.

Unlike many nineteenth-century tales overwritten into "punishment tales" only—"what's done is done and no more chances for you"—in this venerable tale, more chances are ever given: for the old woman is the angel of generosity and carries love for the soul. She is, herself, the Great Woman. Many of the old tales told in our family have at center a radiant woman reminiscent of the folk tellers' many generations of memories about Holy Mother.

CHAPTER THREE **The Drunkard and The Lady**

1. **G!d:** This is a beautiful poetic of the Hebrew way of writing G-d—which is done out of respect. Rabbi Zalman Schacter told me the middle letter in his estimation, since Creator is so—well—creative, could be an exclamation point. I loved the exuberance inferred. And when I told this to the stone-mason who came to help me, it put a lilt in the mind, to lifting of heart, to imagine this way—a kind of joyous mishmash (?) in one beauty word: G!d.

2. This treatment of the indigenous people of Mexico continued for hundreds of years after the conquest. Mexico was a slaver's dream as more Africans were captured and forced to Mexico than ever were forced to all of North America. Add to this the Palacio de la Inquisición, a grand palace built by forced slave labor, in what is now the city of Mexico, in order to execute and burn alive at la quemadera, the burning place, invader-clerics who dared to speak truth or justice to the thousands and thousands of native people over the course of nearly 200 years.

3. In Spanish, we often make an affectionate diminutive of an English or Spanish word by adding *cito,* which means variously, little, dearest, and more.

CHAPTER SIX **The *Memorare,* Remember!**

1. **(And a little woman . . .):** For explication of this ending, please
   see Chapter Twenty-Four, The Highest Prayer.

CHAPTER SEVEN **The Use of the Seven Swords Through The Heart**

1. **"Mater Dolorosa: The Unruined Heart"** ™© 2000, C. P. Estés,
   all rights reserved.

   Prayer Meditation from *La Curandera: Healing in Two Worlds,*
   forthcoming, Texas A & M University Press. Traditionally in the
   Roman Catholic Church, the Sorrowful Heart is understood as
   carrying the seven sorrows of Mary's life on earth. I wrote this prayer
   as I conversed with Our Lady during a time of great piercings in
   my own life. There is no such thing as learning to be whole without
   being tested. Staggering about in pain or bewilderment we are
   learning the choice: to be bitter . . . or to surrender to love.

CHAPTER EIGHT **"Our Lady Behind the Wall"**

1. Throughout this book I use the words Latino, Latina, to
   mean persons from many parts of the world who speak a Latin-
   based language, Spanish in particular, but also Portuguese
   and other languages. Minority and majority groups name
   and rename themselves as they see fit over time. So, we have
   called ourselves Hispanos from Northern New Mexico, and
   the San Luis Valley of Colorado, and Mejicanos from Mexico,
   and there are other words that people use to name themselves
   when they are from other parts of Central and South America,
   the islands of the Caribbean, parts of Europe and Africa.
   Some in the United States, call themselves Chicanos which is
   a movement for justice. Some call themselves Compas, and
   others call themselves Hispanics, which is actually a word
   created by the government census in an effort to create a
   banner word under which many Spanish-speaking people
   could be noted by language of origin. There are also Cholos,
   Vatas y Vatos, Pachucas and other tribal/philosophical groups
   within many Latin-based language communities. Groups often
   name themselves progressively. As time goes on, as struggles are
   engaged, status quos challenged, goals accomplished, thereby
   the names of the group often change—new ones are added,
   old ones may be retired for a time or for all time. In all, groups
   tend to prefer to name themselves rather than be named by

others. This is why I am glad to call each person by whichever heart affiliation they would like, remembering ever that our Holy Mother calls all of us by one name only: Beloved Son, Beloved Daughter.

2. Channel 9 News KUSA (NBC affiliate), A year later, group still wants religious mural of Our Lady of Guadalupe shown, Deborah Sherman, November 23, 2010

Denver Daily News, Church mural frustration grows: Religious procession planned as protest to mural being removed that has significance to Latino community, Peter Marcus, November 23, 2010

Denver Daily News, Mural madness: Group outraged that church won't help police investigate vandalism, Gene Davis, March 11, 2011

The Denver Post, Faithful uprising for Virgin of Guadalupe mural's return, October 1, 2010

The Denver Post, Vandalism of mural of Virgin Mary won't be investigated, Electra Draper, March 10, 2011

El Semanario, Would Jesus hide his mother?, Magdalena Gallegos, June 2, 2010

El Semanario, Disrespect provokes protest, Ramon Del Castillo, June 24, 2010

El Semanario, Straight from my heart: La familia, Magdalena Gallegos, July 22, 2010

El Semanario, Spirit of Guadalupe reins in community, Ramon Del Castillo, December 2, 2010

El Semanario, Hiding of Guadalupe saddens community, December 9, 2010

El Semanario, Straight from my heart: What kind of Church is this?, Magdalena Gallegos, March 10, 2011

El Semanario, Straight from my heart: The last straw, Magdalena Gallegos, April 7, 2011

National Catholic Reporter, Denver Catholics fight to restore Guadalupe mural, Dennis Coday, October 14, 2010

3. **Those who fail to recall their history**: Below is the beautiful quote in context from philosopher Jorge Agustín Nicolás Ruiz de Santayana y Borrás, also known as George Santayana. This means that change is not progress unless it also retains what once was of goodness. To make change alone without the heartbeat of the past is to infantilize all, to keep all ignorant of deleterious matters that occurred in the past that might be prevented or mediated in the present, were the memory of

them present to all. *"Progress, far from consisting in change, depends on retentiveness. When change is absolute there remains no being to improve and no direction is set for possible improvement: and when experience is not retained, as among savages, infancy is perpetual. Those who cannot remember the past are condemned to repeat it."*

4. This letter is one of the most potent of prison prophecies written by those of visionary hearts who were unjustly incarcerated but nonetheless writing and smuggling their words out to the world to help, hold and uplift others. From San Juan de La Cruz (Saint John of the Cross) to Nelson Mandela in our times, there are literally hundreds of names belonging to those who write from prison not to plead their case, but to make the case for others to be uplifted, to be treated justly and well. *Letter from Birmingham City Jail,* is also known as *The Negro Is Your Brother.* This letter was written from city jail in Birmingham, Alabama, on April 16, 1963, by Martin Luther King, Jr. He was incarcerated there after arrest for a planned non-violent protest against racial segregation enforced by the city's government and merchant businesses. Dr. King's letter was smuggled out of jail in a toothpaste tube.

The letter is a response to eight white Alabama clergymen who publicly agreed that social injustices existed for Negroes, but insisted the battle against racial segregation should be fought politely behind closed doors, that is, in the courts, not in the streets. Typical of those trying to hold power, they called King an "outside agitator" who made trouble where there needed to be no trouble over anything. To this, King wrote, "Injustice anywhere is a threat to justice everywhere. We are caught in an inescapable network of mutuality, tied in a single garment of destiny. Whatever affects one directly, affects all indirectly... Anyone who lives inside the United States can never be considered an outsider ..."

King said his group was using nonviolent direct action in order to cause tension that would force the wider community to face the issue head on. They hoped to create a nonviolent tension needed for growth. King responded that without nonviolent forceful direct actions, true civil rights could never be achieved.

The white clergymen disapproved of the timing of the demonstration. King wrote that, "This 'Wait' has almost always meant 'Never.'" King said that they had waited for these God given rights long enough and that "justice too long delayed is justice denied."

5. **Forward for Our Lady**: I have been, perhaps you too have been puzzled when throughout history, opposing sides all claim God is on their side only. Sometimes we humanlings make God far too small. What I prefer to understand instead—and this is why I like Dr. King's exhortation to spiritually self-examine oneself before one launches out into the ether—is that "We are with God. We are with Holy Mother." In other words, our choosing to be "with," means we've managed to not be mired in a far less than divine spark, but to instead stand in and be with the most of the Most, the most creative, the most loving, the most peaceful—and the most determined.

CHAPTER ELEVEN **How the Motherfuckers Became the Blessed Mothers**

1. I told this story using the word "kid," for in our family dialect, a kit and a kid were both names for baby lambs, kittens, and children, even though in standard English, a kid is a goat (much later in life learned).

    We also called green bell peppers, mangoes, and named sundry other creatures, foods, and environs by words I would learn only much later and oft times being called down by others, I would in embarrassment, find that the larger culture used different words for the same things. Eventually, I could see the richness in using many from each, when useful.

CHAPTER TWELVE **The Great Woman Appears to Us Daily**

1. **La Madre, Nuestra Señora, Our Mother, continues**: Sometimes, when I've been on tour to other countries and cities, people ask about Blessed Mother figuratives they've heard have been seen on a tortilla, or about a Blessed Mother-shaped rainbow on a glass building. I do not know that I can gauge all others' experiences. All I know is that Our Lady shows up in ways that have meaning to those who apprehend her.

    I note that media often ridicules or scorns such manifestations. But I think one would have to speak to the people who find meaning there and see what they think firsthand, and weigh it not with a skeptic's heart, but with an open one. I sometimes paraphrase what my own grandmothers said in words like these: "If the message is good, keep it close and work to understand it. If you sense it is not for goodness' sake, then discard it and travel onward. There are many stops on this rail line, many chances to see what can and must be seen, thought, and understood all for the sake of Love."

CHAPTER THIRTEEN **Litany of the Mother Road: Chant of Her Incandescent Names**

1. **Three huge landmasses:** Presently, many geographers divide planet Earth into regions, no longer called "continents." Divided by landmass, there are said to be eight regions: Asia; the Middle East and North Africa; Europe; North America; Central America and the Caribbean; South America; Africa; and Australia and Oceania. It is beautiful to learn that Blessed Mother is known across every one of these enormous landmasses, within all nations and tribes enfolded within each geographic region, and within all manner of families and individuals enfolded within those nations and tribes. She is known everywhere. And often her little Divine Child, as well.

CHAPTER FOURTEEN **Post-Abortion Compassion: "The Children She Got That She Did Not Get . . ."**

1. Recently, a bishop-administrator gave an interview saying, "If . . . youth are willing to go to war and lay their lives down to defend our freedoms, then every bishop should be willing to give up his life, if it meant putting an end to abortion." This took many aback—a bishop-administrator's personalized call for a seeming pre-planned martyrdom for himself and other bishops. It raised many eyebrows, for authentic martyrdom is usually not a do-it-yourself, pre-planned event that I know about.

   The insights and attitudes of our times have to change. Especially amongst leaders, for it seems against life itself, for any prelate to be suggesting his own self-martyrdom when there are legions of already injured and untended souls everywhere to help who are fully alive and needing deep and conscious care. One tiny life already lost, then a second life injured and ignored, while a third life arranges martyrdom? Madness.

2. **Rituals for cleansing the wound of child loss through abortion:** I've prepared many a ritual and offered this to mothers, fathers, grandparents, siblings who grieve having known a souls was trying to come through, but had to turn back. I'd offer here a frame to be filled however you wish, in whatever ways are meaningful and useful to the soul of the mother/father. Many would like to hold ritual out of doors. Some might sit near or in a holy circle of one's choice, or near running water or with an open bowl of water, surrounded with objects from one's life or those provided by a loving other person . . .

these representing the past, the present and one's future life. One might choose those that feel protective and kind to the woman's (and man's) heart. Some like to take off their shoes and sometimes more clothing than that.

Most of all "being with" is the way to hold the holy close. A person can be with others with similar events in life, and their stories often enrich one another. Or one can be with however many one chooses, or not any at all.

Calling on the entrance of the Holy, and/or through Blessed Mother to help in whichever way each person understands best, comes next. Thence, much listening to the story of how all came about, appreciations, regrets, remorse, sense of self.

Then, a small token. Sometimes I have offered a number of items a person can choose from, a soft felt bib, a tiny sleeping baby token that has been decorated, choice of holy cards of Blessed Mother, an image of a bird, an angel, a butterfly, paper to write a hand-written letter as one chooses, or write the name of one's child if one wishes, and various other symbolic things that a person can choose to hold the door between the worlds open while speaking, thinking, being in ways one's spirit feels called to.

A person may want to speak much or little, or not at all. Silence is one of the many languages of Holy Mother, and all will be well in quietude also. The work will progress because holiness has been called to enter, whether one remarks on it or not. The simple way is often the most meaningful. Planting something that will grow in memory of that which is eternal. Placing a treasure of some kind, a simple token of one's love however one wishes, a letter handwritten, a special stone that is symbolic of "earth returned to earth" in sympathy.

One can kneel or sit or stand or dance as one wishes. One can bury, not memory, but ask earth to enclose with tenderness this part of one's life, to hold this sweetness and loss gently and with love. To wash the wound in essence of the Mother, her holy earth. Too, one can bring an image of Holy Mother to leave there or to witness there with oneself. If one weeps, one can weep their tears over the earth there, watering whatever green thing or whatever blessing peace has been given to Earth now to grow there in the name of all. One can just ask in all simplicity that Blessed Mother who knows what to do, who has been ever with us and waiting for us to come to this healing moment, knows what to do. We can ask Holy Mother to please, in our behalf between heaven and earth, deliver our messages for us, to just the right address. We can ask Blessed Mother to give us a sign of her blessing on us, and to take it from here.

3. As one of my friends says, who daily sees the challenges and sufferings of children whose fathers impregnated their mothers, and then left without ever supporting the children: "Planters of seed have to start caring about where it lands." This is true. Specific and ongoing dialogue about these matters certainly occurs between elders and younger men, not as a lecture, but as a character building, ongoing supportive conversation with those the young men look up to. But there need to be far more men involved with young men. I'd just mention the words "millions" more. And far fewer barriers to these discussions. If these matters cannot be discussed at school other than in bio science, which is cut off from young men's feeling and personal experience, if they cannot be discussed at church in honest not hortatory discussion, where can our young men receive these vital transmissions? While women have their own consciousness or lack of same that must be dealt with, here we speak about young men in particular. A father doesn't have to be the same bloodline, rather any honorable man who sets the bar: that it is the mark of a true man to not recklessly nor otherwise impregnate a woman or women, until such is "meant" and the man has the skills to be a "forever father" to his children, and to support them to the best of his ability. The phenomena of men, young and otherwise, who roll about laying down children on as many women as possible because of "male pride," but then abandoning the children and their mothers, appears to be a profound spiritual illness with a huge human price. "What it means to be a man," may not be the question. It may be, "What makes a person faithful to what endures in himself, what is not hurried, what rests on holy ground first and foremost?" There are many issues to this issue, and I ever look to bold men of good heart to lead the way.

4. **"The Mother," by Miss Gwendolyn Brooks:** Born in 1917, she passed from this world in the year 2000. She was the first African American to win a Pulitzer Prize for poetry, and was a winner of a Guggenheim and inducted into the National Women's Hall of Fame, and held many other honors. Yet, she was as earthy and down to earth a woman as one could ever hope to meet; a gentleness about her, along with a fierce set of eagle eyes that saw the larger picture

and the small details all around her. Her poetry books are several, including *Bronzeville.*

CHAPTER SIXTEEN **God Has No Hands: Comforting María,
The Ritual of *Pésame***

1. **little *testudo*, little refugio like a turtle's shell:** The shell of the *tortuga*, the turtle, especially the big sea turtles that wash ashore along the playas in Mexico, are sometimes used as the grotto in which to place an image of La Mujer Grande, The Blessed Mother. There is a reason for this that can be understood archetypally . . . as a way of seeing how to live in, and also for protection of, the softest most critical parts of the psyche and soul . . .

   I'd put it to you this way: soft on one side, hard and durable on the other side. That would be Our Lady and her example to us. The shell of the turtle, the shell of the marble statue, the shell of prayer, are understood as ways to animate our abilities to see that we can, despite all else, stand with such sturdiness against corrosive elements in the overculture.

   This ideal is evident in ancient times too, for the "testudo" was also a way of arming oneself, with shields held overhead, interlocking with all other los soldados y las soldadas, male and female soldiers, in order to run with a protected "shell of shields" overhead toward fortification, or away from fireballs and arrows dropping from the sky. Ancient wisdom for modern souls.

CHAPTER EIGHTEEN **The "Oh Yes, There Is Too Room for You Here"
Ritual of *La Posada***

1. ***El Cristo de La Llave* ex-voto:** The bowers on both side of the Cristocito are filled with locks. I think there are eight of them, for Posada ritual often turns away the Love of the World eight times. The lock and the key are ancient symbols of fertility and childbearing, not only because of one carrying the shape of the treasure casque and one being of the phallic shape, but more so, that these are ancient ideas of hope and holding new life together.

   I made this altarpiece/artpiece as an ex-voto to supplicate and ask Our Lady's intercession for fertility for those who desired to be pregnant, those who longed for a child, but felt "locked out" or not able to "hold within." I am happy to report that in many who've seen this ex-voto, this vigil keeper, such longings have been answered. And I love this little Cristocito with his big wide-awake eyes and his little dress and red painted toenails.

In making this prayer-piece, I was asking, What is a lock? Only to keep a door fastened so what is inside does not fall out? Yes, but also sometimes a lock for privacy. Some locks are filigreed, ornate, with chains, to show that what is here, is loved and treasured. Sometimes, an airlock is created to make a vestibule, a room of a certain pressure, so that one is gradually acclimated to a new way of being, thence, once pressure is equalized, to be born through another door from which the lock has been removed.

Also a lock is a short section of a waterway in which the water level can be raised or lowered by the use of sluices, gates, and temporary damming ... this used to raise and lower a vessel over a span of water that otherwise would be too shallow to pass over.

So, a lock is to hold something, embrace something, equalize something, hold tight to something, and to unlock is to allow something to travel forth, creating conditions just right for the going forth, regardless of the lay of the land. And this felt like a perfect set of attributes to ask for new life for anyone who longs for good in any form.

I also kept in my mind as I worked, What is a key? Often a small, forged shape made of material from the earth, from metal. The metal is cut with flanges or little metal wings to insert in the lock. Inside the lock where matters are hidden, the flanges turn the tumblers so the block that holds the door closed, retreats, and the pathway is either closed tight or else opened for people to enter. A key is also used to tune an instrument, and also a key is an idea or system of thought applied in order to solve a problem or decode a hieroglyph. Some keys are simple as a bolt passed through two rings to hold the vessel shut.

And this is good, too. In the making of walls, the key is the first layer of plaster frosted over between the laths so the subsequent plaster frescos will hold on tight. And the keystone holds the arch in place. And all these, too, seemed as I worked to be good prayers to pray for whichever one was needed most, to make this offering to the Holy Little Child of Love set against the deep red of the rose, so apt a doppelgänger for the juicy layers of nourishment in utero ... all this to pray for those on earth who yearn in their own ways for the Child of Love to come touch their soul to come be their very own.

2. **without being seen:** The ancient writer Lucas relates the story of the birth of the God Child all from Mother Mary's point of view, saying she knew Who she was protecting inside her, that she too could see the hidden Holy while others could not . . . that she hid her knowing of the unseen Immanent One "in her heart." (Luke 2: 19–51)

CHAPTER TWENTY-TWO **Closing Blessing:**
Have You Forgotten? I Am Your Mother

1. On the origin of this ending for our prayers and blessings, please see Chapter Twenty-Four, "The Highest Prayer."

Notes to the Reader

A NOTE ABOUT THE ART HEREIN

Each little artwork I created in *Untie the Strong Woman,* was made as an *ex-voto* in thanks or for help or sustenance or praise, to Holy Mother, and in service of souls, some of whom I knew personally and some were made for those I'd not yet met, perhaps for a soul like you yourself, who was in need of counsel, prayer and healing.

The images I made in multimedia were not made in high resolution, as I do not know how and between my dyslexia and other challenges, the instructions in books made my eyes swim, so complicated it all seemed. So I just cut, glued, trimmed, colored away with the equivalent of child's tools.

In my heart I wanted to lay down the prayer to try to meet the hopeful need, and in so doing, to send my 'prayer-letters' into the place where prayers are given across hand to hand by all that is holy, that juncture where biology, psychology of a person, place and the eternal Creator, might meet as one. Thus, my images or words I placed on and in the ex-votos are technically not sharp focused the way I know and admire that a true professional would be able to do this.

I thought to not place ex-votos in this work, for I know that some are aficionados of printed art pages and would find these not so good. But then I felt a little nudge and maybe saw a little angel's feather flash by, and thought perhaps you would like to see these "painted prayers" with collage elements for health and healing, even though they are softly focused. I would ask only that these ex-votos, as was their original intent, might also bless and be just right for some part of your precious life too, and for those you care about.

A NOTE TO READERS ABOUT WORDS

As a poet, I think we who slug away in the pit of words trying to pry enough loose, hope some will have been made by the angels, even though most have to be sorted and hammered til they are limber and strong even as we are exhausted by the craft of trying to cut the facets while avoiding the schists . . . (that's my idea of poetic humor).

With gravity, I think poets have duty to create new words, to make use of words in new and old ways, to invent words if need be when language does not yet carry a needed conceptual or emotive word, and too, this is why we lapse into poetry when speaking especially about the transformational, the Holy—as mundane prose can convey what occurred, but may not be able to convey the feeling inside what occurred—as well as the lyric line can. I say 'lapse into poetry,' because I think that for many of us, poetics is our first language: It is the way we see the world by what is inside first and outside, second.

Loyal souls have read this manuscript and made notations according to manuals of style, with the premise that I would preserve my own dialect, my own way of writing in my own voice. Thus, you will find in this work some inconsistencies of spelling for instance, as how I learned to spell certain words as a child depended on where our teacher nun was from that year: the United States, or Canada which followed British spelling.

Also, you will find some words which are peculiar to where I grew up in the boondocks of the lakelands and woodlands of the north. I have kept the idiosyncrasies of my 'home language,' and therefore any errors in this manuscript, or seeming errors, are mine alone. I hope you will find my writing follows the way I speak, and in cases of foreign words, those which are not in the common vernacular, are notated in English after the foreign language word.

As you know, words carry stories inside them, stories of the people who use the words regionally for instance, instead of more globally. Thereby even the spelling of words can become discussion points for political views, and certainly about the preservation of languages as well. You will find, for instance, that on the dedication page of this book, the people's dialect of Milano is used to name, as they do, their beautiful Madonna atop the church there, Madunina. She is also called in more global Italian Madonnnina. When making a choice about several ways of referring to an event or person in word or spelling, I tend toward using the dialect of the people in the place where the person or matter exists.

Too, there are some words that I've used, for instance the word religion. I have spoken about this word in its original, meaning, to bind the sheaves together, to stand together in all nourishment and light. I know that for some readers, for their own reasons, this word that derives from relīgare is sometimes aversive, for they have seen crime done by or been hurt by someone claiming they were acting in the name of a religious belief. I would like to return many words to their underlying stories again, and you may find this from time to time in this manuscript.

Also, one of the chapters herein, because of the gritty experience contained, uses a word normally understood as a vulgarity: *motherfucker*. Rather than leaving that transformational event out of the book as some cautioned me, because it literally revolves around a perceived vulgarity, I have shown how it unfolded in context of Our Lady's love, and brought it to you here.

I am sensitive to the fact that some, especially of my own elder generation, may be unused to such words, taken aback or offended by such tough street talk. I am sorry if the word rankles, and those of us from the dirt and who work with those from the ground up do not find such words shocking, rather only as markers of frustration or strivings for power in the moment often. We move to lift the language a bit higher, but more so, the very people themselves, I think. I hope the reader's heart will see that the transformational qualities of the children in that chapter, rise far above this jargonish word.

You'll see an endnote too about what groups of people name themselves versus what others name them, including how the names of groups evolve over time, depending on how they rise up more and more into parity with larger cultures. In this book, I refer to groups by names they currently call themselves, even though those names may change tomorrow, and even though not even all people within the catchment name for the group itself necessarily agree with that particular name. I've been fortunate to have people tell me the old names for many of their groups and subgroups, tribes and clans, and what those names really mean, spiritually, politically, and geographically.

It is beautiful to see how people name themselves both according to what they perceive about themselves now, and also, according to what they hope to become. That last is a very ancient practice: naming oneself or one's group for what one hopes one can/ will become. It is also perhaps one of the reasons Holy Mother has so many names from those who love her so. Not so she can grow into them, but so we can.

Ganz –Votivtafeln

...hese are in the tradition of the minority Swabian tribe my fath...
...es from. These are often called votives in English. On the other...
...ny family, mestizo and Spanish, they are called ex-votos, mean...
...atin, that one has taken a vow to do something, say something,...
..., begin or end something whilst asking with fullest heart for Di...
...stance in a matter related, or sometimes another matter altoget...

...to images are also traditionally painted in order to thank for pe...
...ted. Below are listed many ex-votos out of hundreds I've made...
...decades of my life. They represent my contemplative prayer pra...
...s taught by my father's sisters, my aunts who were old believer...
...h sides of the ocean. They taught me certain tandem prayers to...
...de for each pleading, and exchanges and gifts left for Holy Spir...
..., were I pressed to name this set of practices, perhaps call it exp...
...ayer. But more so, along with our family tradition of spontaneo...
...ake-story," I usually call them by what they are: "prayer-makin...

...me I have made to help and hold those in such need as individu...
...those known to me, and those not known to me, both. And also...
...or what in Hebrew is called, tikkun olam, for repair of the worl...
...oul, meaning I make ex-votos too, to also pray into and for all o...
...humanity who may have need, meaning you also, me too, us al...
...ether. I trust your soul will know when you see each ex-voto he...
...hat challenging event or life passage each is for, and why. Soul...
...tilingual, and one of soul's greatest languages is speaking in im...

List of Illustrations/Credits

Dedication
Photo: La Madunina/Madonnina en Milano, Italia, designed by Giuseppe
    Perego, 1762
    Credit, e grazie tanto: Milano tourist industry

Table of Contents
"M is for Mary, My Mother, My Sister, My Friend"

FIRST WORDS **Opening Blessing:** *Totus Tuus,* **I Belong to You, Blessed Mother**
Ex-voto: "Our Lady's Blessing Quilt for Beautiful Dreams," by Dr. C. P. Estés
The bought quilt I embellished says at the top: Rest, Sweet Sleep, Quiet,
    Peace, Friends, Soothing, Heart, Healing, Beautiful Dreams.
At the bottom, the quilt says: Blessed Mother, Immaculate Heart, Mi
    Madre, Mirror of Heaven, Ivory Tower, Arbol de la Vida, Star of the
    Ocean, Please Pray for Me, Restore Me, Strengthen Me, Heal Me . . .
    My Gratitude Is Yours: Forever, I Am *Totus Tuus* (I Belong to You).

CHAPTER ONE **The First Time Ever I Saw Your Face**
Collage 1: "Red Woman Lake," by Dr. C. P. Estés
Collage 2: "Our Lady of the Mother Lake Michigan," by Dr. C. P. Estés

CHAPTER TWO **Untie the Strong Woman**
Collage ex-voto: "Elder Holy Mother, That She Be Known And
    Shown Unfrozen"
This ex-voto says:
    Blessed Mother, Woman of Many Faces, Many Names: I know you as
    Our Holy Elder, a nearly unheard of depiction of you. But/And in the

old stories, you, as aged Mary, climbed the hills to Artemis' Ephesus where you held forth: "teaching by being." Some old believers report, as at Cana, you continued to enjoin sacred tribal dances.

Today, in June 2011, the day of completing this book, and after near 2 millennia of peoples across the world crying out in pain, it has been decreed worldwide, by Christian authorities, that werewith Christian missionaries are to "reject all forms of violence . . . including the violation or destruction of places of worship, sacred symbols or texts" belonging to others.

If so, true reason for Hallelujah: may it come into being for all groups. All. That all swords are this very day hammered into plow blades . . . to plant new life instead of harming life.

After brutal conquests long ago and uninvited incursions in our own times, these invasions initiating violence and exploitation but said to be in the name of "the Faith"—in June 2011, the World Council of Churches, the Vatican's Pontifical Council for Interreligious Dialogue, and the World Evangelical Alliance—"representing over 90% of the world's Christian population"—has published what I'd call "a remarkable document of conscience." "[T]he first document of its kind in the history of the church . . ." it states clear ethical and humane points: Deception and coercion by missionaries is condemned, as are the destructions of others' cultures and religions. Many of us know "the weeping history" of innocents across the world, and their thousands of religious systems which were egregiously crushed. May a new consciousness about the dignity of persons and groups rise, include awakening any who have wished to press their beliefs on unwilling others "for their own good," including Christians who are brutal to other Christians. May all hearts be unfrozen. May all hearts be made sweet. May all hearts remember the original gift each was born with, that is, to be helpless in love for more than just one's own kind. As has always been meant.

CHAPTER THREE **The Drunkard and The Lady**
Opening image: © Mednyanszky Zsolt/Shutterstock

Artwork: "The Grotto of La Conquista," heroic sculpture, castings, and stonework by Roy Neal

Artwork: "The Well of Mary," sculpture, water features, and stonework by Roy Neal

Photos by Lucy Backus Malloy

CHAPTER FOUR **Guadalupe Is a Girl Gang Leader in Heaven**
Collage ex-voto :"Nuestra Señora de los Cuchillos, Our Lady of the
  Knives," by Dr. C. P. Estés

CHAPTER FIVE **Massacre of the Dreamers: The Maíz Mother**
Collage ex-voto: "Rise Up After Bloodshed" by Dr. C. P. Estés
The words on this ex-voto read:
  "Rise up!
  Even after bloodshed . . .
  Especially after bloodshed,"
  Says La Conquista,
  Our Lady of the Conquered.

Her name associated with the concept of conquering can be understood
  in several ways. She is the mother of those who have been pushed
  down and enslaved by someone or something, whether that be a
  deleterious addiction, or an unjust regime or environs. She is also
  the one who conquers others' hearts, healing the broken heart,
  warming the cold heart, straightening the twisted heart, cooling
  the overheated heart. This title, La Conquista can be understood in
  many good ways.

CHAPTER SIX **The *Memorare,* Remember!**
Collage ex-voto: "Our Lady, Shirt of Arrows: She teaches protection of
  the vulnerable—no exceptions," by Dr. C. P. Estés
This ex-voto, "Shirt of Arrows," reads:
  Memorare

  Because . . .
  She cannot be harmed,
  for She and the Divine Child are Eternal . . .

  Because . . .
  She is certain
  about the Divinity of her own Child
  and the absolute imperishability
  of her Child's teachings . . .

  She ever and immediately moves
  through us,
  to protect every child on earth.

CHAPTER SEVEN **The Use of the Seven Swords Through The Heart**
Collage ex-voto: "Definition of Strength: Pierced but Fierce,"
  by Dr. C. P. Estés

"Pierced But Fierce": this ex-voto reads:

> If it said by the old women of the family
> That the hilts of the swords piercing Our Lady's heart...
> Are shaped like the curling sepals which protect the buds
> of roses ... that with prayer and time, each sword hilt
> will burst into seven fragrant roses, blooming again and
> again, because suffering brings the rain of tears,
> because the rain of tears waters the earth,
> because moisture on dry earth of our being
> is guaranteed to bring forth new life.

> Tears are a river that take you somewhere...
> Somewhere better, somewhere good.*

*This last line is from the book *Women Who Run With the Wolves*.

CHAPTER EIGHT **"Our Lady Behind the Wall"**

"This M Stands For Mother Who Leaps Over the Walls of the Worlds":
   © Phase4Photography/Shutterstock

"Before" Photo: The central altar and "Santo Juan Diego and Our
   Lady of Guadalupe Historic and Sacred Art Mural" painted by
   muralist Carlotta EspinoZa in 1978 at Our Lady of Guadalupe
   Parish, Denver, Colorado.

"After" Photo: The central altar after remodeling, La Señora's mural
   behind the wall

Both photos by Daniel Salazar, Denver, Colorado

Photo: Central Altar at Church of Our Lady of the
   Miraculous Medal

CHAPTER NINE **A Man Named Mary**

Collage ex-voto: "Our Lady Who Glows In the Dark" by
   Dr. C. P. Estés

This ex-voto says:

> Our Lady
> Who glows
> In the dark,
> Exploding swastikas
> Back into meaning
> [the] God of Love.

As many know, the swastika is also called long before it was associated
   to a brutal regime, the whirling logs symbol, the four directions, the
   four winds, the great wheel of life. The use of this most sacred of

ancient symbols was put to use by the Nazis of the twentieth century. They surely made this ancient symbol weep blood from all the murder and mayhem brought about by those who conscripted this as the symbol of their "purity."

My uncle's story of his fleeing from the Nazis is told in the chapter A Man Named Mary. Finally safe in the arms of his relatives in America he told me many times in many ways: Those who murder the innocents, no matter who, no matter when, have no country. Those who save and protect are citizens not of the fatherland, not of the motherland, but the God of LoveLand.

The cross is, in the symbolism of Christ, the promise that Love will prevail, that eternal Love rising not from human beings alone, but from "the source without Source," can never die.

My uncle here, is the same uncle whose much longer story of struggle to survive wartime, and finding the living God in the forest again, is told in the book *The Faithful Gardener: A Wise Tale About That Which Can Never Die.*

CHAPTER TEN **The Black Madonna**
Collage ex-voto 1: "She Who Cannot Be Extinguished"
Collage ex-voto 2: "Sanctu, Sanctu: Standing on the Shoulders of Those Who Stand on the Shoulders of . . ."
Both by Dr. C. P. Estés

CHAPTER ELEVEN **How the Motherfuckers Became the Blessed Mothers**
Collage ex-voto "Our Lady of the Train Trestle" by Dr. C. P. Estés
"Our Lady of the Train Trestle" ex-voto says:
   Our Lady Under the Train Trestle . . .
   A Light Shines Even Brighter
   In the Darkest Dark
Ink drawings: "Tattoocitos: Little Tattoos for Holy Mother" by Dr. C. P. Estés

CHAPTER TWELVE **The Great Woman Appears to Us Daily**
Collage ex-voto: "Mary's Closet" by Dr. C. P. Estés

CHAPTER THIRTEEN **Litany of the Mother Road:**
   Chant of Her Incandescent Names
Collage ex-voto: "Our Lady of the Blue Highways" by Dr. C. P. Estés

CHAPTER FOURTEEN **Post-Abortion Compassion: "The Children She Got That She Did Not Get . . ."**

Collage ex-voto: "La Mariposa: Butterfly Flutter, **Our Lady of New Life**" by Dr. C. P. Estés

"Butterfly Flutter" regarding this ex-voto: When a woman is about four months pregnant or a bit later, one day, so amazingly, we feel a tiny flutter in our wombs: this is the tiny child within, moving inside us. It feels like the flutter of the wings of a butterfly. And for most of us, we stop in our tracks in such holy wonder. In both my eventual full term but difficult (for many reasons) pregnancies I can still remember these many decades later, where I was at that 'butterfly moment,' what time of day or night, the weather outside, what I had been doing, what I was wearing, the state of the day, the smells in the air. Everything stopped in that sacred moment, except for awe, except for such wonder. Life. Moving. Holy. Alive. In my body? To me, with me? Who was coming to me and through me, beginning in butterfly form? Amazing lightness of Being.

CHAPTER FIFTEEN **The Drowning Man**

Collage ex-voto: "The Lasso of Our Lady: For Saving a Life" by Dr. C. P. Estés

This ex-voto says:

　　. . . fierce prayer I sent out with my cry, Mother of God!!
　　And I threw my rosary with all my might across the waves . . .
　　For moments the Lasso of La Virgen hung in the air . . .

　　Oh My Lady, please let the stranger
　　Be held above the water
　　Until help can come.

CHAPTER SIXTEEN **God Has No Hands: Comforting María, The Ritual of *Pésame***

Collage ex-voto: "God Has No Hands But Ours: Las manos de la gente quien la ama, Hands of the People Who Love Her" by Dr. C. P. Estés

Photo: "Before She Was Painted Black: Little Our Lady of Fatima"

CHAPTER SEVENTEEN **The Marys of Mother Africa**

Collage ex-voto: "Holy Mother Africa," by Dr. C. P. Estés

CHAPTER EIGHTEEN **The "Oh Yes, There Is Too Room for You Here" Ritual of *La Posada***

Collage ex-voto: "El Cristo de La Llave: Mary's Miracle Child," by Dr. C. P. Estés

CHAPTER NINETEEN **Our Lady of Guadalupe: The Path of the Broken Heart**

"Letter M Is for La Mystica": © Michael Levy/Shutterstock

CHAPTER TWENTY **They Tried To Stop Her At The Border**

"Letter M is for El Milagro de La María, Miracle of Our Lady": © Mikhail/Shutterstock

Photo of La Señora de Guadalupe and The People who Love Her, Santa Fe, New Mexico

Photo of Nuestra Señora de Guadalupe, Santa Fe, New Mexico

Both by Joshua Trujillo, guadalupejourney.blogspot.com, joshuatrujillo.com

CHAPTER TWENTY-ONE **The Truth about How Very Hard It Is to Get into Heaven**

Collage ex-voto: "A Door To Heaven," by Dr. C. P. Estés

CHAPTER TWENTY-TWO **Closing Blessing: Have You Forgotten? I Am Your Mother**

Holy Card Design: "Blessing of Guadalupe Through Cuauhtlatoatzin, Santo Juan Diego" by Dr. C. P. Estés

CHAPTER TWENTY-THREE **Beautiful Words About The Mother**

"M is for Mi Madre, My Mother": © karbunar/Shutterstock

CHAPTER TWENTY-FOUR **The Highest Prayer**

"M is for Mary, My Mother, My Sister, My Friend"

Notes

Image: Combined works © Anton Novik and LessLemon/Shutterstock

Notes to the Reader

Image: © discpicture/Shutterstock

List of Illustrations/Credits

Photo: "Ganz–Votivtafeln" © Michael Kranewitter, 2007/Creative Commons Copyright

Gratitude and Intercessory Prayer
Image: © Ra Studio/Shutterstock

An Unconventional Biography
Image: Typeface Authentic Ink Initials © Florian Schick/SchickFonts

Additional Works by Dr. Clarissa Pinkola Estés
Image: © jörg röse-oberreich/Shutterstock

Index
Image: © Theo Malings/Shutterstock

Gratitude and
Intercessory Prayer

There's a tale told in our family:

After the war, a peasant woman carried a sack of seeds of golden wheat she'd saved from the rubble. But, she had no land to plant. She sheltered and protected the seeds, and after many years, miraculously, a fertile plot of land was offered to her. Now she could sow her seeds and grow a nourishing field of grain to feed the surrounding villages. But it didn't turn out only as she had planned. For when she began to spade the earth deeply, turning it over, she found gold. The field offered to her, was holding hidden treasure.

Something like this happens sometimes too when people come close to one another in creative work together. I witness: like the peasant in the tale, with each book I've published, I often discover once again new challenges and struggles, but also what I never expected: hidden treasure in and of others who come to walk with me. Some stop for a moment; some only "until the ink dries." And, some bless down hard by being long and loyal fellow travelers who do not turn away during my *luchas,* struggles, during fallow, or storm, or open road-blue skies.

Spending so much time alone toiling in caves of various kinds most of my life, I am grateful for those who have come wanting to help, who knock on the door of my heart whilst I am often flailing about in the far back corner trying to keep the creative fire lit during a crosswind . . .

trying to translate angels, flapping my wings to ward off demons, and just striving hard to lay down line after line, day after day, year after year in the time I've been granted whilst tending to all commitments of heart and soul.

Here are many of "the hidden treasures" who have arrived in full-caped glory and/or who have so sweetly crept near to offer help during my years of life and also the writing of this book. My agent Ned Leavitt who carries rootstock across worlds and in many ways "takes down the stringed instrument to play" daily. **Tami Simon, founder and president of Sounds True, who has developed and sheltered her own field holding hidden treasure, serving others in so many ways: She has ever kept my heart safe.**

My stand-up family who cares about my life. I cherish your lives and talents too. My dearlings, my right and left hands, who have helped whenever I've asked, and often suggested useful things I'd not thought before: To my father Jozsef of beloved memory. To Tiaja, Chicito, Lucy, Teena, Marvell, Martita, Chuck, Nona. Our family has grown tiny as our elders have died: Thus, to all our sweet, strange, harsh, beautiful elders. I've mentioned the reality of our refugee and immigrant backgrounds in many of the stand-alone chapters herein. In the cacophony of "modern times," some forget that many flew overland and underground so hard and so long with at least one broken wing in order for us to be free. We do not forget you. You are our communion of endeared, bedraggled and muddy saints, our tribe of one-of-a-kind souls.

I've been an associate to/with the Sisters of Charity, Leavenworth Kansas for nearly fifteen years now, an order of nuns who are healers, hospital-makers, educators, fierce and focused women who can pray the paint off walls. They live in many nations, including China, and we share study time, and pray together daily. My sisters strengthen me that we work with and love "the least of the least," whom we know for certain, are in so many ways, really, "the most of the most." *National Catholic Reporter:* three brief posts there became three long chapters here. Gratitude for carrying my column "*El Rio Debajo del Rio,* The River Beneath the River" about my views on justice, culture and spirit. To Sister Mary Madeleva, poet, who took the time when I was sixteen years old, to send an annotated letter encouraging my lyric work. And to the young nun who took my poetry to Sister Madeleva; we called you Sister Mary Magnolia, for you had the most beautiful southern accent. To all Sisters and Brothers of the Congregation of the Holy Cross for teaching us social justice; the one "first thing" that must last.

Marilyn Auer, publisher, *The Bloomsbury Review,* who gladly allowed Blessed Mother into pages writ by wondrous desperados, laser-minded geniuses and authors strangely and wondrously gifted. Those "dear brave souls" in "the sudden villages," that are formed on my Facebook pages and other forums, who have supported this work with such heart and excitement: it means a lot to the lonely writer, always.

To all the Truers whose forbearance and loving-kindness is so appreciated. It may seem a book is a simple thing; write, edit, print, distribute. But/and, nearly one-hundred souls at and associated with Sounds True touched this work in some way so we could gladly bring it to you. To senior editor Haven Iverson, a young mother who gives the same kind of care to books as to her actual children. Karen Polaski, managing art director, a rare talent—both acute and kind, who understands the electricity of words and images. Other smart and patient souls in art and editorial departments: Lisa Kerans, Levi Stephen, Beth Skelley. Proofing: the good many-eyed Arguses: Rachel Shirk, Florence Wetzel, Allegra Huston. Lucy Malloy, **Dr. Martha Urioste, Rachael Patten; Jeff Hoffman, Indexer. Others in love-service as clarions of books who let others know the book is on its way and what it is about: In copywriting and caravanning, Chantal Pierrat, Shelly "Emotikins" Francis, Wendy Gardner, Grayson Towler. Good map-makers for logistics: Wendy Albrecht, Jaime Schwalb, Jenifer Wolinski, Rebecca Chenoweth. My hobbitzim, so unusual of heart, and loyal. These are the engineering men who bring my voice to you with such exquisite clarity of sound and with beautiful images for the worldwide Live online events we do, including** *Untie the Strong Woman:* **Aron Arnold, Stephen Lessard, Hayden Peltier, Josh Wright.**

To all my colleagues who contribute so much to the world in their own so very original voices, and to those who encouraged this last forty years of the "pinkola-estésian" marque: my development of a branch of archetypal psychology spring-boarding from Jung's profound delivery of such, based on my understandings of the root carriers of archetype: all our ethnic people's practices and oral traditions. Rafael López Pedraza, Thomas Kirsch, Renos Papadopoulos, Andrew Samuels, Joyce Meskis, Molly Moyer, Spence Backus, Virginia Sumners, Jan Vanderberg, Craig M., the "Willow" family, J.Cupcake, Dana Pattillo, charlie merhoff, *Las Marias,* "The Women in White," *mis Guadalupañas* worldwide, Ana Castillo, Demetria Martinez, Claribel Alegria, Maestra Elena, Eduardo Galeano, Steve Rush, Mike Wilzoch, Alice Walker, Maya Angelou—*mis comadres y compadres* mentioned here and prior who made the walk and the walker stronger—*Todos se refugian en El Corazón,* all of us seeking sanctuary in The Heart.

To all innocent souls imprisoned in thought, memory, or behind bars of any kind across the world. Do not lose heart. Holy Mother knows you are alive, and we, "the old believers, and the old women in black," daily pray for your freedom in every way—soul, spirit, mind, heart, body. Promise. Too, for the Soul, whom I consider the most endangered species on the face of this earth: That you endure, Soul! And to Holy Mother, *La Entrada,* the Entryway, to whom it is not too much to say, I owe my life. *Totus Tuus ego sum Maria.* I belong to you. You belong to us. All of us. All.

An Unconventional Biography

Clarissa Pinkola Estés, PhD, is an American poet, post-trauma specialist, social activist, and diplomate psychoanalyst certified by charter of the C. G. Jung International Association of Psychoanalysts in Zurich, Switzerland.

"I was raised in the now nearly vanished oral and ethnic traditions of my families. I'm a first-generation American who grew up in a rural village, population 600, near the Great Lakes. Of Mexican mestiza and majority Magyar and minority Swabian tribal heritages, I come from immigrant and refugee families who could not read or write, or who did so haltingly. Much of my writing is influenced by my family people who were farmers, shepherds, hopsmeisters, wheelwrights, weavers, orchardists, tailors, cabinetmakers, lacemakers, knitters, horsemen and horsewomen from the Old Countries. We also say we love so much to dance ourselves into the ground at any opportunity, that we get up to dance even when someone slurps their soup too loud. Excesses and poverties of many kinds were often somehow considered necessarily complementary."

Estés' poetry is used throughout her psychoanalytic books, spoken-word audios, and stage performances as *remedios,* medicines offered for others.

> *"Since I began creating spoken-word series in the Sounds True studios in 1989, and since I was a kid, I call my family stories 'stories as medicine,' and my poems I call, cuentitos, my little stories. I carry some charisms in the old traditions of healing: the sound of la voz, that is, voice, and las palabras de la chupatinta, words from my ink-stained writing hand; and pláticas, which means a conversation in which both persons' hearts might begin to beat with the same rhythm, together. Such healing ways can be soft, but are more so, often, walking the rough road where as the beautiful Yeats put it in a most treasured line: 'All ladders start . . . In the foul rag and bone shop of the heart.'"*

Author of many books on the life of the soul, her work has been published in more than thirty languages. Her book *Women Who Run With the Wolves: Myths and Stories of The Wild Woman Archetype* was on the *New York Times* bestseller list for 145 weeks. She speaks as a visiting scholar at universities, is a diversity teacher drawing from her biracial and tri-heritage backgrounds.

> *"My doctoral degree and post-doctoral diploma were so hard-won, raising kidlettini, working several jobs, holding body and soul together somehow. I've such gratitude to have been allowed to not just learn, but to study, to create in my doctoral concentration, a discipline area that did not exist before: ethno-clinical psychology; the study of the journey of the soul in tribes, corporate groups, family groups, religious life, cultural groups from tiny to large, a group being anywhere 'two or more are gathered in the Name.' Even though my university life was humble in terms of not being at the most famous name colleges—as important, my own family was the completely outfitted rustic and wondrous underground laboratory. Too there was a venerable university I'd so admired but knew I'd no chance of attending for lack of everything. It was called the 'oldest institution of higher learning in the USA' under the motto 'Veritas,' Truth. For me growing up as wild child of the woods and water—though Cambridge, Massachusetts, was out of my reach utterly—I think the great Mother Lake, Michigan, became my Harvard."*

She has taught memoir, e-book writing, and storyteller critique and performance at many institutions and private facilities. Her teaching of writing in prisons began in the early 1970s at the men's penitentiary in Colorado, and in other locked institutions throughout the West and the Southwest.

> *"Some of the greatest conceptual writers are those who are in prison. Writing can be, in many ways, the survival mechanism of Spirit. Most all us poets say that writing and poetry saved our lives. This is not a puff statement. It is a truth about the paucity of real nourishment inside or outside iron bars in our times. Poetry and writing, are bags of blood for the hungriest arterial system we possess that can so easily wither when restricted unjustly— meaning, the animating one Spirit."*

Estés is also a post-trauma recovery specialist and psychoanalyst who has practiced clinically for forty-one years. Her doctorate is from the Union Institute & University.

> *"I began my work as a post-trauma specialist in the 1960s at Edward Hines Jr. Veterans Hospital in Hines, Illinois. There I worked with World War I, World War II, Korean, and Vietnam War soldiers who were living with quadriplegia or incapacitated by loss of either/or, both arms and legs. I also heart-broke myself working at other facilities caring for severely injured children—it was a time when middle-class and upper-class parents were told to put their injured or special needs children 'away' in institutions. I also worked closely with war veterans and their families, all having their own version of what was then called shell-shock, today called post-traumatic stress disorder. I'd learned from my own refugee family, that when one is taken to war, all who love that one are taken to war also. All are worthy of care."*

Estés continues to minister to those who have experienced childbearing loss and to surviving families of murder victims. She has served at disaster sites and has developed post-trauma recovery protocol for earthquake survivors in Armenia. Since then, her protocol has been translated into many languages and is used to deputize citizen helpers to do post-trauma work on site and for the months and years yet to come. She served Columbine High School and community after the massacre in 1999, and she continues to work with 9–11 survivors and survivor-families on both the East and West coasts.

"There is no such thing as a life without suffering, I wish there were. So much. But also there is much goodness, including calling, that can come from even the worst suffering. I don't say it lightly. My home, as a child, was filled with the war-torn, fresh from being run over by two different brutal war-hardened armies who cared nothing for purity nor precious life. I saw up-close the terrible open wounds: I also saw the amazing forms of new life that were born from the wound's edges over and over again. Like a cut-down tree growing ten strong saplings straight out of its hewn trunk. It is the same for those who have been hurt hard: they walk wounded, but with new life learning to leap outward again and again."

Estés served as appointee by two governors to the Colorado State Grievance Board (1993–2006) where she was elected chair. She is a board member of the Authors Guild, New York; a contributing editor to *The Bloomsbury Review;* and a member of the National Association of Hispanic Journalists. She is managing editor of the political news site TheModerateVoice.com and also writes there on news, politics, and spiritual concerns. Her column *El Río Debajo del Río*, the River Beneath the River, is archived at *National Catholic Reporter,* ncronline.org.

"One of the endeavors I have loved most is to help mothers learn to read and write in their mother tongue. Thus, in a mothers' literacy project in Queens, New York, I went to tell our family stories, and all the moms then wrote stories from all their home countries. They were so excited to practice their writing and reading with their own stories from their parents and elders, which they suddenly revalued (and sent their stories to me all printed out by hand as a so touching set of hand-written sheaves). In Madagascar, we were able to help provide adult literacy help by encouraging the printing of local folktales, health care and hygiene information, for people in their own language. These texts were then used for learning to read and write. To me, to learn to read and write is miraculous: To help others learn these two magics is to give others soul-to-soul resuscitation. Reading alone puts the entire universe right into a soul's hands. Writing makes the gate fly open for that soul to say what the universe looks like to them in their own one-of-a-kind voice. Miraculous Mother smiles."

Estés testifies before state and federal legislatures on welfare reform, education and school violence, child protection, mental health, environment, licensing of professionals, immigration, and other quality of life and soul issues. She is the recipient of numerous awards for her life's work, including the first Joseph Campbell Keeper of the Lore Award for her work as La Cantadora. For her written work, she received the Gradiva Award from the National Association for the Advancement of Psychoanalysis, the Catholic Press Association award for her writings on spirit and religion, and the Las Primeras Award, "The First of Her Kind," from the Mexican American Women's Foundation, District of Columbia. She is a 2006 inductee into the Colorado Women's Hall of Fame, which celebrates women of international influence who are change agents.

> "*I think being a change agent could be like being Santa Sombre, Saint Shadow, the one we call as such in our family as one who just blesses whatever can be blessed, clears whatever can be cleared, seeds whatever can be seeded, and moves onward, not looking back at outcome. Do we ever know the good we hopefully will be able to lay down in la semilla form, as just a tiniest seed, even randomly dropped or perhaps placed purposely? Probably not most of the time. Ours is to carry the planting stick, to wash the seed, to choose which ones, and to lay the seed, sometimes one to an opening in this or that yielding earth. Sometimes, to plant strong in hostile ground, five or ten seeds to a single rocky aperture. Then, we move on to the next ground, hard, stony, soft, doesn't matter. What is faith, but that we can, will follow, follow, follow—stumbling, striding doesn't matter as much as following the sight lines that grow wider, deeper as we grow older. The work may be only this: the next, the next, pouring the seed through the next aperture, with as much love as possible, failing, standing, falling, pulling forward again . . . following La Sembradora, She, the Sower who knows the way.*
>
> "*This work,* Untie the Strong Woman, *is the continuation of all my other works, looking at the largest archetype of the Holy and integral Woman, from many different angles. Wild Woman, Wise Woman, Holy Woman. They share the same heartbeat. As I wrote in* Women Who Run With the Wolves, *the wild woman archetype is not a savage nor out of control essence imbedded in the psyche: it is a natural instinctual set of longings and knowings within the psyche. As I say in the audio series,* The Dangerous

Old Woman *about the wise woman archtype: Wisdom is not a condition, it is a holy endeavor. As I wrote in* Women Who Run With the Wolves *... eat nourishing food, rest in peace, follow calling, render loyalty, love the children, dance with joy, tune your ears, attend to death and resurrection, create love in the world in all ways, pray by speaking truths that will raise yourself and others. You will find these premises in all my work,* Women Who Run With the Wolves *about the Wild Woman Archetype,* The Dangerous Old Woman *about the Wise Woman Archetype, and* Untie the Strong Woman *about Holy Mother."*

Additional Works by
Dr. Clarissa Pinkola Estés

BOOKS

La danza delle grandi madri [The Dance of the Grand Grandmothers].
  Milan: Sperling & Kupfer / Frassinelli, 2006.

*Women Who Run With the Wolves: Myths and Stories of the Wild Woman
  Archetype.* New York: Ballantine, 1995. First edition, 1992. Also
  published in more than thirty other languages.

The Faithful Gardener: A Wise Tale About That Which Can Never Die.
  New York: HarperOne, 1995.

The Gift of Story: A Wise Tale About What Is Enough. New York:
  Ballantine, 1993.

Campbell, Joseph. *The Hero with A Thousand Faces: Commemorative
  Edition.* Bollingen Series XVII. With an introduction by Clarissa
  Pinkola Estés. Princeton: Princeton University Press, 2004.

Brothers Grimm. *Tales of the Brothers Grimm.* Edited by Clarissa
  Pinkola Estés. Rantoul, IL: Quality Paperback Book Club, 1999.

AUDIOBOOKS, LIVE RECORDINGS, AND PROFESSIONAL TEACHING PROGRAMS

Estés is an award-winning spoken-word artist in poetry, stories, blessings, and psychoanalytic commentary. Her many audio works published by Sounds True are available as CDs and MP3s, and have been broadcast over numerous National Public Radio and community public radio stations throughout Canada and the United States.

Untie the Strong Woman: Blessed Mother's Immaculate Love for the Wild Soul. 2011

The Joyous Body: Myths and Stories of the Wise Woman Archetype. Vol. 3 of *The Dangerous Old Woman* series. 2011

The Power of the Crone: Myths and Stories of the Wise Woman Archetype. Vol. 2 of *The Dangerous Old Woman* series. 2010

The Dangerous Old Woman: Myths and Stories of the Wise Woman Archetype. Vol. 1 of *The Dangerous Old Woman* series. 2010

Mother Night: Myths, Stories, and Teachings for Learning to See in the Dark. 2010

Seeing in the Dark: Myths and Stories to Reclaim the Buried, Knowing Woman. 2010

The Beginner's Guide to Dream Interpretation. 2003

Bedtime Stories: A Unique Guided Relaxation Program for Falling Asleep and Entering the World of Dreams. 2002

Theatre of the Imagination, Volume One. 1999, 2005

Theatre of the Imagination, Volume Two. 1999, 2005

Warming the Stone Child: Myths and Stories about Abandonment and the Unmothered Child. 1997, 2004

In the House of the Riddle Mother: The Most Common Archetypal Motifs in Women's Dreams. 1997, 2005

The Red Shoes: On Torment and the Recovery of the Soul. 1997, 2005

How to Love A Woman: On Intimacy and the Erotic Lives of Women. 1996, 2005

The Faithful Gardener: A Wise Tale about That Which Can Never Die. 1996, 2005

The Boy Who Married An Eagle: Myths and Stories About Men's Interior Lives. 1995

The Radiant Coat: Myths and Stories about the Crossing Between Life and Death. 1993, 2005

The Creative Fire: Myths and Stories about the Cycles of Creativity. 1993, 2005

The Gift of Story: A Wise Tale about What Is Enough. 1993, 2005.

Women Who Run With the Wolves: Myths and Stories about the Wild Woman Archetype. 1989, 2001. Audio underground bestseller, published before the completed manuscript found its publisher.

Index